Economics of
Shipping Practice and Management

To
Jeremy and Linda

Economics of Shipping Practice and Management

Alan E. Branch
F.C.I.T., F.I.Ex., A.I.T.A.

Shipping Executive/Lecturer/Chief Examiner Shipping and
Export Practice/Shipping and Export Consultant

Author of *Elements of Shipping, The Elements of Export Practice*
and *A Dictionary of Shipping/International Trade Terms and
Abbreviations*

Chapman and Hall
LONDON   NEW YORK

387, 51
B 81 a

First published 1982 by
Chapman and Hall Ltd
11 New Fetter Lane, London EC4P 4EE
Published in the USA by
Chapman and Hall
733 Third Avenue, New York NY 10017

© 1982 A. E. Branch

Typeset by Inforum Ltd, Portsmouth
Printed in Great Britain by
J. W. Arrowsmith Ltd, Bristol

ISBN 0 412 23580 3 (cased)
ISBN 0 412 16350 0 (paperback)

British Library Cataloguing in Publication Data	Library of Congress Cataloging in Publication Data

Branch, Alan E.
  Economics of shipping practice and
  management.
1. Shipping
I. Title
387.5   HE571
 	
ISBN 0-412-23580-3
ISBN 0-412-16350-0 Pbk
	Branch, Alan E.
	  Economics of shipping practice and management.
	
	  Bibliography: p.
	  1. Shipping. I. Title.
	HE571.B669 387'.0068 82-6438
	ISBN 0-412-23580-3 AACR2
	ISBN 0-412-16350-0 (pbk.)

Foreword

Sir Frederic Bolton, M.C.

*Chairman of F. Bolton Group Ltd, Director of Sealink Ltd
and a past President of the General Council of British Shipping*

The shipping industry has always lacked a body which can confer professional status on would-be practitioners: in that sense, unlike those closely allied to his responsibilities – the marine engineer, the shipowner or manager is obliged to remain an unqualified amateur.

The latest addition to Mr Branch's list of titles goes a long way towards correcting this position: a proper study of the material in his book would clearly go far to confer the status of 'complete ship operator' upon anyone who was examined on its contents. Knowledge as comprehensive as that acquired through Mr Branch's book must provide a sound base on which to build the experience of practice.

Contents

Preface

This book has been written to provide a practical, overall understanding of the economics of shipping practice and the management of a competitive, profitable shipping company. It reflects the author's many years of experience in ship management, international trade and education. It deals in simple language with the economics of ship operation, the freight market, ship investment criteria, ship management, the economics of design, the finance and economics of international trade, the combined transport concept, marketing and budgetary control, shipboard management, political factors, the role of international organizations, the principles of freight forwarding, the economics of chartering, the services rendered by sea transport to international trade and many other aspects of this extensive subject. The importance of complete professionalism in all areas of shipping practice as a means of providing the viable, high quality service required to sustain and expand international trade cannot be overemphasized. This book will help towards establishing that professionalism.

The material assembled here is intended not only for students preparing for shipping examinations but also for persons employed in shipping companies, ashore or afloat. In short, it is an *aide-mémoire* to those engaged in the industry throughout the world and may be regarded as 'the shipping executive's handbook'. Readers who wish to know more about the basic elements of the subject should also study the companion volume *Elements of Shipping*, the fifth edition of which is now available.

The book is particularly commended to students taking shipping, export and transport examinations under the aegis of the Institute of Chartered Shipbrokers, the Institute of Freight Forwarders, the Institute of Export, the Institute of Transport Administration, the Institute of Materials Handling, the Chartered Institute of Transport and the Society of Shipping Executives. It is ideally suited not only for university and polytechnic courses in the United Kingdom – but also for courses offered in Hong Kong, Nigeria and Malaysia. The book will also assist students or shipping executives taking a short shipping course, or the Foundation Course in Overseas Trade.

I am greatly indebted to the various organizations listed in the Acknowledgements for the assistance they have given so enthusiastically; the fact that many of them are situated overseas is reflected in the international content and market of the book.

At my request, Mr H. B. Jackson, B.Sc. (Econ), F.I.Ex., F.I.B., former Chief Executive of Barclays Export and Finance Co. Ltd, wrote Chapters 2 and 8 on the economics and finance of international trade. Mr A. J. Rogan, B.Sc., C.Eng., F.R.I.N.A., and Mr O. R. Norland, F.I.B., a director of Hambros Bank Ltd, contributed to Chapter 3 on the economics of ship design and Chapter 4 on ship investment criteria, respectively. Similarly, Danish Seaways-DFDS contributed to Chapter 11 on shipboard management. Mr D. B. Cox was responsible for the diagrams. I am most grateful to all of them for their very significant contribution, which has enriched the contents of the book.

Finally, I should like to express my grateful thanks for the considerable secretarial help given by my lifelong family friends Mr and Mrs Splarn, who have undertaken similar tasks for my other publications. As always, I wish to record with gratitude the help rendered by my wife in proof reading and to pay tribute to her tolerance and enthusiasm during many a lost weekend.

A.E.B.

19 The Ridings,
Emmer Green,
Reading,
Berkshire.
April 1982

Acknowledgements

The author wishes to acknowledge the generous assistance provided by the following companies and institutions:

Baltic and International Maritime Conference
Baltic Exchange
Council of European and Japanese National Shipowner's
  Associations
Danish Seaways (DFDS)
European Ferries Ltd
General Council of British Shipping
Inter-Governmental Maritime Consultative Organization
International Association of Independent Tanker Owners
International Cargo Handling Co-ordination Association
International Chamber of Commerce
International Labour Office
International Monetary Fund
Nigerian National Shipping Line
Organization for Economic Co-operation and Development
Organization of the Petroleum Exporting Countries
Sealink UK Ltd
United Nations Commission on International Trade Law
United Nations Conference on Trade and Development

Diagrams

CHAPTER 1

Services Rendered by Sea Transport to International Trade

Function of shipping and its relationship to international trade. Balance of trade and balance of payments. Relationship between world seaborne trade and world mercantile fleet.

FUNCTION OF SHIPPING AND ITS RELATIONSHIP TO INTERNATIONAL TRADE

Transport is an essential facility for the exploitation or development of economic resources on a national or international scale. It allows articles or materials to be conveyed from areas of low utility to areas of high utility.

The reasons for the provision of transport may be economic, social or political. For example, the presence of a steel works in South Wales is due to a number of factors, including the local availability of coal and labour and the existence of reliable, cheap sea transport, which allows the importation of iron ore through Port Talbot. Ore mined in South Australia, where it has little local value, is shipped to an area of steel production such as South Wales, where the industry originally developed owing to the proximity of high grade iron ore mined in the local coal measures. Efficient shipping has enabled the industry to remain in the locality despite the exhaustion of local ores, and the development of huge iron ore carrier vessels has made South Australian ores competitive with Swedish, Algerian and Canadian ores in spite of the longer distance over which the ores must be carried. Similarly, rail and sea transport enables Canadian wheat growers to ship substantial quantities of grain from the prairies to processing and consuming areas such as India or the United Kingdom and allows cars manufactured in Japan to be sold at competitive prices in the United Kingdom and the USA.

Generally speaking, the demand for shipping is derived from the demand for goods. Certain forms of transport, such as pleasure cruises and holiday travel, may be regarded as 'consumer services', but the basic function of shipping involving economic, social or military needs is the creation of utilities of place.

1

In a society where transport costs are relatively high, the need for a balanced social policy is paramount if isolated communities are to remain in existence. Thanks to liner conference services and, more recently, the introduction of containerization and specialized bulk carriers, shipping has facilitated the development of world resources in terms of both raw materials and manufactured goods. The exchange of goods has brought countries with a high level of industrial advancement, such as those in Europe, into contact with nations at a lower level of industrialization such as India and other countries in the East. In so doing, it has helped nurture community life through the development of local industry producing goods for overseas markets.

Shipping therefore allows economic resources to be developed to the full. It permits specialization in economic activity, whether it be mining, car-making or farming. Without cheap, reliable and well managed shipping services, the exchange of goods and services would be far smaller, to the serious detriment of living standards worldwide.

BALANCE OF TRADE AND BALANCE OF PAYMENTS

When a country engages in international trade there emerges what is called the 'balance of payments'. The people of every country eventually require that payment for the goods they make or the services they render to be made in their own currency – which is normally the only legal tender in their own country. If we buy goods or services from the USA we must pay in dollars; if we buy from Germany we must pay in deutschemarks. The best way to obtain these currencies is to sell some of our own goods and services to the USA and to Germany. If we can sell to them just sufficient to cover the cost of our purchases from them, then our payments with those countries will be in balance. In practice, of course, trade does not work out as simply as that, as we may want more, or less, from a country than it requires from us, so that our balance of payments with that country will be in disequilibrium. Fortunately, in most cases we can overcome the problem by paying in some other currency acceptable to them, as explained in Chapter 2. Because our balance with different countries may be in our favour or in theirs, we have to consider our balance of payments against all the other countries of the world in total. The balance of payments is composed of three elements: the balance of trade, the balance of invisibles and the balance of capital items. The balance of trade is quite simply the difference between the total of 'visible' items exported and those imported, that is, items which can actually be seen passing through the docks and airports. The 'invisible' items are services rendered to foreigners or services received from foreigners. The chief invisibles are banking, shipping, insurance, air transport, tourism and income from foreign investment. To these can be added remittances home by emigrants, the cost of maintaining diplomatic posts and troops abroad, brokerages, specialist fees, etc. The balance of trade and the balance of invisibles together make up the 'current account' of the balance of payments as distinct from the capital account.

In the past capital items formed an insignificant portion of the balance of payments, but this is no longer the case. Today, thousands of millions of pounds are on the move in search of a secure investment with a high return. This is known as 'hot' money. As the term implies, it moves easily and quickly in response to economic conditions and, exchange control permitting, can leave a country as quickly as it entered. Other capital items arise from government loans to other countries and long-term borrowing by the government, local authorities and large corporations.

At the end of the year a balance is struck, if this shows a deficit the government has to borrow enough money from other financial bodies around the world to keep the account straight. If the balance is in surplus, the excess may be placed in the reserves or lent to countries in deficit.

The problems arising from the balance of payments are a matter for the government and the Treasury, which dictate policy; the exporter and importer can merely operate within the framework laid down. Basically, the only way for a country to eliminate a balance of payments deficit is to increase its income and reduce its expenditure, that is, increase its exports of goods and services and curtail its imports; moreover, it must take whatever internal measures are necessary to bring that about and encourage the inflow of capital by maintaining economic stability and attractive interest rates.

The large sums of money that are today transferred around the world have upset the once orderly conduct of international trade and exchanges. On the one hand this has led to restrictive measures which have hindered the growth of trade and, on the other, it has resulted in the formation of various international organizations with a view to controlling these measures, as described in Chapters 12 and 13.

The need to preserve a healthy balance of payments occupies an important place in every country's international trade policy, and accordingly governments must adopt appropriate measures to realize this objective. The techniques employed may include import restrictions, exchange control and, in some countries, the practice of flag discrimination; political factors of the latter kind are described more fully in Chapter 14.

The UK balance of payments on current account for recent years is shown in Table 1.1.

In reviewing these results and the contribution shipping makes to the UK economy, we must bear in mind that the United Kingdom adheres to the principle of commercial freedom of the seas and does not practise flag discrimination to sustain its fleet.

In 1980, the latest year for which detailed statistics are available, shipping made a net contribution of over £1000 million to the UK balance of payments. This sum represents receipts from abroad less payments abroad for such necessary items as bunkers and port and cargo handling charges. A large part of these export earnings came from trade between overseas countries, known as the cross trades. In addition, the fleet saved a further sum of about £300 million net

Table 1.1   Invisibles in the UK balance of payments 1976–80 (£m)

	1976	1977	1978	1979	1980
Net private invisibles	+5151	+4815	+5497	+6028	+5306
(of which UK owned ships)	(+1014)	(+1025)	(+ 975)	(+1144)	(+1150)
Net general government transactions	−2103	−2572	−3016	−3433	−3278
Total net invisibles	+3048	+2243	+2481	+2595	+2028
Total net visible trade balance	−3929	−2284	−1542	−3458	+1178
Current net payments balance	− 881	− 41	+ 939	− 863	+3206

Source: *UK Balance of Payments*, 1981 edition.

by carrying imports which would otherwise have come in foreign ships.

The importance of UK shipping may also be judged from the so-called Sea Transport Account, the balance sheet drawn up by the government to show the overall cost of Britain's shipping services. It comprises the balance of payments transactions for UK ships, foreign ships on charter to UK operators and overseas operators. The net figures for recent years are: 1975, plus £56 million; 1976, plus £48 million; 1977, plus £60 million; 1978, minus £27 million; and 1979, plus £63 million. The Sea Transport Account thus moved into deficit in 1978. A major cause of the decline in 1978 was the decrease in the UK owned and registered fleet – which fell by over 4.5 million deadweight tons in 1978 – and the large amount of tonnage laid up in that year. With the fleet continuing to decline, there seems no prospect of a substantial improvement in the near future despite the improved 1979 results.

It is important, however, not to underestimate the contribution of the UK owned fleet; without it the deficit on the Sea Transport Account would have been around £1100 million higher. It is a matter of speculation whether the government will embark on some form of subsidy or flag discrimination. One must bear in mind that other contributory factors are also involved, particularly the development of fleets in developing countries, the eastern hemisphere and Comecon, the question of flags of convenience and the longer-term implications of the UNCTAD V Conference, which are described on pp. 218–224.

RELATIONSHIP BETWEEN WORLD SEABORNE TRADE
AND WORLD MERCANTILE FLEET

Table 1.2 gives an analysis of major merchant fleets during the period 1970–79. The following points are significant:

(a) The largest mercantile fleet is Liberian, sailing under a flag of convenience. Its growth has been dramatic since 1970, particularly in the tanker sector (see Table 1.6).

(b) An even more stunning increase during the period 1970–79 occurred in the Japanese fleet, particularly in tanker tonnage, as a reflection of the increase in Japan's worldwide industrial import-ance.

Table 1.2   Major merchant fleet figures at 1st July of each year (in thousands of deadweight tons)

	1970		1975		1977		1979*	
	Dry	Wet	Dry	Wet	Dry	Wet	Dry	Wet
UK	15 778	20 370	21 917	30 780	21 542	29 119	18 463	28 744
Liberia	23 153	35 482	41 936	84 075	49 199	106 549	52 871	103 632
Japan	22 264	4 593	29 906	33 439	31 281	33 417	30 667	33 127
Norway	14 329	15 617	18 858	26 566	19 245	29 627	13 885	27 747
Greece	10 829	7 171	22 419	15 106	31 215	18 069	40 375	20 311
USA	13 883	8 155	10 881	9 424	10 303	11 326	10 337	13 915
Panama	3 570	5 756	11 388	10 560	18 227	12 905	21 678	12 926
France	3 158	5 812	4 452	13 473	4 912	14 862	5 130	15 714
Italy	5 197	4 593	8 101	7 410	8 721	8 919	9 183	9 772
World	172 850	148 391	242 258	286 472	294 263	342 964	315 990	347 572

* Figures for 1st January 1979.
Source: GCBS based on Lloyd's.

(c) There are six flag of convenience fleets, namely those registered in Liberia, Panama, the Somali Republic, Cyprus, Singapore and the Sultanate of Oman; it is significant that two feature in Table 1.1.

(d) In 1970 total dry cargo tonnage exceeded the wet tonnage fleet, but by 1979 the reverse applied owing to the enormous growth in the tanker fleet, particularly through the construction of VLCCs and ULCCs. However, wet tonnage remained practically stable between 1977 and 1979, whilst the dry cargo fleet continued to grow as a result of the expansion in the international general cargo market, primarily under cargo liner terms.

(e) The Greek fleet expanded rapidly during the period, particularly in the dry cargo sector, where a fourfold increase was recorded. In contrast, the dry cargo sector of the UK fleet grew only modestly during the period 1970–77 and actually recorded a decline between 1977 and 1979.

(f) The UK fleet expanded between 1970 and 1977 but then began to decline again; in the three and a half years to late 1979 it contracted by nearly 25 per cent. The decline can be attributed to the expansion of the Eastern bloc fleets, the growth of flag of convenience fleets and general trade depression.

One aspect not apparent from Table 1.2 was the dramatic growth in the combined Arab fleet, which rose from 1 to 7 million gross register tons (grt) between 1970 and 1977. The fleet composition was very diverse; in 1976 it included 400 general cargo vessels, 110 tankers, 5 bulk carriers and 500 smaller vessels. By 1978 the Arab nations generated 25 per cent of world seaborne tonnage, including 52 per cent of all seaborne crude oil, but still owned only 1.8 per cent of the world mercantile fleet. The phenomenal expansion in the fleet, which will undoubtedly continue, was greatly facilitated by the purchase of second-hand vessels when laid-up tonnage was at its peak in 1977–78 and shipowners were anxious to sell at much depressed prices in order to finance mortgage repayments. Much of such tonnage was relatively modern and could be converted cheaply. An analysis of the merchant fleet sailing under Arab flags is given in Table 1.3.

International seaborne trade measured in tonne-miles grew at an annual average rate of 13 per cent between 1964 and 1973, but during the period 1974–78 it declined substantially (see Table 1.4).

Table 1.3   Arab flag merchant shipping, 1977 (gross register tons)

	Total	Oil tankers	Bulk carriers	General cargo	Other
Kuwait	1 831 194	1 078 775	12 860	673 033	66 526
Iraq	1 135 245	978 664		80 898	75 684
Egypt	407 818	126 887		227 048	53 883
Algeria	1 055 962	623 203	63 094	123 034	246 631
Libya	673 969	595 381		36 332	42 256
Lebanon	227 009			221 989	5 020
Saudi Arabia	1 018 713	839 216		113 132	46 365
Morocco	270 295	105 582	32 494	75 456	56 763
Sudan	43 375			42 255	1 120
UAE	152 100	77 899		64 353	9 848
Tunisia	100 128	26 827	20 157	46 552	6 592
Bahrain	6 409	931		1 943	3 553
Syria	20 679			19 043	1 636
Oman	6 137			4 573	1 564
Yemen	1 463			1 260	176
Qatar	84 710	72 571			12 142
Jordan	696			496	200

Source: *UNCTAD Review of Maritime Transport*, May 1978.

Table 1.4 International seaborne trade and deadweight tonnage of the world fleet at 1st July of each year (in millions of deadweight tons)

	1971	1972	1973	1974	1975	1976	1977	1978
Dry Cargo								
World dry cargo tonnage	196.9	214.4	230.4	242.3	257.7	272.7	294.3	310.4
Combination carriers in wet trades	15.8	23.2	29.4	24.8	22.5	23.6	27.3	26.7
Dry tonnage	181.1	191.2	201.0	217.5	235.2	249.1	267.0	283.7
US reserve fleet	5.8	4.3	3.2	2.8	2.4	2.2	2.2	2.1
Great Lakes ships	4.8	4.8	4.8	4.7	4.8	4.7	3.2	5.3
Tonnage laid up at 1st July	1.4	3.1	0.7	0.5	6.0	7.0	6.0	13.5
Total active tonnage	169.1	179.0	192.3	209.5	222.0	235.2	255.6	262.8
International seaborne trade MMM (tonne-miles)	352.0	340.9	353.2	330.9	316.5	325.0	323.7	335.6
Tanker								
World tanker tonnage	172.9	191.5	213.2	242.3	286.5	325.7	343.0	348.3
Combination carriers in wet trades	15.8	23.2	29.4	24.8	22.5	23.6	27.3	26.7
Wet tonnage	188.7	214.7	242.6	267.1	309.0	349.3	370.3	375.0
US reserve fleet	0.3	0.4	0.3	0.3	0.3	0.1	0.1	0.1
Great Lakes ships	0.2	0.2	0.2	0.2	0.2	0.2	0.3	0.2
Tonnage laid up at 1st July	0.2	4.1	0.5	0.2	27.4	42.5	31.1	43.5
Total active tonnage	188.0	210.0	241.6	266.4	281.1	306.5	338.8	331.2
International seaborne trade MMM (tonne-miles)	923.9	922.9	1060.6	1068.8	817.6	685.3	531.9	538.2
Total								
World tonnage	369.7	405.9	443.6	484.6	544.2	598.4	637.2	658.7
US reserve fleet	6.2	4.7	3.5	3.2	2.8	2.4	2.4	2.2
Great Lakes ships	5.0	5.0	4.9	4.9	5.0	4.9	3.5	5.5
Tonnage laid up at 1st July	1.6	7.2	1.2	0.6	33.4	49.5	37.1	57.0
Total active tonnage	356.9	389.0	434.0	475.9	503.0	541.6	594.2	594.0
International seaborne trade MMM (tonne-miles)	1276.0	1263.8	1413.7	1399.7	1134.1	1009.5	855.6	873.8
Combination carriers in wet trades (%)	85.0	87.0	84.1	62.3	52.5	51.9	57	55

By contrast, between 1st July 1970 and 1st July 1978 the world merchant fleet doubled in size to 659 million dwt. During the period 1970–74 the annual increase in the world merchant fleet closely matched the annual increase in international trade, particularly where dry cargo was concerned. Between 1972 and 1974 world tanker demand actually exceeded capacity, and remedial action had to be taken. From 1975 onwards, however, the disparity between world merchant fleet capacity and the level of international sea-borne trade widened annually as a result of the marked slowdown in world trade and the completion of vessels that had been ordered up to five years earlier, when forecasts of world trade growth had been more favourable.

Table 1.5 gives details of laid-up shipping during the period 1971–79. The following points may be made:

(a) The level of laid-up tonnage seems to have reached its peak in 1978 and to have declined markedly since then.

(b) Tanker tonnage laid up far outweighs laid-up dry cargo tonnage, reflecting the vast increase in the tanker fleet during the past decade, which substantially outstripped the world demand for energy and hence for international oil distribution.

(c) The fall in laid-up tonnage in 1979 reflects improved trading opportunities and a rise in the number of vessels sold to emerging maritime nations, including Arab states, China and Comecon

Table 1.5   Laid-up shipping at mid-year (in thousands of deadweight tons)

	World		United Kingdom	
	Dry cargo	Tanker	Dry cargo	Tanker
1971	1 396	199	106	1
1972	3 087	4 119	167	377
1973	674	481	31	–
1974	475	157	–	–
1975	5 992	27 431	861	1 816
1976	7 026	42 513	448	4 602
1977	6 009	31 112	153	2 260
1978	13 492	43 521	2 260	3 996
1979	4 927	16 533	116	2 445

Source: GCBS based on Lloyd's.

countries (see p. 194). In addition, many owners sold their vessels for scrap as they saw no opportunity to trade again on viable terms within a reasonable period.

(d) The excess tonnage in the tanker sector will probably not return to the 1977–78 level in the foreseeable future because tanker owners are likely to be more cautious in future investment, particularly as world demand turns to other forms of fuel, such as coal.

Our study of the world mercantile fleet would not be complete without examining the growth of the flag of convenience fleets as shown in Table 1.6. This calls for the following comments:

(a) The capacity of the Liberian tanker fleet grew threefold between 1969 and 1979 and the non-tanker sector expanded by over two and a half times. The growth of both sectors had stabilized by 1979, with the tanker division actually showing a decline.

(b) The total capacity under flags of convenience rose nearly three and a half times during the period under review.

(c) The Panamanian fleet also expanded dramatically between 1969 and 1979; in particular, the non-tanker sector showed a sevenfold increase in capacity.

Table 1.6   World fleets: Growth of tonnage under flags of convenience (in millions of deadweight tons)

Date (mid-year)	Liberia		Panama		Other*		Grand total	% of world fleet
	Tankers	Non-tankers	Tankers	Non-tankers	Tankers	Non-tankers		
1969	30.5	20.9	5.3	2.8	0.4	1.6	61.5	19.8
1970	35.3	23.2	5.8	3.0	0.5	2.3	70.1	21.1
1971	41.6	27.4	5.7	4.0	0.5	3.3	82.5	22.3
1972	48.7	32.4	7.2	5.1	0.8	4.6	98.8	24.3
1973	56.9	35.4	8.1	7.1	1.7	8.1	117.3	26.4
1974	66.4	37.3	8.7	8.7	2.5	9.7	133.3	27.5
1975	84.1	41.9	10.6	11.4	3.7	10.0	161.6	29.7
1976	97.3	44.9	11.5	13.7	6.2	10.1	183.8	30.7
1977	106.5	49.2	12.9	18.2	6.5	9.1	202.4	31.8
1978	105.9	51.2	12.8	20.2	6.4	9.8	206.2	31.3
1979 (at 1st Jan)	103.6	52.9	12.9	21.7	6.1	10.4	207.7	31.3

* Comprises Cyprus, Singapore, the Somali Republic and the Sultanate of Oman.

(d) The fleets of the other countries offering flags of convenience, that is Cyprus, Singapore, the Somali Republic and the Sultanate of Oman, also showed substantial growth, but they remain small in relation to the total, accounting for about 8 per cent of all flag of convenience tonnage in 1979.

(e) In 1969 the flag of convenience fleet accounted for 19.8 per cent of the world mercantile fleet. By 1979 the figure was 31.3 per cent, confirmation that in the intervening decade it had grown at a faster rate than the world fleet as a whole; nonetheless, from 1977 onwards its share of the total had remained more or less stable owing to the world trade recession.

A number of salient points emerge from our examination of Tables 1.2 to 1.6 and the picture they present:

1. The impact of the foreign flag of convenience fleet has grown considerably; it now accounts for nearly one-third of the world mercantile fleet capacity.

2. The level of laid-up tonnage seems to have reached its peak by 1977–78. It is to be hoped that, as a result, shipowners will be less speculative in their tonnage provision and an endeavour will be made to correlate total mercantile fleet capacity more closely with world trade demand. Much will depend on the political motivation of fleet development.

3. One aspect not specifically illustrated by the tables is the fact that in mid-1977 the fleets of the major shipbuilding nations accounted for about 40 per cent of total gross registered tonnage. Shipowners in the traditional maritime countries will thus be at pains to prevent the total eradication of shipbuilding in their countries at a time of much reduced world demand for new tonnage. The possession of a modern shipbuilding industry holds many advantages for such countries in that they can develop a modern fleet and ensure the efficient maintenance of existing vessels. Furthermore, it should facilitate closer co-operation between shipowners and shipyards with regard to viable fleet size and shipyard capacity in order to provide continuous employment for both.

4. The dramatic fall of 25 per cent in the UK fleet capacity in the period 1977–79 serves to emphasize the difficulties experienced by an established maritime nation adhering to the principle of the commercial freedom of the seas in the face of competition from fleets operating under political motivation.

5. During the past decade there has been a dramatic increase in the size of fleets operated not only by developing nations but also by those countries in the Orient whose trade has expanded rapidly. This is true of many of the Far Eastern countries, especially Japan, and has shifted the centre of gravity of the world fleet from the Western to the Eastern Hemisphere.

6. The growing practice of oil-producing countries to possess fleets of their own will have a profound effect, as has been seen in the expansion of the Arab fleet (Table 1.3).

There is every reason to suppose that the composition of the world mercantile fleet will continue to change, with state-run fleets growing at the expense of the free enterprise sector. Much will depend on the attitude of governments and the incentives that they offer shipowners for the provision of new tonnage in a period when world shipbuilding is depressed. This could involve the scrap and build technique, with shipowners building less tonnage than they demolish. As trade expansion and depression tends to be cyclical, ship operations should be much more profitable by the mid-1980s.

CHAPTER 2

Economics of International Trade

Function of international trade. Survey of international trade. Commodity trades. Flow of manufactured goods. Multinational companies. Freight forwarding. Major trading areas of the world. Preferential trading groups. International exchange rates.

In our examination of the economics of shipping, it is important that we view the industry against the background of international trade and thereby place the role of shipping in perspective. One must bear in mind that ships carry some 99 per cent of world trade in volume terms and almost 80 per cent in value terms, the remainder being conveyed primarily by air. Moreover, there is evidence of a trend towards more political involvement in the international exchange of goods and less freedom of commercial trade, while fiscal policies are becoming more prevalent in the attitude of various governments towards world trade. Factors such as these influence the economics of international shipping.

FUNCTION OF INTERNATIONAL TRADE

Trade among nations began for a variety of reasons. The haphazard distribution of natural resources around the world is one reason: some nations possess natural ores and chemical deposits in excess of their own requirements while other nations have none. For example, Britain has large reserves of coal but lacks many minerals such as nickel, copper and aluminium, and the Arab states have vast oil deposits but little else. The effects of climate on the cultivation of natural products is a second reason; some products will grow only in the tropics whereas others, such as citrus fruits, require a Mediterranean climate. Thirdly, some nations are unable to produce sufficient of a particular commodity to satisfy home demand; this is true of Britain's wheat requirement. With the development of industry and technology, however, there arose another incentive for nations to exchange their products. It was found that it made economic sense for a nation to specialize in certain activities and to produce those goods for which it enjoyed the greatest advantages; these were then exchanged for the products of nations which had advantages in other fields, giving rise to trade based on the 'law of comparative costs'.

Economists maintain that it will be advantageous for mankind if people specialize in those occupations in which they have the greatest comparative advantage or the least comparative disadvantage, leaving the production of goods and services for which they have little aptitude to others. This principle of specialization in certain trades and occupations is paramount in the theory of international trade. Nevertheless, complete specialization may never occur even if it is economically advantageous. For strategic or domestic reasons, a country may continue to produce goods in which it does not have an advantage. The benefits of specialization may also be affected by transport costs: the expense of moving goods and raw materials around the world narrows the limits within which it will be profitable to trade. Another impediment to the free flow of goods on the basis of comparative advantage is the possible introduction of artificial barriers to trade, such as tariffs or quotas.

The benefits deriving from the development of international trade are (a) a reduction in the cost of goods owing to the advantages possessed by the supplying country, (b) a greater variety of products, (c) wider markets for the producing country, thus leading to economies of large scale production, and (d) the overall growth of trade owing to reciprocal advantages.

SURVEY OF INTERNATIONAL TRADE

There is evidence of trading between nations as far back as the sixth century BC. In those early days the exchange of goods was conducted on a 'barter' basis now known as 'compensation trade'. For example, Solomon supplied food to the Lebanon against delivery of timber with which to build the Temple and early Phoenicians brought fabrics and dyestuffs to Cornwall in exchange for tin. A medium of exchange in the form of coins was introduced early in the fifth century BC; these were exchanged weight for weight where sufficient trust could be placed on their metallic values. This was not a foreign exchange system in the modern sense, however. By Roman times some trading was being conducted by exchange of coin, the first evidence of a foreign exchange system. Money changers such as those ejected from the Temple in Jerusalem were carrying on the dual functions of bullion dealing and foreign exchange that now form distinct but related markets. Upon the decline of the Roman Empire there was a widespread reversion to barter or the exchange of metallic coin by weight, but by the eleventh century AD money changing had once again become an important profession.

In the thirteenth century bills of exchange began to displace coin for trade purposes, creating a financial market that remained almost unchanged until the end of the eighteenth century. The importance of London was increasing throughout this period, although in the sixteenth and seventeenth centuries Antwerp and Amsterdam were probably more important. In the sixteenth century there evolved a system for forecasting future exchange rates, which in Holland, Belgium and Spain mainly took the form of betting. Mail transfers came into being after the French Revolution, but did not dislodge bills of exchange from their dominant position. Forward exchange dealing was developing throughout the nineteenth century, although in this regard London lagged behind such centres as Vienna, Berlin, Trieste and St Petersburg. With the growing influence of Great Britain in world trade, a large proportion of transactions was expressed in sterling, so that London merchants had little cause to buy or sell currencies, whilst abroad there was obviously need for a market in sterling against other currencies. Meanwhile, banks were developing techniques and services to facilitate the smooth conduct of international trade by establishing worldwide networks for the rapid transfer of funds and providing economic and credit information.

Just as the means of payment developed, so did the means of transport. With clippers giving way to steamers and ultimately oil-fired vessels and with the more recent advent of container transport, the transfer of goods around the world became quicker and safer. Cargo insurance underwent a parallel development.

As the basic requirements for the growth of international trade were met, there then developed a variety of methods and expertise to assist in the conduct of that trade, for example the services of export houses specializing in certain markets, the appointment of agents overseas, direct selling by travelling sales staff, the establishment of branch offices or subsidiary companies abroad and group marketing to share expenses.

Everything would suggest that the 'law of comparative costs' could operate to its fullest extent to the benefit of all. Unfortunately, the economic and political pressures to which individual nations are subject have tended to create barriers to the free flow of goods. These include the protection of home industries by means of tariffs and quotas, the imposition of customs duties to raise revenue, the prohibition of trade with certain countries – for example, the Arab nations' boycott of firms selling to Israel – and the formation of customs unions such as EFTA and the EEC. On the other hand, the more prosperous countries have also attempted to facilitate the sale of primary products by developing countries.

COMMODITY TRADES

Any article of commerce, that is to say anything offered for sale, may be regarded as a commodity. In modern marketing, however, the term is used in a more restricted sense to describe any primary product or raw material marketed internationally, either in its original state (e.g. mineral ores, corn, cotton) or after initial processing to make it acceptable as an industrial raw material (e.g. metal ingots); this definition therefore excludes manufactured goods.

As mentioned above, the essential factors of climate, topography and accessibility have led certain areas of the world to export commodities produced in excess of local requirements. Primary producers are increasingly aware of the importance of studying the requirements of their customers and adjusting their products accordingly. Whereas producers of manufactured goods are involved in the marketing of their wares and often deal direct with retailers, very few primary producers go further than to place their produce on the market through intermediaries such as merchants, brokers or jobbers. Moreover, the 'market' for manufactures is the nationwide chain of retailers, but for commodities there are market places where buyers meet the sellers (or the merchants or brokers acting on their behalf) and bargains are struck in conformity with the self-imposed rules of the market.

Some of the most important commodity markets of the world are situated in Great Britain, and particularly in London. The prices fixed in the London markets are reported daily in the financial press, which also comments on dealings in foreign terminal markets such as New York (e.g. coffee).

Three different types of sale are practised in the London markets:

sale of actual bulk of physical goods, sale by sample and sale by specification. Fruit, fish and other perishables are sold in bulk after inspection; imported frozen meat is sold by auction against sample at Smithfield; wool from Australia and New Zealand is auctioned on the Wool Exchange after inspection at the warehouse; and at the daily meeting of the London Metal Exchange members buy and sell such metals as copper, lead, tin and zinc by specification. The bullion market meets twice daily, with dealers both buying and selling gold and silver on behalf of their clients; all orders are tabled and the price is fixed to reflect the forces of supply and demand.

In markets where sale is by specification, the members' associations have devised standard specifications for various commodities. On the Metal Exchange lead is defined as 'good soft pig lead' and on the Baltic Exchange there are international standards for grain. Rubber is in the form of 'latex' or 'sheet' conforming to standards laid down by the Rubber Trading Association.

Members of any of these exclusive markets are required to comply with an established code of conduct, which takes the following form:

1. Transactions are conducted verbally, but where the commodity is not immediately transferred to the buyer against payment, written confirmations are exchanged. These take the form of standard 'contracts' that have evolved over time and must be employed by all parties.

2. Any dispute between buyer and seller is submitted to arbitration as laid down by the market authorities.

3. Where any commodity is sold by specification, the actual consignment is inspected and the price adjusted to take account of any divergence from standard.

Many of these markets have evolved an important form of 'futures' contract, usually for three months ahead. A 'future' is a contract by which the seller undertakes to deliver and the buyer undertakes to accept a stipulated quantity of a standard commodity at a future date, the date and related price being fixed at the time the contract is concluded, thus enabling dealers to guard against the risk of price fluctuations.

Two types of intermediary operate in the markets – the merchant and the broker. The merchant buys from one or more suppliers and on-sells to his clients in the same way as an export merchant, whilst the broker buys and sells on behalf of a principal and is paid a 'brokerage'. In some markets there are separate brokers for buying and selling. Where the commodity is sold by auction, the auctioneer is considered to be the agent of both buyer and seller. In many commodity transactions the goods are sold while still in transit, so that in effect the buyer purchases the documents of title and not the goods themselves. The main document involved is the bill of lading (for further details see *Elements of Shipping* and *The Elements of Export Practice*).

FLOW OF MANUFACTURED GOODS

As the developed countries began to specialize increasingly in manufacture, they reached a point where they no longer produced enough raw materials for their industries or food for their peoples. In consequence, they exported manufactured goods in exchange for raw materials and foodstuffs. The increase in specialization and the growth of technology resulted in the exchange of technical products between the more industrialized countries, so that manufactures were exported not only to buy raw materials and food but also in exchange for other technical products.

Scientific research and technological development have brought about an enormous increase in the volume and variety of manufactured goods. This has led to a rapid growth in the exchange of manufactured goods between industrialized countries, but it has also resulted in the development of synthetic substitutes for many natural products, such as synthetic rubber, plastics and man-made fibres. As a consequence, many primary producers have sought to acquire manufacturing expertise and to become at least partly industrialized.

The growth and direction of international trade are thus influenced by a multiplicity of factors: comparative advantage, which will encourage a country to specialize in certain products; political factors, where governments seek to control the movement of goods either to protect the value of the currency or for strategic reasons; the desire to diversify the economy, especially where the country has been dependent on a single product; and finally, a monopoly of the supply of an essential product by one country.

MULTINATIONAL COMPANIES

As world trade and its attendant risks increased, many firms realized the need to adopt an international strategy. Whereas previously they had built plant overseas whenever an export market reached sufficient size to support the investment, now they ensured that they had a plant wherever market analysis indicated a potential need. This change in policy has led to the creation of large multinational companies. As one company put it, 'We are no longer a British company with some international business but a British-based international organization'. The economic factors which have influenced the development of multinational corporations are (a) the use of local products, (b) savings in freight costs, (c) the availability of cheaper local labour, (d) tax concessions and available finance, (e) technical collaboration to spread development costs and secure new products, (f) the provision of more reliable demonstration, installation, delivery, repair and maintenance services from local facilities and (g) higher profits. These are coupled with strategic considerations such as (i) the need to control facilities of a certain size so as to gain market power and avoid the dispersion of resources, (ii) economies of scale in central services and research, (iii) fiscal advantages obtained by transferring goods at the most advantageous prices in order to minimize taxation, (iv) the existence of investment grants and (v) the possibility of shifting liquid capital to hedge against currency devaluations. Host countries welcome the establishment of subsidiaries of multinational companies because they bring employment, new technology and increased growth. They may or may not increase exports or imports. At the same time, host countries are wary of the possibility of price manipulation between members of the group, particularly in order to show profits where tax is lowest.

Shipping has played a major role in the development of multinational companies. Many such companies own or charter their own fleet so that they may convey raw materials and/or manufactured goods at cost rather than at liner conference rates. Moreover, they have complete control over schedules, with many of them owning or operating their own maritime terminals. All these factors aid the competitiveness of the product in the international market-place. The development of new activities and the expansion of existing ones by multinational corporations have added the exchange of skills and technology to the exchange of goods and services which make up international trade.

FREIGHT FORWARDING

This section will describe developments in the freight forwarding industry in broad terms and will leave aside the techniques of such matters as documentation and the processing of export consignments, which are fully treated in *The Elements of Export Practice*.

Since the early days of international trade there have been entrepreneurs who have arranged the transport of goods from one country to another. Eventually they came to be known as shipping and forwarding agents. Their modern counterparts, now termed freight forwarders, may still work as sole traders as their forebears did, but they are just as likely to be sizable companies with a worldwide network of offices and several thousand employees. In recent years mergers have led to the formation of larger companies able to raise capital more easily and to offer a wider range of services. Some freight forwarding organizations are now owned partly or wholly by major shipping companies, an arrangement which benefits the one through the provision of capital and the other through the direction of cargoes to the company's ships.

Since the late sixties the freight forwarding industry has undergone considerable change in line with innovations in the transport field and the growth in world trade, which the industry has helped to foster. The provision of warehousing facilities, a long-established part of the freight forwarder's business, has permitted the development of freight consolidation, the practice of combining consignments into standard load units. This has gone hand in hand with the introduction of packaging services and integrated transportation involving several modes of transport. Freight forwarders were in the forefront of the development of Ro/Ro road haulage services in short sea trades and containerization on deep sea services. Many now own or lease ISO containers and road haulage vehicles. More recently they have begun to promote the carriage of unaccompanied trailers in deep sea multi-purpose services.

Since 1977 freight forwarders have considerably expanded their business in the consolidation of air freight. Airlines belonging to IATA had previously marketed most of their cargo space themselves, but they have now practically abandoned the field to the freight forwarders, to whom they allocate space on freight aircraft. Freight forwarders are thus able to offer a complete service covering collection of the goods, documentation, packaging, carriage by air, customs clearance and delivery by their agent or representative abroad.

Freight forwarders tend to specialize in a particular trade, such as livestock, dangerous cargoes, art, bullion, household effects or indivisible loads. By acquiring specialized expertise they are able to raise the standard of service and realize economies of scale, thus ensuring that goods are conveyed under conditions of reliability and efficiency.

The main services offered by modern freight forwarders are the following:

(a) Evaluation of all the factors affecting a proposed international transit, including rates, transit times, schedules, documentation, packing, customs, statutory obligations, finance and insurance. On the basis of this the freight forwarder produces a transport distribution analysis outlining alternative services to enable the shipper to decide which transit to adopt, bearing in mind the terms of export sales contracts and any conditions imposed by the shipper himself.

(b) The collection and delivery of consignments, where required.

(c) Acceptance of the merchandise and either its conveyance throughout the transit (e.g. by TIR road haulage between the United Kingdom and continental Europe) or its sponsorship for carriage by container, air freight or road haulage. The freight forwarder may be responsible for documentation, clearance through customs, financial settlement and transit arrangements, depending on the extent to which the exporter wishes to make use of these services.

(d) Packaging. This facility, which forms an important part of the international forwarding business, is offered by many large agents.

(e) Consolidation of consignments for conveyance by container, air freight, train ferry or road haulage. The inclusive tariffs are lower than the cost of despatching the goods as break bulk consignments. Moreover, consolidation affords better protection to the goods, permitting lower insurance premiums.

(f) The simple booking of individual consignments on specific sailings or flights where consolidation is not desired.

(g) Arrangements with shipbrokers for chartering a vessel or aircraft to transport an indivisible load.

(h) Development of international trade for airlines, shipowners and road haulage operators. Freight forwarders earn commissions on the volume of traffic generated.

There can be no doubt that freight forwarders are making a very significant contribution to the development of world trade and, in particular, are facilitating the flow of manufactured goods. The complexity of world trade today calls for a high standard of service and a deep understanding of the trade and its associated distribution arrangements to ensure that the flow of goods is subject to no impediment. The recent tendency for freight forwarders to provide their own international transport facilities, such as road haulage vehicles and containers, is to be welcomed as it enables them to have closer control over operations and to achieve greater competitiveness, which itself aids the development of trade.

MAJOR TRADING AREAS OF THE WORLD

There are three main types of economy:

1. Free enterprise economies, where government control is at a minimum and trade and industry are largely run by private enterprise; the best example is the USA, but many of the developing countries also have this type of economy.

2. Mixed economies, where some industries are state-owned but many others and most trading activities are in the hands of private firms. The United Kingdom provides a good example of this type, although in fact all advanced nations and many developing countries have at least some state-run industry.

3. Planned economies, where the state runs all industry and commerce except for tiny pockets of free enterprise such as the smallholdings on which peasants are allowed to grow a few vegetables to sell for cash. This sort of economy is generally communist controlled and its international trade is conducted by state trading enterprises.

Trading patterns have gradually changed since the end of the Second World War. In the past, Western nations specialized in industrial products to exchange for the raw materials and food they required, whilst primary producers relied upon their sales of natural produce to buy industrial goods. Some countries with a favourable climate were able to combine industrial growth with the production of much of their food requirement.

The United Kingdom is probably the best example of a country which relied almost entirely on the export of its manufactures in exchange for raw materials and food. Under the colonial system this was a very satisfactory arrangement for Britain, but with the end of the Empire the newly independent nations began to cast their net more widely in seeking buyers for their produce and suppliers of their industrial needs. At the same time they sought to diversify their economies and develop some industry.

The basic geographical pattern of produce remains largely unchanged for reasons of climate and the location of raw materials – that is, Western Europe and North America for industrial goods; South America for coffee and rubber (Brazil), wheat and beef (Argentina) and minerals such as copper (Peru); the Near East for rubber and tin; Australasia for wool and mutton; and Africa for timber, cocoa and vegetable oils. However, these divisions are no longer as sharply defined as they were previously. Japan has entered the list of manufacturing countries in a big way; the Arab nations have developed their oil production; and countries in South America, Africa and the Near East have begun to establish industries. At the same time, the Western nations have attempted to come closer to self-sufficiency in food and to intensify the search for minerals at home; examples of this are the encouragement of agriculture and the search for oil in the United Kingdom and the development of fruit and vegetable cultivation in countries bordering the Mediterranean. The interchange of goods between nations is thus expanding, diversifying and moving away from the previous clearly defined paths.

PREFERENTIAL TRADING GROUPS

Since the very beginning of international trade, certain trading groups have felt a desire to join together for mutual protection and assistance. An early example of this was the Hanseatic League founded in northern Germany during the thirteenth century, an arrangement that came to an end upon the disintegration of Germany as a result of the Thirty Years' War (1618–48).

The more important preferential trading groups of modern times may be summarized as follows.

British Commonwealth
This was a free trade area of considerable importance, comprising the members of the British Commonwealth of Nations. As their economies became more highly developed, however, member nations ceased to maintain the system of preferences and sought a wider sphere of trading activity. The vestiges of the Commonwealth preference system disappeared when the United Kingdom joined the European Economic Community in 1973.

European Free Trade Association (EFTA)
The United Kingdom was disinclined to join the EEC at its inception in 1957, as the member states wished to go far beyond the removal of customs barriers. Accordingly, Great Britain, Norway, Sweden, Denmark, Portugal, Austria and Switzerland signed the Stockholm Convention in 1959 establishing the European Free Trade Association, whereby they agreed to reduce import duties among themselves and to maintain their individual tariffs towards non-member countries. Finland became an associate member in 1961 and Iceland a full member in 1970. Now that Denmark and the United Kingdom have joined the EEC, the significance of EFTA has declined considerably.

European Economic Community (EEC)
As the reconstruction of Europe was beginning after the end of the Second World War, there emerged the idea of a supernational European community based initially on economic union but developing towards political union. It evolved through the following stages:

(a) Belgium, the Netherlands and Luxembourg formed the Benelux customs union in 1948.

(b) The European Payments Union was set up in 1950 to help solve the balance of payments problems of individual countries.

(c) In 1952 six countries – Belgium, France, West Germany, Italy, Luxembourg and the Netherlands – joined together to form the European Coal and Steel Community.

(d) In 1957 these six nations signed the Treaty of Rome by which they agreed to form the EEC, which came into existence on 1st January 1958.

The Treaty provided for the removal of customs barriers and

other obstacles to trade between member states, the introduction of a common external tariff towards third countries and common policies for agriculture and transport. Plans were also made for the harmonization of taxation; for example, the French VAT system was to be adopted by the other members.

On 1st January 1973 the United Kingdom, Denmark and Ireland became full members of the EEC. Greece joined in 1981 and Spain and Turkey have also made application for membership.

Council for Mutual Economic Aid

Set up in 1949, the Council for Mutual Economic Aid (CMEA or Comecon) groups together the USSR, Poland, Romania, the German Democratic Republic, Czechoslovakia, Hungary, Bulgaria, Mongolia, Cuba and Vietnam. Although not a member, Yugoslavia enjoys special status that enables it to participate in certain spheres of Comecon's activities. The Council aims to attain self-sufficiency through the complementary development of member countries' economies on the basis of central planning. In its early years it contented itself with co-ordinating the foreign trade of member countries, many of which have been reluctant to agree to further proposals for integration.

The benefits to be derived from free trade areas stem from the increased market opened to members, especially where the area has an affluent population. Their advantages were soon appreciated, and free trade areas have been set up in various parts of the world; it is estimated that about two-thirds of world trade is already conducted between such groups.

Besides EFTA, the EEC and Comecon, the following free trade areas have been created:

(a) Latin American Free Trade Association (LAFTA), comprising Brazil, Bolivia, Mexico, Argentina, Colombia, Peru, Venezuela, Chile, Ecuador, Uruguay and Paraguay; in 1983 LAFTA will be replaced by the Latin American Integration Association (ALADI), a less ambitious and more flexible form of co-operation.

(b) Central American Common Market (CACM), whose members are Guatemala, El Salvador, Honduras, Nicaragua and Costa Rica.

(c) Caribbean Free Trade Association (CARIFTA), the fore-runner of the present Caribbean Community and Common Market (CARICOM), which comprises Antigua, Barbados, Belize, Dominica, Grenada, Guyana, Jamaica, Montserrat, St Christopher-Nevis-Anguilla, St Lucia, St Vincent and the Grenadines, and Trinidad and Tobago.

The activities of these various trading groups (with the exception of Comecon) have to conform to the principles laid down in the General Agreement on Tariffs and Trade (GATT), which requires it signatories:

1. To concert together to achieve a mutual reduction of tariff barriers and preferences;
2. To avoid discrimination by means of tariffs against foreign products which compete with home products;
3. To abolish quantitative controls; and
4. To remove existing restrictions imposed by exchange control.

Although several of these rules have been given practical application as trade has been liberalized, it is unlikely that the general requirements of GATT will be implemented in the present state of world trade.

INTERNATIONAL EXCHANGE RATES

The subject of foreign exchange relates to the exchange of various currencies one for another. On the practical side it concerns the methods of settling foreign debts, the means of payment and the services of banks and brokers. Settlement of debts between parties in the same country is quite simply effected by the payment of money, which the creditor is prepared to accept as it is the legal tender of the country. Where the payer and recipient live in different countries and use different currencies, however, there arises the need for a system of conversion – the foreign exchange market. Unlike the markets in commodities or stocks and shares, the foreign exchange market has no centre but consists merely of telephonic communications between dealers (at the banks) and brokers.

Rate of exchange
The price of one currency in terms of another is called the rate of

exchange; it is the number of units of one currency that will be exchanged for a given number of units of another currency. Hence rates against sterling are the number of foreign currency units to the pound. A glance at the financial press shows that two closing rates are quoted for each currency; the higher is the market's buying rate for that currency and the lower the market's selling rate. Transactions between dealers are conducted at approximately those rates. A banker who is asked to buy or sell foreign currency relies upon the market for cover, and the prices at which he can obtain this cover are market rates. Hence in quoting to his customer he bases his rates on those ruling in the market, adjusted to make provision for profit.

The market rates quoted in the press are 'spot' rates, i.e. those applied to transactions for completion immediately or at the latest within two working days from the date of the deal. As currency is a commodity like any other, its price will be governed by the interaction of demand and supply and hence by short- and long-term factors influencing buyers and sellers. The short-term factors fall into two categories – commercial and financial.

Commercial operations relate to trade in goods and services which, as we saw in Chapter 1, make up the current account of the balance of payments and give rise to payments and receipts in various currencies, thereby determining supply and demand in the foreign exchange markets. Where a country's total purchases exceed its sales, there will be an excess supply of its currency, which will cause its price to decrease, in other words the rate of exchange will fall. Expectations of future movements in exchange rates give rise to 'leads and lags'; a debtor will pay a foreign currency debt before it is due if he expects that currency to appreciate in value (lead) or delay payment if he expects it to depreciate (lag).

Financial operations come under a variety of headings:

(a) Stock Exchange operations: the purchase of securities on foreign stock exchanges (bourses) by private or corporate investors in order to yield a return or in the expectation of a capital appreciation. These are portfolio investments as opposed to 'industrial' investments, which represent capital placed by manufacturers in subsidiary or associated enterprises abroad.

(b) Banking operations: the transfer of funds by bankers for investment or deposit in foreign centres.

(c) Speculation: transactions based on the expectation that the exchange rate of a particular currency will change in response to some political or natural event. Whether the operator buys or sells a currency depends on whether he anticipates a rise or fall in value.

(d) Interest payments: interest on loans and dividends from investment.

(e) Loan payments: the issue of a loan in one country on behalf of a borrower in another gives rise to a payment across the exchanges from the country of the lender to that of the borrower which will have an adverse impact on the exchange rate of the lending country's currency and cause that of the borrowing country to appreciate. This effect would be offset if the proceeds of the loan were used to purchase goods or services from the lending country. Upon repayment of the loan the reverse effect will occur.

(f) Inter-governmental transfers: governments borrow from and lend to each other in the same way as private individuals and trading companies; the payments resulting from such loans have the same effect as that outlined above.

(g) Exchange stabilization: official operations in the foreign exchange market in order to control exchange rate movements by varying the relation between supply and demand. These operations are usually directed at keeping fluctuations to a minimum, although sometimes a government may deliberately seek to raise or lower the exchange rate of its currency.

Forward exchange
In view of the increasing amount of business conducted on credit terms, it is quite likely that a merchant will be liable to pay his supplier in the latter's currency at a future date or to receive foreign currency at a future date from a buyer. With exchange rates floating at present, he is vulnerable to any changes in currency values that may occur in the interval between conclusion of the contract and the date on which payment is due. It is to provide cover against such exchange risks that the 'forward exchange' market came into existence. The merchant contracts with a bank to purchase or sell one currency in exchange for another at a predetermined rate on an agreed future date. He thus knows how much he will eventually pay or receive in his own currency, and any intervening fluctuations in the exchange rate will not affect him.

Forward contracts may be 'fixed' or 'option'. A fixed forward is a contract with a specific performance date. A forward option stipulates a period of time during which performance is to take place, the actual date then being chosen by the customer. It should be clearly understood that the 'option' is not whether the customer deals or not – he is fully committed to the transactions: it relates only to the date on which he takes or delivers the currency concerned.

Forward rates

The rates for forward exchange deals are quoted as a premium or discount on the spot rate, i.e. an amount above or below spot; sometimes they are at 'par' with spot. For example, if the forward dollar/sterling rate is quoted at a discount on the spot rate (measured in the conventional way as the number of dollars to a pound), then in terms of dollars sterling is cheaper forward than spot. Conversely, if the forward rate is at a premium, sterling is dearer forward than spot. In calculating the rate for a forward deal, a premium is added to the spot rate, whereas a discount is deducted from it. Forward margins (discount or premium) are determined by interest rate differentials and by market expectations of future spot exchange rates. Currencies in which interest rates are relatively low tend to be dearer forward than spot in terms of currencies in which interest rates are relatively high. The press usually quotes forward margins for one, three and six months forward, but by arrangement with the bank it is possible to cover for longer periods, depending on the currency concerned.

A customer who has contracted to buy foreign currency but finds that he no longer requires it will still have to take delivery of the currency at the agreed forward rate; he can then sell it back to the bank at the ruling spot rate. Similarly, if the customer has not received the foreign currency he has contracted to sell, he will have to buy the amount required at the ruling spot rate for delivery to the bank. In practice, the bank may merely debit or credit the difference to the customer's account. Where circumstances cause a delay in fulfilment of a contract it may often be extended at an adjusted rate by arrangement with the bank. In the United Kingdom the Export Credits Guarantee Department (ECGD) will cover not only losses due to the failure of a foreign buyer to pay but also the cost, if any, of closing out forward exchange contracts made in connection with the commercial transaction (see *The Elements of Export Practice*, Chapter 10).

From the above it will be seen that the forward exchange market enables the ordinary merchant to protect himself against fluctuations in exchange rates. Problems can still arise, however, where expenditure and receipts are expressed in a number of different currencies. One example of this is found in connection with freight charges. For the sake of convenience a conference's rates of freight are expressed in a single currency called the 'tariff currency', usually the US dollar. Nevertheless, freight can be paid in another currency, so that agreement has to be reached on the basis for conversion of the sum involved. Where adjustments in relevant currency values have resulted in a reduction in the rates of freight or increases in shipowners' operating costs, it has been the practice of conferences to increase tariff rates of freight or to introduce or increase a 'currency adjustment factor' (CAF).

A shipowner naturally calculates in terms of his own currency and if it depreciates against the tariff unit he seeks to impose a surcharge to protect the real value of his revenue in relation to his expenditure, which may be in a variety of other currencies.

There has been a tendency to regard the CAF as a means of keeping ratios of past rates of exchange fixed for all time. Changes in the terms of trade owing to the different rates of inflation in various countries have not been taken into account when calculating sea freights. Relationships between currencies have, however, changed considerably. When the value of sterling was falling the system favoured the British exporter in terms of freight rates; when sterling began to appreciate, however, shipowners in other countries applied a currency adjustment. The situation became more complicated when rates of exchange were allowed to float and the dollar was effectively devalued. The system which had stood the test of all the upheavals in exchange rates began to show signs of strain. The heart of the problem is that if there were a parity of CAFs it would be to the disadvantage of British shippers, but continental European shippers argue that if basic rate parity is maintained then CAF parity should also be the rule. If the present CAF disparity is permitted then basic rate disparity should also be introduced. The various conferences serving different areas of the world have reacted to changing circumstances in different ways and a final solution to the problem has yet to be found.

CHAPTER 3

Economics of Ship Design

Influence of cost, construction and safety factors. Ship design criteria.
Economics of ship propulsion.

This chapter outlines the basic factors likely to influence the design
of a modern vessel compatible with the market needs of the 1980s
and beyond. It is not a technical assessment but primarily an
evaluation of the economic and related factors relevant to efficient
ship design; it should be read in conjunction with Chapter 4, which
deals with ship investment criteria.

INFLUENCE OF COST, CONSTRUCTION AND SAFETY FACTORS

Let us first review the trends stemming from developments of the
past decade that will influence ship specifications in the 1980s and
beyond.

(a) Extensive legislation regarding the construction of ships has
been adopted during the past decade, as may be seen from the list
of conventions sponsored by IMCO (see *Elements of Shipping*).
Particular emphasis has been placed on ship safety, crew accommodation as prescribed by the ILO and the control of pollution.
Moreover, bulk carriers conveying dangerous classified cargoes are
strictly regulated to reduce the risk involved.

(b) Manning levels on vessels are likely to fall during the next
decade, with greater emphasis on crew versatility. This will entail
raising the standard of crew accommodation, introducing more
labour-saving devices, particularly in the galley, and employing
better ship maintenance techniques based on improved marine
technology. Moreover, passenger and crew accommodation will be
finished with a decor that is easy to clean, largely maintenance-free
and, of course, fire resistant.

(c) Requirements concerning the range of life saving equipment
and its survey are likely to become more stringent.

(d) The question of fuel costs is one of increasing concern to
shipowners and will be a major consideration in the choice of
propulsion units and hull lines in the 1980s. It is also a major factor

31

behind the development of long lasting anti-fouling systems to counter marine growth and the use of self-polishing copolymer paint, which has proved particularly popular with ULCC and VLCC tonnage. The subject of ship propulsion is considered separately at the conclusion of this chapter.

(e) A greater degree of nationalism and trade protectionism will emerge in the next decade. Accordingly, governments will become increasingly involved with shipping practice and management and with the financing of fleets. Such countries might impose certain ship design criteria, such as a particular form of propulsion to reduce their heavy fuel import bill. International politics will play an increasing role in shipping in the long term, as emphasized in Chapter 14.

(f) The range of navigational equipment and shipboard facilities to speed up cargo transhipment and provide quicker access to and from ports will increase. Examples include the bow thruster, auto-pilots, greater use of computers, bridge control and the automated monitoring of machinery. Electronics – particularly micropro-cessors – will play an increasing role in the day-to-day operation of the vessel, with more emphasis on automation as an aid to reducing crew manning levels.

(g) The more intensive use of vessels will tend to shorten their depreciable life to twelve years in the case of bulk carriers and fifteen in that of general cargo vessels. Hence the greater the range of sophisticated equipment, such as aids to the transhipment of cargo and more rapid manoeuvring in port, the more emphasis will be placed on the cost effectiveness of such facilities.

(h) The commercial managers of shipping companies are exerting growing pressure to reduce the time spent conducting ship surveys, as the immobilization of vessels for periods of between ten days and a month is not only costly in terms of replacement but also tends to reduce service quality, which today is the shipper's prime consider-ation in selecting a particular service. Advances in ship design and the development of in-water survey and inspection in order to dispense with periodic dry docking promise to bring major im-provements in this regard.

(i) In the bulk carrier sector speed will become less important, in contrast to liner services, where shippers place a premium on rapidity. A service speed of 13 knots may become more common.

(j) The trend towards the construction of larger vessels to exploit the economies of scale and improve crew productivity is likely to continue in certain categories of tonnage, particularly those below 100 000 dwt. Much will depend on the basic economics of each ship investment and the availability of the infrastructure, particularly ports, to handle the increased ship capacity and still maintain a steady improvement in ship turnround times. However, in the bulk cargo field, particularly the tanker sector, it is possible that very few VLCCs or ULCCs will be built. Experience has shown that they are not the ideal size ship in periods of fluctuating demand and that they tend to be rather inflexible in operation as few ports have the resources to handle them fully laden. Vessels of between 100 000 and 200 000 dwt are more likely to produce optimum results.

(k) The 1970s were a time of unpredictable market trends and volatile fluctuations in some trades owing to a variety of political, financial and economic factors. The ship operator of the 1980s will thus need a fleet of versatile vessels capable of meeting varying market requirements. This will call for multi-purpose vessels of optimum specification, examples of which are to be found on pp. 229–235. The more complex designs required to meet varying and sometimes conflicting needs in terms of layout and equipment will undoubtedly increase the initial capital cost, but should significantly improve profitability.

(l) Maritime canals and inland waterways are likely to play a more important role in the 1980s. Maritime canals will enable deep sea vessels to save distance and thus fuel, while the further development of inland waterways will encourage an extension of the feeder type tonnage into this market and promote the expansion of the LASH and BACO barge carrier concepts explained on pp. 127–128.

(m) The development of more economical shipbuilding techniques will undoubtedly continue throughout the 1980s. Continual improvements in design techniques are facilitating construction, the use of flat plate instead of rolled curved plate can reduce building costs and the use of prefabrication is now universal. More recently, savings have been made by installing equipment and piping at the building stage rather than during fitting-out. Computerized techniques have also aided design and production, including substantially reducing construction man-hours in many areas.

(n) Shippers will place increasing emphasis on service quality, involving such factors as reliability, competitive tariffs and attractive transit times. Tonnage built in the 1980s must reflect these requirements. Combined transport operations will continue to expand.

Other considerations will undoubtedly emerge as the 1980s proceed. Nevertheless, it is essential that the foregoing factors be borne in mind in evolving the optimum ship design of the future.

SHIP DESIGN CRITERIA

The scope for making the wrong decision in ship design has increased greatly in recent years with the increase in the size of vessels and the expansion in the range of types available. It is axiomatic that a ship design must be the best for the job, but technical criteria such as minimum resistance are not enough. It is now generally accepted that the main criterion must be an economic one that gives full weight to technical factors. To design the optimum ship, the influence of different design features on initial cost must be evaluated in depth; the shipbuilder is much better able than the shipowner to quantify accurately the cost of alternative hull proportions, materials or machinery arrangements. However, initial cost is only part of the overall picture. As shipowners become more ready to apply the principle of minimum cost over the life of the vessel rather than minimum initial cost, shipbuilders and naval architects will have to show not that their designs are the cheapest, but that they are the most profitable.

Investment in a ship of a given specification usually involves four main factors, namely (1) the shipbuilding cost, (2) the operating expenses in the trade in which she will be engaged, (3) the cargo and passenger traffic volume, and (4) the level of tariffs applicable to the traffic forecasts. The summation of such data will make it possible to draw up a cash flow statement for the entire depreciable life of the vessel and from this derive a profit and loss statement showing the rate of return on the investment. Such an exercise, which is beyond the scope of this book, is usually undertaken by specialist investment accountants in the shipping company using the techniques of discounted cash flow (DCF) and net present value (NPV). Many such calculations are made to devise the vessel which will produce the most favourable investment return overall having regard to all the circumstances. A further point to bear in mind is the most economic deployment of the ship's capacity. It is not necessarily correct to assume that the vessel is operating at her optimum level when she is down to her loadline, especially in the case of general cargo vessels conveying a variety of cargoes rated according to volume or weight. It is usually a mixture of such rated traffic that produces the most favourable financial result.

There are two main design options: one is the preliminary or tender design, which comprises a rough estimate of price from the shipbuilder in response to a simple indication of requirements from the shipowner. The other is the detailed or contract design worked up by the shipbuilder on the basis of a fuller statement of requirements. The latter technique is more common and involves close collaboration between the shipbuilder and the shipping company, which might engage naval architects as consultants if such expertise is not available in the company itself.

After a number of such competitive tenders from shipyards at home and abroad have been evaluated, the contract should be awarded at a fixed price to the yard offering the best deal bearing in mind factors such as price, delivery date, credit availability and standard of workmanship. Provision for arbitration should be made in order to settle any likely disputes; the contract should also include the usual guarantee of materials and workmanship and adequate penalty clauses to cover failure to deliver the ship on the specified date. In the case of overseas shipyards the price may be based on a composite currency unit to safeguard the shipowner's financial situation.

Working in close liaison with the shipbuilder, the naval architect will be expected to undertake the following tasks:

(a) Assess market demand for the new tonnage by means of market research and other management techniques, taking particular account of long-term needs.

(b) Ascertain possible ship types, overall dimensions/capacity and optimum speed related to market needs.

(c) Draw up a preliminary technical specification, giving a range of alternative ship designs. Computer-based procedures will often be used.

(d) Make a broad estimate of the cost of the ship and evaluate her operating expenses and earning potential therefrom. Such an evaluation would be carried out in respect of all the ship design options.

(e) Select the optimum design of vessel. This could involve the use of mathematical programming techniques and should allow for intangible factors.

(f) Finally, process the detailed ship design and submit the final specification for evaluation.

The foregoing evaluation will make it possible to compile a detailed quotation for the specified vessel. This will comprise the following elements:

1. The actual hull form
2. The general arrangement plan of the ship
3. Draught, length and beam
4. Total ship capacity, including cargo and/or passenger accommodation
5. The trading pattern forecast for the vessel's entire operational life. For example, the ship may be earmarked for two trades, spending the first five years of her assignment carrying high volume break bulk cargo in one trade and the following ten years carrying containerized general cargo in another. This will influence the ship design.
6. Freeboard
7. Optimum speed
8. General ship structure, including scantlings
9. Actual displacement of the vessel and tonnage (GRT or NRT)
10. Longitudinal strength of the vessel
11. Ship's machinery – an important element in optimum ship performance
12. Lightweight, cargo deadweight and volume requirements
13. Stability and trim of the vessel in accordance with her trading limits
14. The ship's powering, which will be largely influenced by the hull form and the optimum speed dictated by the market need
15. The general fitting-out and equipping of the vessel
16. General bunkering and stores needs. For example, low fuel consumption lengthens the passage between bunkering calls.
17. The general economic evaluation. This involves producing perhaps three options within different initial cost and optimum results bands. For example, of two ships with the same broad profile, the faster vessel may require greater provision for bunkering owing to increased fuel consumption and will consequently have a smaller cargo capacity.

Let us now examine the broad factors influencing ship size. As these will vary according to circumstances, they should be regarded as no more than general guidelines.

(a) Longer voyages tend to favour larger vessels as they can exploit the economies of scale in the trade, thereby maximizing revenue at the expense of only a marginal increase in cost elements such as crew complement.

(b) Situations where cargo is shipped in only one direction and the vessel returns in ballast also favour larger vessels on account of the economies of scale.

(c) Times of high interest rates favour smaller vessels, mainly because they are more flexible in operation. Moreover, smaller ships are usually able to find cargoes more easily in times of depressed trade and so attain economic payloads to fund the investment. This explains the popularity of parcel tankers and the use of partially laden VLCCs and ULCCs on a multi-port schedule to keep them in operation.

(d) Larger vessels such as ULCCs or VLCCs are limited in the range of ports where they may call fully laden owing to their draught and overall size.

(e) The frequent service favours smaller vessels, as they can achieve a rapid turnround more easily than can large ships. This disadvantage of size can be mitigated, however, by loading and discharging cargo simultaneously, as is now possible with some modern tonnage, particularly two-deck Ro/Ro vessels.

(f) The more efficient and faster the cargo transhipment arrangements, the further the pendulum of advantage swings in favour of larger vessels. The reduction in port turnround time helps maximize a vessel's revenue through improved utilization. Obviously, the larger the vessel the greater the revenue benefit.

(g) The smaller vessel is better equipped in economic terms to carry more valuable cargoes as it is less expensive to operate at the higher speeds demanded than a ship of larger capacity.

We shall now turn our attention to the factors that will influence the ultimate ship design. It will be appreciated that a number of options in outline ship design are usually evaluated before the final selection is made. Remember, too, that the ultimate consideration is not the initial cost of the ship but its profitability throughout its operational life.

The basic parameters of ship design for a particular trade or trades are the following:

1. The vessel size. This involves her overall length, draught, beam and other dimensions including her tonnage, which may vary from one voyage to another.

2. Size of the crew and the scope for rearranging crew duties in order to reduce the complement.

3. Maximum and economical speeds of the ship and overall transit time. The tendency is not to build faster vessels but to improve overall transit time by reducing the time spent in port.

4. Fuel consumption, both on passage and in port, fuel cost per tonne and the likely trend; an increasingly important aspect at a time of high bunker prices. The tendency is to provide machinery that burns low grade fuel, such as diesel engines.

5. Number of operational days per year; survey periods are tending to be reduced to an acceptable minimum.

6. Anticipated operational life of the vessel and its components. Nowadays vessels are operated more intensively, so that a period of fifteen years is regarded as an optimum life.

7. Load factor, which may vary according to the trade and season.

8. A broad appraisal of the cargo specification in terms of quantity, shape, stowage factors, packaging, handling, cargo value and volume. An analysis would be required if cargo shipments varied markedly in the course of the year.

9. Variations in cargo specification available for shipment. In the summer perishable cargo might predominate whereas in the winter a higher proportion of consumer goods might be carried. The more versatile the vessel, the more favourable will be the load factor and the financial results. However, the benefits of adaptability must be weighed against the additional cost of such tonnage.

10. Details of cargo stowage arrangements. Ideally these should be made as flexible as possible and have regard to future trends.

11. The method of shipment. This includes Ro/Ro units, containerized cargo, bulk cargo (dry or liquid) and ocean barges as found in LASH.

12. The prospect of balanced cargo flows. With the growing practice of flag discrimination, shipowners are finding the imbalance of trade in their services more difficult to resolve. (See pp. 199–219).

13. The level of competition and alternative services, particularly

from the point of view of designing a vessel that will be more attractive to the market than existing tonnage.

14. Features of the route of trade, embracing its physical characteristics, length, number of ports of call and general bunkering pattern. This involves making provision for any particular navigational aids, adequate bunkering capacity, facilities to cater for any variation in crew or cargo needs according to the season and the possibility of operating the vessel in a variety of trades at different times of the year.

15. The actual time in port, a factor of increasing importance as greater emphasis is placed on rapid turnround in order to improve overall transit times.

16. Restrictions or constraints imposed by the port or terminal. This will involve draught, beam, cargo, transhipment arrangements and other factors.

17. Shore investments, such as berths and handling equipment. This can prove very costly, particularly if a purpose-built bulk cargo vessel requiring capital intensive transhipment facilities is to call at several ports.

18. The volume of cargo loaded or discharged per hour. This calls for particular attention in order to reduce the time spent in port.

19. Initial cost of the vessel. This requires careful evaluation in the light of the investment budget and the return on capital.

20. Financial conditions, comprising general funding arrangements (see pp. 47–51), the availability of subsidies for building or operating vessels (see pp. 44–45), short and long-term tax concessions, depreciation allowances, provision for inflation and prospective revenues, taking account of freight rebates and the payment of commissions.

21. The direct operating cost of the ship in terms of crew wages, fuel, stores, maintenance and port dues; with regard to the latter, particular attention should be paid to net register tonnage/gross register tonnage.

22. Fixed overheads such as depreciation, interest on loans and survey costs.

In practice, many of the foregoing parameters will remain constant for various ship designs while others may necessitate extensive technical calculations; for example, payloads (effective deadweight) require the accurate estimation of deadweight and power from principal main dimensions. Estimates of both initial and operating costs must also reflect the differences between the alternative designs.

A dynamic view should be taken of physical restrictions, by assessing the possibility of changes during the ship's life. This is particularly true in the case of draught; it may be worth paying a little more for a deeper draught ship, even though the vessel may not be able to operate fully laden on more than a small percentage of voyages during her life. If there are no restrictions on length or beam, a larger ship operating at reduced draught may well have a greater payload and offer lower freighting costs per tonne than a smaller ship down to her marks. Choice of optimum size is therefore a trade-off between the known costs of greater size and the chances of being able to use the additional capacity sufficiently often during the ship's life.

To sum up, therefore, we have seen that marketing requirements, overall trade demand, service frequency and route characteristics (such as route length and the number of countries to be served) will be the prime considerations in the shipowner's choice of design. Ship speed will be a significant factor, but must be viewed in the context of overall transit time and, in particular, time spend in port. Greater emphasis will be placed on the versatility of ship deployment, which will be essential in overcoming trade fluctuations over the life of the vessel. The manager with a fleet of multi-purpose vessels will be better able to ensure full ship deployment than one with an excessive proportion of highly specialized tonnage. More attention will also be paid to increasing the ship payload through increased deadweight capacity; this will involve more skilful hull design and the use of lighter construction materials. Much progress has already been made in this area during the past two decades.

The importance of ship design in ensuring that the optimum vessel is built will undoubtedly increase, thus further enhancing the role of the naval architect within the ship management team. He will provide many of the innovations from which the improved profitability of the fleet will flow.

ECONOMICS OF SHIP PROPULSION

Ship propulsion is becoming an increasingly important aspect of ship design, as economic fuel consumption is clearly bound up with the optiumum vessel configuration. Shipowners are extremely eager to reduce fuel consumption but at the same time sustain or even improve existing speeds and overall transit times by means of more efficient hull design, better hull coatings and quicker turn-round in port. Although much will depend on the vessel type, trade and schedules, there are many factors conducive to the design of vessels with a high optimum speed:

(a) Valuable cargoes demand fast transits, whereas low value cargoes tend not to be able to bear the higher freight charges. In broad terms, higher value cargoes are normally conveyed in the liner cargo trades, while lower value cargoes are found primarily in the bulk carrier market, some of which operates under tramp conditions.

(b) Faster ships tend to be able to charge a higher rated tariff. In short, they are able to generate more income on a quicker sailing than a vessel with a similar specification but slower speed and conveying lower rated cargo. It may be argued that the higher construction cost per deadweight tonne of a container vessel offering fast schedules justifies the higher tariff it can command.

(c) Faster vessels draw greater advantage from rapid turnround in port than does slower tonnage.

(d) Most new tonnage is financed by raising loans. As a vessel of moderate speed makes more voyages a year than a slower ship, it can have a higher revenue earning potential and thus a better prospect of meeting the capital charges.

(e) With crew costs continuing to escalate, the faster vessel can make more productive use of the crew as it can make more voyages a year.

(f) Vessels with high speed potential are able to operate at two levels; in peak periods they can run at high speed, thus providing extra capacity by making more voyages, while at other times they can operate at a slower speed. This avoids the heavy expense of chartering additional tonnage to provide extra ship capacity in peak periods.

(g) In times when capital to finance new tonnage is in short supply a faster vessel would be more productive but would incur higher fuel costs. Two faster vessels are likely to produce a better investment return overall than three slower vessels each of equal capacity and would absorb less capital. Likewise, in the event of a shortage of shipyard capacity, two faster vessels would involve fewer shipyard resources than three slower ships of similar capacity.

(h) Faster vessels tend to give improved sea performance in adverse weather.

It must be stressed that these points in favour of speed are generalizations and that in practice no two situations are likely to be identical. Nor do they sanction speed for its own sake – an increase of one knot beyond a vessel's optimum speed may raise initial machinery costs by up to 20 per cent – 6 to 7 per cent on the total ship cost – and will undoubtedly bring a substantial increase in fuel consumption. In addition, the more powerful machinery and larger fuel requirements associated with higher speed will occupy a larger proportion of the vessel's total capacity.

Ideally, the shipowner should aim for the vessel with the maximum economic speed compatible with the optimum ship design, a combination likely to proclude the most favourable investment return. As already stated, much will depend on the trade in which the vessel is engaged, which will determine her broad specification.

In technical terms one must bear in mind that a vessel's resistance to many forms of motion varies approximately as the square of the speed and that installed power and fuel consumption vary as the cube. Moreover, if turnround time is left out of account, ship productivity can only increase in direct proportion to the speed. Hence there is an optimum speed which reconciles both technical and economic factors, at which point the increased capital and operating costs of additional speed outweigh the increased revenue. The equation is complicated by the relationship between hull fullness and the speed/length ratio; bulk carriers have relatively low speeds, partly because of the need for large deadweight and high block coefficients.

The choice of propulsion unit will become a significant factor in the 1980s. At present the diesel engine is the natural choice of most shipowners in view of its low fuel consumption and initial cost. In addition, diesel-powered vessels can travel further without refuelling than can steam turbine ships. Alternatively, the relatively short distances between bunker ports mean that less shipboard bunkering space need be provided, thereby releasing more for cargo accommodation. Some owners are converting diesel units to burn low grade bunker fuel. The problems that still arise with diesels relate mainly to noise, vibration and the relatively high maintenance costs. Research is being conducted to overcome these difficulties.

The steam turbine, with high initial outlay, low maintenance cost and exceptional durability, was the first choice for passenger tonnage, mammoth tankers and many deep sea container vessels until 1978. For passenger vessels it has the added advantage of being vibration free. Regrettably, however, such machinery has a higher specific fuel consumption and is therefore uneconomical compared with the diesel engine. As a result, many owners are now replacing their steam turbines by diesel engines, thereby prolonging the useful life of the vessels. Similar remarks apply to gas turbines, although vessels with this means of propulsion are relatively few.

Over the next few years the fuel bill is likely to become more stabilized but the incentive will remain to improve propulsion techniques and give more attention to hull form and coating techniques. It has been predicted that modern reheat turbine plant, perhaps with fluidized bed combustion, will be competitive with diesel engines by the end of the decade. The possibility of alternative fuels must not be discounted; for example, within ten years nuclear power may be a commercial proposition in mercantile tonnage, although its introduction will probably be a slow process owing to the opposition it engenders. A more likely occurrence is the development of coal-fired propulsion, a method that may be attractive in conjunction with the turbine engine, which has a thermal efficiency of about half that of the diesel engine. A recent study predicts fuel savings of up to 70 per cent – based on 1979 oil prices – using finely powdered coal as fuel on a 120 000 dwt coal carrier of 23 500 horsepower between Japan and Australia. On such a voyage the collier would consume about 700 tonnes of coal; about 17 per cent of this weight would remain in the form of ash, which could give rise to problems of disposal. Another research project conducted in the United States involving the use of coal or coal based fuels in diesel powered electricity generators has demonstrated the suitability of the valveless, crosshead, two-stroke machine for such purposes. The fuel used was de-ashed coal liquid, a solvent refined coal in liquid form at normal ambient temperature. It was found that the injection of a small amount of diesel oil gave thermodynamic results practically equal to those obtained from normal diesel fuel. Further research is being carried out with 'slurry C', a mixture of diesel oil and pulverized coal solids.

In conclusion, it may be said without hesitation that fuel economy will feature prominently in ship design and specification throughout the 1980s.

CHAPTER 4

Ship Investment Criteria

*Economics of new and second-hand tonnage. Methods of finance. Factors
determining investment criteria.*

Ship investment has an important influence on ship management
today and involves the consideration of many factors. This chapter
attempts to examine the various aspects of ship investment in a
practical way.

ECONOMICS OF NEW AND SECOND-HAND TONNAGE

As the 1980s proceed, many shipowners will weigh the relative
merits of new and second-hand tonnage in a wide range of situations. Let us consider the factors involved and the way in which
they affect the choice made.

(a) *Capital requirement*
A new ship is far more expensive to purchase than a second-hand
one, but financial aid such as building or shipyard subsidies or grants
will probably be generous and readily available. Furthermore, in
many countries the tax relief benefits on new tonnage tend to be
very favourable, as for example in the United Kingdom, where
there is a system of 'free' depreciation. An increasing number of
shipowners nowadays alleviate the capital burden of new tonnage
by leasing the vessel from a consortium of banks; title remains with
the bank (the lessor), but the ship operator has full use of the vessel.
The buyer of a second-hand vessel, on the other hand, may not be
able to obtain credit or government subsidies for the purchase and
modification of the ship and will therefore have to finance the entire
sum from his own resources. If the available capital is limited this
may nevertheless be an attractive option in view of the much lower
cost and the fact that the prices of second-hand vessels are not static
but are determined by the forces of supply and demand. Hence,
when many vessels are laid up in times of depression – particularly
for an extended period – prices tend to fall as owners in financial
difficulties sell in order to clear their mortgage repayments. A good
illustration occurred in the period 1978–80, when the Chinese fleet

was built up by purchasing relatively modern ships – many no more than five years old – at prices considerably below the cost of new tonnage. A further advantage of the relatively low capital cost of a second-hand vessel is the possibility of using her in a new trade to test the market and establish the viability of the route. Alternatively, she may be acquired for use during seasonal peaks and as a relief ship to obviate the need for chartered tonnage, which may prove more expensive. Much will depend on the market situation and charter rates in relation to the purchase price of the ship under consideration.

(b) *Time scale*
Depending on the specification of the vessel, a period of between two and four years may elapse between the decision to build a new ship and the vessel's maiden voyage. The shipowner might be required to fund the vessel throughout the period of construction, which may take up to three years; in practice, many shipowners nowadays obtain a preliminary loan. In addition, during that time the trade may have diminished, as occurred in the tanker market after the mammoth rise in the price of crude oil in 1973, or the character of the trade may have changed, for example owing to the introduction of Ro/Ro vessels on a route previously served exclusively by container ships. Fortunately, unforeseen shifts such as those outlined here are not common. A second-hand vessel presents the advantage that it is available almost immediately. Delay caused by modification work will not extend beyond a few months at most. This aids cash flow, as a second-hand ship begins to earn her keep relatively quickly.

(c) *Ship specification*
A major advantage of new tonnage is that the vessel can be tailor-made to suit the market and so take advantage of modern marine technology. The benefits that accrue could include the entire range of factors that influence operational viability discussed in Chapter 3. Second-hand tonnage naturally tends to be more vulnerable to the risk of obsolescence as marine engineering technology develops and new regulations on ship specification and equipment are introduced. Hence, accommodating a second-hand vessel in the trade for which she is earmarked may involve converting the vessel to the new owner's requirements or to meet IMCO standards, the cost of

which can sometimes prove difficult to ascertain merely from an inspection at the time of purchase. The transfer of the vessel from one register to another may also make the cost of conversion uncertain, as regulations concerning ship construction and equipment vary from one country to another. From a financial point of view, the more modern the vessel the more likely it is that modification will prove attractive or that the cost thereof can be amortized over a longer operating life. It would probably be difficult to justify any major alterations to a vessel built more than ten years ago. Naturally, not all ships will require modification, and the more acceptable the second-hand ship's specification, the more likely it is that the vessel will be viable and fit in with the overall fleet composition.

(d) *Operating expenses*

A modern vessel is likely to be cheaper to operate than her predecessor on a strict payload comparison basis. For example, a vessel conveying 60 000 tonnes of iron ore is more economical than a ship of 30 000 tonnes capacity. As experience of containerization has shown, the substantial economies to be derived from the operation of new vessels could bring about a reduction in fleet size, as modern vessels would be capable of operating more intensively than their predecessors. Second-hand tonnage tends to be more costly in terms of crewing, fuel consumption and general ship productivity than a vessel of modern specification. Moreover, her transhipment arrangements are likely to be somewhat sluggish, so that the vessel will spend longer in port than a modern ship. Overall she tends to provide a poorer service at higher cost to the shipowner. It must be stressed that this is not always the case; much depends on the age of the vessel and the trade. The older the vessel, the less attractive it is to shippers; moreover, underwriters tend to decline insurance cover on the hull and machinery of vessels more than fifteen years old.

(e) *Maintenance costs*

The survey and maintenance costs of a vessel tend to increase in real terms annually and usually rise significantly beyond the tenth to twelfth year, according to ship specification and use.

METHODS OF FINANCE

In evaluating the methods of funding new and second-hand tonnage, it is important to bear in mind the three major problems besetting the shipping industry in the early 1980s – excess shipbuilding capacity, state involvement in shipowning and protectionism. These factors, which are treated at some length in Chapters 1 and 14, clearly have an impact on ship finance; in this section, however, we shall examine aspects of the subject that are immediately relevant to shipping investment.

Certain information is required before funds are committed to finance investment in a ship, namely:

(a) The shipowner's fleet composition and cash flow projection for the next five years.

(b) An assessment of the quality of management in the shipping company, with particular emphasis on the ability to accept and anticipate change.

(c) An evaluation of the shipping company's long-term business plan, embracing predictions of revenue, expenditure and investment over the next seven to ten years. This will portray the overall cash flow situation and indicate the way in which the company intends to develop the various activities in which it is engaged. A sound shipping company will protect itself against emergencies by building up a modern diversified fleet, by having a basis of sound and profitable contracts and by preserving adequate liquidity. In general terms, a financial institution will be looking for qualitative rather than quantitative growth.

If all is well in these regards, the shipping company will have the scope to take fast and decisive action when necessary. Moreover, whilst financing institutions will have to pay close attention to the quality of management in shipping companies, they will themselves have to be able to work with management of a high calibre and to understand the problems and complexities of the shipping industry. The conditions for loans and their legal documentation will need careful formulation to allow room for flexibility and rapid action without the necessity for time consuming referment procedures or complicated addenda. Particular attention should be given to regular control and information procedures. Over the longer term, co-operation between shipping companies, shipyards, bankers, lawyers, accountants, insurers and brokers could well lead to new forms of agreement to meet the changing situation as the decade proceeds.

Nowadays new tonnage is financed from three main sources:

1. The shipping company's own funds, raised through the liquidation of reserve capital and possibly the sale of displaced tonnage.
2. Government grants and subsidies.
3. Loan capital obtained on the open market, including bank mortgages, which may be provided at very low interest rates.

Shipowners are unable to finance new tonnage entirely from their own resources owing primarily to the low capital return on existing tonnage and the high rate of inflation in shipbuilding costs. Many shipowners supply up to one-third of the capital for a new project from their own funds and raise the residue externally. Such external finance may take several forms:

(a) Subsidies provided by governments or government agencies to domestic yards or shipowners. Such subsidies, which would be repayable only in exceptional circumstances, are commonly granted when shipyards are hungry for orders, the particular nation's fleet is in a depressed state or there is a desire to inject new tonnage into the fleet.

(b) Domestic loans granted by governments or government agencies for the construction of new ships in domestic yards; such finance must be repaid.

(c) Foreign loans provided by governments or government agencies for the construction of new ships in foreign yards; these too must be repaid.

(d) Grants provided by governments or government agencies in the form of subsidies, incentive grants or loans for the modernization and/or expansion of domestic shipyards.

(e) Export credit. Governments and government agencies may themselves provide export credit schemes or may guarantee credit provided by some other institution for new vessels, thus enabling domestic shipyards to compete favourably in foreign markets by offering comparable credit facilities. (See *The Elements of Export Practice* for an explanation of the role of the Export Credit Guarantee Department in the United Kingdom.)

(f) Bank loans. In the 1980s banks and other leaders will probably become involved on an increasing scale in the ownership and operation of modern tonnage through the use of arrangements including special credit terms, profit sharing and sale/purchase options. A mortgage on a modern ship represents a sound investment for the bank provided the owner, the ship and its trading prospects have been appraised correctly. The advantage for the shipowner lies in the fact that he can begin to develop his own business at low initial cost and with good, competitive vessels, a point of especial relevance to the small companies with wide experience and skill in ship management that a healthy independent shipping industry needs as a counterweight to the large shipowning groups.

(g) Leasing or sale/leaseback arrangements over fifteen years or longer with commercial banks. These are attractive to shipping companies as they release financial resources but allow them to retain the use of the asset concerned. The tax incentives available in some countries such as the United Kingdom and the USA apply only if the ships are new and a genuine third-party deal is involved. Sale/leaseback provisions may be incorporated into package deals, especially where the ship is firmly committed to a long-term contract with a first-class charterer.

(h) Loans from specialized institutions such as ship mortgage banks, which raise the necessary long-term funds by means of private placings or the sale of bonds.

(i) Long-term loans provided by insurance companies, pension funds and certain private lenders for first-class borrowers.

Certain special factors apply to the funding of second-hand tonnage. For example, in recent years purchasers have been able to buy vessels at prices far below the actual cost of replacing such ships; most financial institutions have been reluctant to finance such acquisitions unless the buyer is of undoubted strength and able to put up substantial equity. Most shipping companies recognize the mutual advantage of full financial disclosure to their bankers, the exchange of ideas and the availability of modern banking expertise. Loan agreements will increasingly make provision for consultation between lender and borrower before the latter assumes new commitments that would affect his debt/equity ratio.

The need for financial assistance is not confined to the purchase of vessels; it may also arise when a shipping company runs into difficulties for a variety of reasons, such as the unforeseen rise in the price of oil in 1973 and the consequential downturn in trade. As liquidity problems become acute, lending institutions are faced with the choice of restructuring loans, precipitating the bankruptcy of the company concerned or requiring immediate sale of the asset held as security for the loan. They are particularly loath to forego interest on loans; the whole point of lending against security is the knowledge that, if necessary, the security can and should be realized under the terms of the loan agreement.

It should be borne in mind in this connection that the debt mortgaged on ships throughout the world is not purely and simply a commercial risk. The report prepared by the Shipping Finance Study Group of the International Maritime Industry Forum in October 1976 on the financial implications of excess capacity in the shipping and shipbuilding sectors suggested that some $38 million (over 50 per cent) of the global debt on large ships afloat and on order in July 1976 was probably a direct or indirect government risk. In many cases the government credit or guarantee bears a high degree of risk insofar as the security ranks after first mortgage loans granted by commercial lenders. Moreover, the government pro-portion of total credit is growing as the majority of new shipbuilding orders placed in recent years have been financed to a very large extent by means of government-backed credit; by 1981 it accounted for more than 70 per cent of outstanding debt. A recent examin-ation of just a portion of the mortgage debt – which is a commercial risk – reveals that it is widely dispersed, involving syndicates of ten, twenty or more banks.

In the short term at least, credit provided or guaranteed by government will dominate the finance of new vessels. Commercial institutions will therefore be confined to a secondary role, providing credit against guarantees, arranging package deals and assisting in negotiating and completing the required documentation, licences and authorities. They will also be in a position to arrange bridging finance and to grant loans against security ranking ahead of gov-ernment risks, or against separate security. Banking expertise will be particularly valuable when multi-currency options are required and bankers should have a useful role to play as intermediaries, agents, trustees or 'buffers' between official lending agencies and shipping companies.

It will be clear from what has been said above that governments are now highly involved in the provision of shipping. This involve-ment is not, however, always beneficial to the industry as a whole.

Some of the ways in which their action has harmed or might jeopardize the prospects of a free and competitive international shipping industry are examined in Chapter 14.

The need to fund new tonnage on a sound basis cannot be overstressed; if the basis is sound there will be a favourable correlation between available shipping capacity and international trade prospects.

FACTORS DETERMINING INVESTMENT CRITERIA

The following factors must be borne in mind as criteria for investment in new vessels, the conversion of existing tonnage or the purchase of second-hand ships:

(a) The actual market prospects of the trade or route, in both the short and the long term. Trade prospects are most difficult to forecast, as international trade is unpredictable by nature and susceptible not least to the political climate, which can change the whole pattern of events within the time scale of the project. A good example is the tanker market in the 1970s, as mentioned above. Nevertheless, the market can be assessed by means of commercial research in the widest relevant sphere possible; trade statistics published by governments and international organizations should be studied and contact made with trade associations, chambers of commerce, governments, shippers' councils and international organizations such as UNCTAD and the OECD. Consultants may even be engaged for the purpose; the fee involved may be high, but it is small in relation to the capital cost of the project.

(b) Commercial factors in the context of maintaining or increasing the company's market share on the route. The new ship must convey cargo profitably, perhaps by means of improved handling techniques such as a switch to containerization. This may attract new flows of traffic but lose existing customers whose goods are unsuited to the new method. Modern tonnage generally stimulates overall traffic and thus captures an increased share of the market.

(c) An analysis of the existing vessel covering her age, her general suitability to both her current trade and expected short and long-term trade developments, voyage and survey/maintenance costs, the resale value of the vessel (inasfar as this can be determined) and finally the residual life of the vessel as an economic unit employed elsewhere in the fleet, possibly testing the viability of a new service. This analysis will involve the departments of the marine engineer, the marine superintendent, the traffic manager and the accountant.

(d) An assessment of present and future competition in the widest sense of the term. It should therefore cover not only direct competition from other shipping lines as expressed in service quality, rates (particularly rebate levels), transit times, type of tonnage, range of facilities, fringe benefits for Ro/Ro drivers (for example, some operators include the driver's meal and cabin in the rate) and the period of credit afforded to shippers in regard to the payment of accounts; it should also extend to subversive competition – as found in flag discrimination practices, flags of convenience and the activities of mercantile fleets from Eastern bloc countries, particularly the USSR, in capturing a proportion of the cross trade flow – and to the competition offered by alternative carriers such as the railways (the example of the Trans-Siberian Railway is described on pp. 121–122) or the airlines, particularly in passenger trades on short sea routes between the United Kingdom and the continent of Europe.

(e) Any credit facilities, grants or tax concessions offered by government. Further details in this regard are to be found in the preceding section.

(f) Capital availability and methods of finance; these factors are also discussed above. The cost of the capital ultimately sought must be closely evaluated. The technique generally used is that of discounted cash flow, which relates the cash flow generated annually by the new vessel to the situation that would prevail if no investment were undertaken; initially there may be a loss, with profit appearing in later years.

(g) The economics of the new tonnage (see Chapter 3 for a detailed treatment).

(h) Closely allied to the preceding point is the return on the investment. The appraisal should cover the options available: the effect of making no investment, investment in the new proposed vessel and alternatives such as ordering one large vessel instead of two small ones, converting existing ships, buying second-hand tonnage and chartering a vessel with perhaps an option to purchase on completion of the charter. A return of new investment of between 10 and 15 per cent should be sought, although today many shipowners achieve a yield of only 5 per cent.

(i) Available shipyard capacity and the time scale of the project. Tentative enquiries are made of suitable shipyards likely to tender for such a project and the time scale each would recommend having regard to existing commitments. A project involving two or three sister ships brings cost savings if all the vessels are built in the same yard. The saving must be weighed against the time implications; a single yard is likely to take longer than three separate yards, which could build the vessels almost simultaneously. A further point to bear in mind is that the delivery date does not entirely rest with the shipyard, as up to 80 per cent of a vessel's components are supplied by outside contractors, many of which could be situated overseas. Payment to shipyards is usually made in five instalments each representing 20 per cent of the value of the vessel. Substantial cost savings can be realized by having an option on a further vessel of similar design with the shipyard. It is desirable that the option be exercised in the early stage of the first vessel's construction, thereby ensuring continuity of work.

(j) The manner in which the new investment fits into the company's five-year business plan, if any.

(k) Any effects the new tonnage will have on other services within the company, such as the possibility of traffic diversion or tariff adjustments.

(l) Policies laid down by the OECD, particularly credit terms and any scrap and build schemes with which a particular government may be associated.

(m) The invisible export earnings of particular services. For example, a loss-making service may generate 70 per cent of its income by carrying other countries' cargo; closure of the service would result in the loss of such invisible exports, but modernization by the provision of new tonnage could transform the route into a potentially profitable operation.

(n) Depreciation of the new vessel over its estimated useful life. The ship's residual value is reviewed annually and a portion written off in the accounts. In the United Kingdom a system of free depreciation applies. Container ships, tankers, gas carriers, oil/bulk/ore carriers, oil/ore carriers, Ro/Ro vessels and broadly similar tonnage tend to be given a depreciable life of fifteen years. The life of offshore supply ships is put at twelve years and other vessels, such as tugs, are allocated a twenty-year life.

(o) An increasing number of services are operated by consortia, as found in the deep sea container services, by two operators jointly providing a service between their countries or by shipowners collaborating under liner conference conditions. The existence of such arrangements will affect the investment and may require submissions from the other operators involved.

To conclude our review of the factors influencing investment, it is relevant to draw attention to the report of the Morpeth Committee in the United Kingdom, which concluded that historical cost accounting is positively misleading in periods of rapid inflation. Service profitability is distorted if depreciation allowances are based on the original capital cost of the vessel rather than her current replacement cost. A good example is that of Overseas Containers Limited and its associate AJCL, which commissioned thirteen new vessels between 1969 and 1973. By early 1977 the original capital cost was about one-third of the current replacement value. This disparity, which is continuing to widen, gives an increasingly false impression of the real earnings of assets more than four or five years old. Many shipowners bridge the gap by making provision out of after-tax profits or become dependent on future loan finance. Calculation of the depreciation gap depends on a prediction of replacement costs, which will be influenced by factors such as the timing of replacement, technological change, exchange rate fluctuations and the world index of shipbuilding prices.

Finally, as we have seen in the past, the successful shipowner is the one who anticipates and adapts to change. The current decade will see the emergence of problems in abundance, but equally it will present a multitude of opportunities to the investor and good shipping entrepreneur.

CHAPTER 5

Economics of Ship Operation

Economics of ship manning. Factors to consider in planning sailing schedules. Surveys and maintenance. Problems caused by fluctuations and imbalances in trade. The relative importance of speed, frequency, reliability and cost of sea transport. Port operation.

The economics of ship operation today warrant close attention by management to ensure that the service provided is viable, competitive and best suited to the market requirements, having regard to safety, statutory obligations and service standards. This entails careful evaluation of a wide range of elements.

Let us first place the subject in perspective by examining Table 5.1 which gives an analysis of a voyage estimate, based on 1980 prices, for a typical 60 000 dwt modern bulk carrier with a 16 knot service speed.

The constituents of the voyage estimate can vary by some 10 per cent owing to price changes and will differ according to the type and age of the ship and the country of registration. For example, a passenger vessel will have a larger crew than a cargo ship, so that crew costs will account for a greater proportion of the total. Nevertheless, the following points emerge from the table:

(a) The cost of fuel oil is the largest item in our example, almost 30 per cent of the total. Fuel economy is therefore a crucial consideration in scheduling. In the next few years further research will be undertaken to devise more economical ship machinery and hull

Table 5.1

Items	Percentage of total costs
Fuel oil	29.6
Lubricating oil	0.9
Engine maintenance	1.2
Hull maintenance	3.9
Crew costs	24.2
General administration	0.4
Insurance	7.6
Capital cost (depreciation, interest charges, etc.)	28.2

55

designs to produce the optimum speed compatible with the most favourable fuel consumption level. (See Chapter 3 for a treatment of the economics of ship propulsion.)

(b) In the example, capital charges come to about 28 per cent of the total. Shipowners from countries that offer loans at low rates of interest and subsidies for building or operating vessels will not face such a heavy burden; this applies especially to the Eastern bloc and developing countries.

(c) Crew costs represent almost one-quarter of total costs. This important subject is treated at greater length in the following section.

It is apparent from this brief analysis of the table that vessels operating in subsidized fleets and/or paying lower wages have significantly lower voyage costs and are therefore at a competitive advantage. Moreover, many of the rapidly expanding fleets that fall into this category – particularly those of India and China – have been built up by purchasing second-hand modern tonnage at low prices, a fact which further boosts their competitiveness. Against this background it is essential that the fleets of the Western hemisphere operate on the principle of the 'commercial freedom of the seas'.

ECONOMICS OF SHIP MANNING

The crewing of vessels today is a cost element to which shipowners are devoting increasing attention in order to achieve the lowest crew complement compatible with statutory requirements, safety and market needs. This entails not only reducing the volume of shipboard work, but also adapting the methods employed.

Before examining the factors which influence crewing levels, it is appropriate to deal briefly with the existing crew structure, shipboard organization, legislation, crewing agreements, the role of the National Maritime Board in the United Kingdom and the part played by international organizations.

The master has overall charge of the ship. Beneath him, duties are generally divided among three departments: the deck, the engineer's department and the catering department.

The deck department is the responsibility of the chief officer or first mate, who supervises the handling of cargo and is responsible for the upkeep of the ship and her equipment, excluding the engine room and auxiliary power gear. The deck department includes junior seamen, seamen grades I and II, petty officer (deck) and chief petty officer (deck).

Radio officers are specialists either engaged by the ship's owner or employed by a company that installs radio apparatus, such as the International Marine Radio Company Ltd or the Marconi International Marine Communication Company Ltd. Statutory provisions require British vessels of between 500 and 1600 grt to have either radiotelephony or radiotelegraphy. All vessels exceeding 1600 grt must have the latter. The number of certificated radio officers aboard ship varies between one and three, depending on the size and type of ship. In some vessels conveying a relatively small number of passengers the radio officer also acts as purser, for which he receives additional remuneration.

The engine room is in the charge of the chief engineer, who is responsible to the master for the main propulsion machinery and the auxiliaries, comprising the electrical plant, cargo winches, refrigeration plant, steering gear and ventilation system. In recent years the electrical plant has increased in importance, a trend that is reflected in the training now given to engineering officers and ratings. The engineer officers on a typical cargo vessel comprise the chief engineer, the first engineer and second, third and fourth engineers. The ratings of the engine room department include junior motormen, motormen grades I and II, petty officer (motorman) and chief petty officer (motorman).

The catering department is under the control of the chief steward or catering officer, who is responsible for catering, the galley, galley stores and ship's linen. He is assisted by cooks, bakers and assistant stewards. The number of catering personnel is tending to fall with the increased use of ready prepared foods and labour-saving devices such as tea-making machines and disposable utensils.

In the UK shipping industry the conditions of employment are set out in a crew agreement between the seafarer and the shipowner in accordance with the Merchant Shipping Acts of 1970 and 1979. The agreement may take the form of a contract of service established under the Merchant Navy Established Service Scheme initiated by the General Council of British Shipping. The scheme, which is applicable to both officers and ratings, provides for company service contracts with a particular shipping company and general service contracts with the industry as a whole. When a seafarer with the latter type of contract is not employed on a ship he receives establishment benefit and is required to hold himself available for posting to any vessel designated by the establishment. The scheme is financed by a general levy on shipowners employing seamen on general service contracts. Seamen holding a company service contract must receive benefit on terms at least equal to those provided under general service contracts. These two forms of agreement are very common and are much preferred to casual employment arrangements.

The National Maritime Board (NMB) is a forum for negotiations between shipowners and seafarers on matters affecting pay, hours of duty, manning, leave and travelling expenses. It is composed of six panels, each representing a seagoing department with its own particular problems and requirements, that is to say masters, navigating officers, radio officers, engineer officers, catering staff and finally sailors and motormen. Each panel has twenty-four members drawn equally from shipowners and employees, with a chairman from each side. Negotiations on matters within the Board's field of competence may be conducted by any of the panels, whose decisions are binding. The NMB is administered by a permanent independent staff and is financed by a proportionate levy on shipowners and seafarers. The organization and negotiation of seafarers' conditions of employment are similar in other maritime countries and reflect IMCO and ILO conventions.

The Merchant Shipping (Certification of Deck and Marine Engineer Officers) Regulations 1977, which came into effect on 1st September 1981, prescribe the minimum number of deck officers and marine engineer officers to be carried by UK registered ships. The scale varies according to the tonnage or power of the ship, the area in which the voyage takes place and whether passengers are carried. Similar requirements also apply to ships registered outside the United Kingdom which carry passengers between places in the UK, between the UK and the Channel Islands or the Isle of Man or on voyages that begin and end at the same place in the UK without calling anywhere outside the UK. Tugs and sail training ships are subject to special requirements. The regulations make provision for short-handed operation if one officer is absent owing to illness or incapacity. Certain officers in ships carrying bulk cargoes of specified dangerous chemicals or gases have to undergo additional training.

Table 5.2 Minimum number of deck officers to be carried in ships of 80 grt and over, other than passenger vessels and tugs

Trading area	Description of ship	Minimum number of certificated deck officers to be carried				
		Class 1 Cert.	Class 2 Cert.	Class 3 Cert.	Class 4 Cert.	Class 5 Cert.
Unlimited	1600 grt and over	1	1	1	1	–
	80 grt but under 1600 grt	1	1	1	–	–
Middle trade	5000 grt and over	1	1	1	1	–
	1600 grt but under 5000 grt	–	–	1*	1	1
	Under 1600 grt	–	–	–	2*	1
Near continental	10 000 grt and over	1	1	1	–	–
	5000 grt but under 10 000 grt	1	–	1	1	–
	1600 grt but under 5000 grt	–	–	–	2*	1
	800 grt but under 1600 grt	–	–	–	–	3*
	200 grt but under 800 grt	–	–	–	–	2*
	80 grt but under 200 grt	–	–	–	–	1*

* Subject to special provisions.

Table 5.2 shows the minimum number of deck officers prescribed in the Merchant Shipping (Certification of Deck Officers) Regulations 1977.

The 'near continental' area is bounded by a line drawn from a point on the Norwegian coast in latitude 62° North to a point 62° North 02° West; thence to a point 51° North 12° West; thence to Brest, but excluding all waters which lie to the eastward of a line drawn between Kristiansand, Norway and Hanstholm lighthouse on the northern Danish coast.

The 'middle trade' area (which includes places in the Baltic Sea) is bounded by the Northern shore of Vest Fjord (Norway) and a line joining Skemvaer lighthouse to a point 62° North 02° West; thence to a point 58° North 10° West; thence to a point 51° North 12° West;

thence to a point 41° 9′ North 10° West; thence to Oporto but excluding the 'near continental' area.

The unlimited trading area comprises the rest of the world.

Certificates of Competency (Deck Officer) are awarded to deck officers who meet the standards laid down by the Department of Trade, which broadly reflect the outcome of discussions within IMCO. There are five new classes of certificate. Class 1 is the Master Mariner level, equivalent to the Master Foreign-Going Certificate prescribed under the Merchant Shipping Act of 1894; similarly, classes 2 and 3 are equivalent to the First Mate Foreign-Going Certificate and Second Mate Foreign-Going Certificate respectively.

The Certificates of Competency required for appointment as ship's master are shown in Table 5.3.

Table 5.4. shows the minimum number of marine engineer

Table 5.3 Certificate of competency required for appointment as ship's master

Certificate of Competency (Deck officer) or certificate of validity	Command endorsement	Description of ships and areas
Class 2 or class 3	Master (middle trade)	Ships (other than passenger ships) of less than 5000 grt going between locations in the combined near continental and middle trade areas
Class 4	Master (middle trade)	Ships (other than passenger ships) of less than 1600 grt going between locations in the combined near continental and middle trade areas
Class 2, 3 or 4	Master (near continental)	Ships (other than passenger ships) of less than 5000 grt going between locations in the near continental area. Passenger ships of less than 1000 grt going between locations in the near continental area
Class 5	Master (near continental)	Ships (other than passenger ships) of less than 1600 grt going between locations in the near continental area. Passenger ships of less than 200 grt going between locations in the near continental area.

Table 5.4 Minimum number of marine engineer officers to be carried in ships of 350 kW and over, including sail training ships with a propulsion engine

Area	Registered power of ship (kW)	Minimum number of certificated marine engineer officers to be carried			
		Class 1 Cert.	Class 2 Cert.	Class 3 Cert.	Class 4 Cert.
Unlimited or middle trade	3000 and over	1	1	–	2
	746 or more but under 3000	–	1*	1	1
	350 or more but under 746	–	–	1*	1
Near continental	6000 and over	1	1	–	1
	3000 or more but under 6000	–	1*	1	–
	746 or more but under 3000	–	–	1*	1
	350 or more but under 746	–	–	–	1 and 1*

* Subject to special provisions.

officers laid down in the Merchant Shipping (Certification of Marine Engineer Officers) Regulations 1977.

There are four Certificates of Competency, that of Marine Engineer Officer Class 1 corresponding to the First-Class Engineer Certificate prescribed under the Merchant Shipping Act of 1894. Certificates of Competency of Classes 1, 2 and 4 are issued for motor or steam machinery or a combination of the two; Class 3 certificates are issued for motor machinery only. Table 5.5 shows the certificates required for appointment as chief engineer officer.

IMCO and the ILO have also had a profound influence on the manning of vessels. The function of these organizations is described in Chapters 12 and 13; a detailed treatment of the IMCO requirements relating to watch-keeping, training, certification and the continued proficiency of seafarers' knowledge and the resolutions adopted at the 1978 International Conference on Training and Certification of Seafarers are to be found in *Elements of Shipping*.

We are now in a position to consider the factors relevant to the setting of crew levels:

(a) Statutory obligations. In the case of vessels registered in the United Kingdom the relevant legislation comprises the various Merchant Shipping Acts.

(b) Regulations laid down by shipping industry bodies. For example, the NMB sets a maximum period for continuous duty on board British registered ships and also regulates such matters as overtime rates, leave arrangements, liquidation of leave, consolidation and relief crews.

(c) Terms and conditions negotiated between shipowners and trade unions; these may constitute local variants of provisions laid down by bodies such as the NMB.

(d) The type, age and classification of the vessel. Modern vessels require a smaller crew owing to the reduced workload and the use of more modern equipment. This applies particularly to automation and, in some cases, the use of computers in the engine room; improved décor, reducing cleaning work; the greater use of ready prepared foods to reduce catering personnel and improved ship maintenance techniques. The introduction of more multi-purpose vessels has brought about greater manning flexibility, not only in dry cargo liner vessels and bulk carriers but also in multi-purpose passenger vessels conveying Ro/Ro, accompanied cars and pass-

Table 5.5 Certificates of Competency required for appointment as chief engineer officer

Class of certificate of competency or service	Description of ships and areas
Class 2	Ships of 746 kW or more but under 3000 kW registered power going to, from or between any locations
	Ships of 3000 kW or more but under 6000 kW registered power going between locations in the near continental area
Class 3	Ships of 350 kW or more but under 746 kW registered power going to, from or between any locations
	Ships of 746 kW or more but under 3000 kW registered power going between locations in the near continental area
Class 4	Ships of 350 kW or more but under 746 kW registered power going between locations in the near continental area
	Sail training ships of less than 350 kW registered power going to, from or between any locations

engers as found in the short sea trades. One interesting development in this regard has been the use of lower passenger certification levels for the winter than those applied in the summer, allowing a considerable reduction in the crew. The vehicle deck load factor is unaffected by this change in certification and may thus be used to the full to meet the heavier demand from road hauliers outside peak holiday periods. It should be noted that vessels may carry up to twelve passengers without conforming to the more stringent regulations concerning surveys and crew accommodation that apply to passenger vessels.

(e) The trade in which the vessel plies and the degree of competition. Under liner conference arrangements where shipowners of various nationalities with similar vessels each bear their own operating costs, there is intense pressure on vessels from high wage countries to have smaller crews than those from countries with lower wage scales. This helps make crew costs more compatible and equitable.

(f) The scope for reducing demarcation between the three departments – deck, engine room and catering – and especially the scope for dovetailing the duties of the first two.

(g) Wage costs. Countries with high wage costs are continuously striving to reduce crew complements to remain competitive. Much progress has been made in this respect, particularly in the Federal Republic of Germany, the Netherlands and Scandinavian countries. The following example shows the 16 man complement of a Danish registered 'omni carrier' vessel of 8000 dwt operating on the route Gulf of Mexico/US East Coast–Mediterranean–Caribbean/Central America/Mexico:

Master	Second engineer
Chief mate	Third engineer
First mate	Electrician
Second mate	Purser
Radio officer	Cook
Chief engineer	Four trainees
First engineer	

The ship has a total container capacity of 516 TEU and vehicular deck space of 1416 square metres. Heavy lifting gear for loads of up to 120 tons is also provided. A profile of the vessel is to be found in Diagram X. A number of maritime nations, such as the Netherlands and the United Kingdom, have long employed non-domiciled ratings in their mercantile services. In recent years the British merchant navy included some 11 500 non-domiciled ratings, many of them from the Indian subcontinent. Their rates of pay and conditions of service tend to be inferior to those of British seamen; however, the disparity is now declining, and so too is their proportion of the fleet's complement of seafarers. Similarly, under arrangements agreed with the five UK maritime unions, by 1979 there were about 1100 UK seafarers serving in 112 foreign flag ships managed by UK companies.

(h) Where it has been impractical to reduce the crew complement, shipowners have endeavoured to improve crew productivity by increasing the workload at less busy times during the voyage, particularly on ship maintenance. Increasing the maintenance undertaken while at sea can reduce the time spent on surveys.

It will be appreciated that the relative importance attached to the factors listed above will vary according to the circumstances of each ship. Nevertheless, shipowners will all have the same aim – to set a crew level compatible with statutory requirements and considerations of viability, market demand and safety. The question of manning levels will undoubtedly become a major issue during the present decade. It is to be hoped that in the long term the differences in manning levels between industrialized nations and developing countries will narrow; consultation through the International Labour Organization could help achieve this objective. Much will depend on the ability of third world countries to finance new vessels and train crews to man them. The shipping industry must become more capital intensive if fleets from different countries are to compete on equal terms.

FACTORS TO CONSIDER IN PLANNING SAILING SCHEDULES

It is of the utmost importance that a vessel be fully employed whenever she is available. The very large capital investment she represents gives rise to heavy financial charges, so that periods in which she is laid up – and thus earning no revenue – must be kept to an absolute minimum. If a ship is in commission only during peak periods, there may be good reason to reduce the size of the fleet by concentrating cargoes on a smaller number of vessels on lengthening passage times in order to keep the fleet fully employed. The latter short-term solution, which would be appropriate in times of trade depression, may prove cheaper than either laying up a number of vessels or selling them and chartering tonnage when traffic improves. It is a question of examining the economics of the particular situation.

The shipowner must also ensure that a profitable load factor is continuously realized. With the development of multi-purpose vessels able to take a mixture of traffic, it is most desirable that the actual mix be profitable. For example, on the vehicular deck of a vessel conveying container and vehicular traffic, preference should be given to the high rated Ro/Ro traffic rather than to trade cars or caravans, which are often regarded as filler traffic in liner cargo services.

There are basically two types of service: the regular service and sailings provided to meet a particular demand. The former is usually associated with cargo liner trades and bulk carriers, integrated into an industrial production flow, whilst the latter is mostly confined to tramp vessels.

The sailing frequency of cargo liners is determined months in advance within the conference. Liner services attract a wide variety of cargoes, including machinery, steel rails, foodstuffs and motor vehicles. At certain times and in various trades there is naturally a need for increased sailings to cater for seasonal increases in traffic. The required additional tonnage is sometimes chartered, thereby ensuring that the shipowner is not burdened with excess capacity at other times of the year. Wherever practical, surveys and overhauls are undertaken outside peak periods. Many container vessels and specialized bulk carriers are on continuous survey to ensure that the frequency of dry-docking and the time spent out of commission are kept to a minimum.

A large number of factors influence the formulation of sailing schedules. The most important are listed below:

1. The overall number of ships and their availability.
2. The types of ship available, in particular their size (length, beam and draught) and any special characteristics, such as the need for special equipment for loading and discharging cargo. Some ships may be suitable for cruising; others, by virtue of their size may be able to operate only between ports with deep water berths. Hence, in general a large fleet of small vessels has more operational flex-

ibility than a small fleet of large vessels restricted to a limited number of ports able to accommodate them. This problem is particularly important in the case of VLCCs and ULCCs, which account for some 200 million dwt of the world tanker fleet totalling about 325 million dwt. With multi-purpose vessels conveying road haulage vehicles, passengers and accompanied cars, the mix of vehicles shipped can vary according to the season and the time of day. Such variations in demand are accommodated by the use of vehicle decks that can be adjusted hydraulically, so that for one sailing a vessel may accommodate 50 cars and 20 large road haulage vehicles while on another occasion it may carry as many as 300 cars but nothing else. Another aspect of this factor is the operation of ships of different specifications on the same service. For example, two container ships may have a 20 per cent capacity variation and a service speed difference of 2 knots. Ideally, all the vessels on a particular service should be nearly identical, particularly in terms of speed and capacity.

3. The plying limits of individual ships and, in the case of liner tonnage, any conditions imposed by liner conference agreements. It is the practice for liner conference members to agree the sailing programme and the allocation of sailings per member in accordance with the availability of berths at the ports and ship disposition having regard to surveys and market demand.

4. The volume, type and characteristics of the traffic. This requires very close analysis, and options must be examined to establish whether the service could be improved and capacity utilized more productively if the distribution method were changed. For example, the development of containerization has transformed many traditional distribution methods and thereby raised the demand for such services. In the cargo liner trade the situation should be examined in the context of combined transport. Furthermore, an analysis of the origin and destination of cargoes in a liner trade may suggest the rationalization of ports of call and thus promote the use of feeder services centred on key transhipment ports.

5. Seasonal traffic fluctuations. This subject is discussed separately on pp. 71–72.

6. Maintenance of time margins where services connect. For instance, a passenger vessel may be served by a connecting rail service. The schedule must provide adequate time to ensure that connections are maintained and make allowance for delays caused

by bad weather, service disruption or other factors. Inland surface transport is generally more flexible than sea transport; with the development of combined transport, this apsect is becoming more important.

7. The availability of crew and suitable change-over ports. A shortage of key certificated personnel could delay the ship's departure; fortunately this is a rare occurrence. The shipowner has to decide the most suitable ports for crew change-over, bearing in mind the need for easy access by air and the wishes of the crew.

8. Arrangements for dealing with emergencies. All ship operators must lay down the procedures to be followed in the event of a service disruption, which may be classified as a major or a minor incident. Few shipowners nowadays have standby vessels, particularly in peak periods, so that in the event of a major incident involving the withdrawal of a vessel, they may charter a replacement ship, increase the service speed of remaining vessels in the fleet and/or speed up port turnround time, divert traffic to another operator or switch a vessel from elsewhere in the fleet. The choice made will depend on cost, service quality, resource availability and, not least, the expected duration of the disruption. If it will last a few days, fairly simple measures can be introduced, such as giving urgent or perishable commodities priority over other traffic; if it will continue longer, some of the more extensive measures will have to be taken.

9. Climatic conditions. Some ports are ice-bound at certain times of the year, thus preventing the movement of shipping. This is particularly relevant to the St Lawrence Seaway, Arctic regions and the Baltic Sea. In recent years the Russians have developed nuclear-powered ice-breakers to keep their shipping lanes open as long as possible in winter. When a port is closed, ships will obviously sail to the nearest port and the cargo will complete its transit overland, usually by rail.

10. Competition. Liner conferences were developed to restrict competition to service quality rather than rates, which were standardized. This has greatly facilitated the elimination of under-cutting, although the fierce competition that remains in many trades tends to lead to overcapacity, with the attendant risk that operators will offer unprofitable services. In order to counter competition and generate market goodwill, shipowners may feel obliged to provide additional services and in so doing occupy berths that could other-

wise be allocated to competitors in the port. In recent years increasing competition has come from the Eastern bloc and flag of convenience fleets, which have operated on more favourable financial terms than those found in liner conference trades. An operator providing services to match those of his competitor must carefully evaluate the voyage costs in relation to revenue and consider all the options, including the possibility of a gentleman's agreement with the competitor.

11. General availability of port facilities and dock labour, and any tidal restrictions affecting times of access and departure. This is a critical factor which requires particular attention if a vessel is switched from one service to another involving different ports. In devising any service of a regular nature reliability is a paramount consideration, so that it is important that the port facilities provided are adequate and reliable and that the tides do not seriously impair continuous access. As the cost of fuel continues to rise, increasing attention is being paid to reducing port turnround time in order to allow slower passages. Much can be achieved in this regard through the advance planning of transhipment arrangements and development of the stowage plan. Many major ship operators are using computers to determine shipboard stowage and to produce the cargo documentation. The ship operator or his agent should maintain close liaison with shippers, customs, rail and road operators and port authorities, including dock labour, to ensure maximum co-operation and adherence to schedules. A port liaison committee often helps solve problems rapidly.

12. Time required for terminal duties at the port. This will embrace such activities as discharging, loading, customs procedures, bunkering and victualling and should also leave a margin to allow for reasonable delays.

13. Voyage time. This is primarily a market consideration. Relatively fast schedules are costly in terms of the initial capital expense of the machinery and fuel consumption. An increase of 1 knot above an optimum speed can increase both initial cost and fuel consumption by up to 25 per cent. The trend towards faster schedules in the late 1960s and early 1970s, which reflected the development of containers and VLCCs, will not persist in the 1980s. Slower schedules are already finding acceptance, mainly on account of the escalating cost of fuel. The benefits of faster schedules require very careful consideration in both cost and marketing terms.

14. Any hostile activities taking place or expected along a vessel's route. Hostilities tend to increase insurance rates and thereby overall voyage and freight costs. The implications of re-routing the services must be carefully examined; in many cases a diversion will be unavoidable.

15. The use of canals such as the Suez and Panama Canals as alternative routes. There is a growing tendency to route services via maritime canals in order to save passage time and fuel. The canal dues have to be set against the cost of taking the longer route in terms of additional fuel consumption, longer passage time, crew cost and less favourable fleet utilization.

16. Estimated voyage cost and expected traffic receipts. This is a very important item in the increasingly cost-conscious shipping industry. It would not be practicable to cost individual voyages separately on a liner service, but a fairly reliable financial statement of anticipated expenses and revenue on a twelve-monthly or seasonal basis should be drawn up. Within a liner conference variation of the schedules would require agreement with the other members. Such a financial exercise is also relevant when consideration is being given to chartering tonnage to supplement sailings in peak periods.

17. Imbalance in trade. This factor is examined in greater depth in a subsequent section (p. 71).

18. Bunkering requirements and the location of bunkering ports. Advantage should be taken of favourable bunkering prices and payment terms; consortia of shipowners may be able to negotiate concessionary terms.

19. Any sailing programme should reflect traffic growth and the likelihood of securing new flows of traffic. For example, a new factory may be opening in a particular country that may generate an inward flow of component parts and an outward flow of the finished product.

20. The dates and expected duration of surveys.

To conclude, the formulation of sailing schedules merits considerable management attention to ensure that the optimum service is provided. Costs and revenue should be monitored constantly and a profit and loss statement covering a period of between two and five years should be produced in order to ascertain the most favourable service schedule compatible with market considerations and overall company policy. Schedules should be kept under constant review so that they may be modified to meet changing circumstances.

SURVEYS AND MAINTENANCE

In some trades vessels are now entering dry dock for loadline surveys at intervals of two years or longer; indeed, some VLCCs and ULCCs are dry docked only every four years. This has been made possible by the adoption of shipboard management techniques (see Chapter 11) and the practice of spreading survey work over a number of years. The use of better paints and anti-fouling systems and the move towards in-water survey and inspection have also contributed to lengthening the period between visits to the dry dock.

The choice of shipyard for survey work should be based on a careful evaluation of competitive tenders. The three prime factors to consider are total fixed contract costs, the time scale and the standard of workmanship. However, attention should also be paid to the capacity and adequacy of yards – in particular their technical ability to undertake the work – general productivity, their record of industrial relations; the shipowner's previous experience with yards; exchange rates and the effect of any exchange rate variation on fixed cost contracts; the cost and duration of voyages to and from the yard and crew expenses during the survey period; any national or international policies towards particular countries undertaking ship survey work; the insurance provisions; arbitration terms in the event of a dispute; the availability of credit and the terms of payment.

In order to reduce costs, a few shipowners have decided to maintain their vessels only to the statutory obligations laid down by the country of registration rather than to the voluntary standards of ship classification societies. It should be noted that P and I clubs and insurance underwriters usually insist on vessels being maintained to classification society standards. The annual survey costs of passenger vessels can also be reduced by having a passenger certificate valid for only six months. This applies mainly to estuarial services, where services are either severely curtailed or discontinued in winter.

PROBLEMS CAUSED BY FLUCTUATIONS AND IMBALANCES IN TRADE

Fluctuations and imbalances in trade are common to all forms of transport, and particularly difficult to overcome satisfactorily in shipping. They are caused by economic, social and political factors, with the latter apparently growing in importance. The main circumstances in which trade imbalances occur in shipping are set out below.

1. One of the most extreme cases of imbalance is to be found in the shipment of the world's oil. Tankers convey the oil from producing to consuming countries and return in ballast. This is an extremely difficult problem to solve. To lessen the impact of the unproductive ballast voyage, tankers tend to return at a slightly higher speed than when laden.

2. An abnormal amount of cargo in a particular area – owing to an unusually large harvest, for example – or an exceptionally high demand for imports – caused perhaps by famine or shortages – can give rise to an imbalance in traffic. Ships will be fully laden in one direction but sailing in ballast in the other. This problem, which arises in the tramp market, can be mitigated by the use of multi-purpose dry cargo vessels that can carry a different commodity to or from a nearby port and thus reduce the voyage in ballast to a minimum.

3. Government restrictions might be imposed on the import and/or export of certain goods. Import restrictions may be necessary to protect home industries and help maintain employment, to combat a persistent trade deficit or to preserve a country's holdings of hard currency. They may be temporary or permanent, depending on the circumstances in which they were introduced. Official trade restrictions are tending to increase in spite of the development of free trade areas and bilateral agreements aimed at reducing the practice.

4. Other political factors, such as flag discrimination, distort the volume of cargo freely available for carriage. Further information will be found in Chapter 14.

5. Seasonal fluctuations in traffic can cause the industry difficulties. Peak traffic flows tend to inflate the fleet complement and foster uneconomic operation. They are particularly evident in the

tramp markets, although they will become less prevalent as modern technology permits the processing and storage of commodities, leading to more even demand for ship capacity. Seasonal fluctuations in traffic flows can be smoothed out by varying charges according to the season, diverting traffic from popular routes to less busy ones, offering shippers advantageous rates on such items as warehouse storage and developing closer liaison with shippers through trade associations and shippers' councils. Methods of coping with the peak volume that will remain include increasing sailing speeds, switching vessels from a less busy trade, chartering additional tonnage, carrying more deck cargo when weather permits, returning empty containers and trailers by a different route, improving the planning of shipboard stowage in order to reduce loading time and generally improving port turnround.

6. Passenger services are obviously subject to seasonal fluctuations. Shipowners often organize cruises to fill unused capacity during the off-season.

7. The flow of traffic between two countries may be balanced, but difficulties may still arise owing to differences in the characteristics and stowage factors of the commodities to be carried in the two directions. Problems of this nature involving break bulk cargo in 'tween deck vessels have been overcome by the construction of shelter deck vessels (see *Elements of Shipping*) Such disparities may have been accentuated by the development of containerization, although the problem is now diminishing as the range of container types increases. For example, in one direction the cargo may comprise a very large proportion of perishable goods requiring refrigerated accommodation or containers, while in the other direction manufactured items such as machinery, consumer goods or trade cars might be carried. A problem then arises with regard to the return of the refrigerated containers; they could either be shipped empty, which might leave insufficient space for the return cargo, or adapted to take refrigerated or non-refrigerated dry cargo of a limited commodity range. Collapsible containers have been introduced in a few trades, but they have met with limited success and are unlikely to gain ground.

The larger the fleet, the greater the opportunities to combat trade imbalances. The operator of a large fleet is generally engaged in a number of different trades and is thus able to switch some of his vessels to the trades where demand is greatest. Cargo liners are more vulnerable to imbalances than tramp vessels, as unlike the latter they cannot normally change from one trade to another. This may be overcome by operating a liner as a tramp vessel on certain runs, which necessarily entails a short voyage in ballast to link up with one of the tramp trades. Liners can switch trades in certain circumstances, thereby ensuring maximum use of the vessels; one example is that of ships within a consortium serving a group of trades.

Technology has helped smooth out some of the imbalances and fluctuations in trade. For example, modern techniques allow the distribution of certain bulk foodstuffs to be spread over a longer period and the development of multi-purpose vessels has brought greater flexibility of operation. Some vehicular ferries in the short sea trades have as many as four hydraulically operated decks to permit a variable combination of cars and road haulage vehicles to be carried. Likewise, some container ships have an integral ramp so that they can accommodate both containers and vehicles, an arrangement that permits great flexibility and independence of port operation. Such multi-purpose vessels are more expensive to build but offer greater opportunities for profitable operation in the changing context of international trade.

Finally, operators faced with a severe imbalance of trade may endeavour to resolve the problem by means of the price mechanism; this is particularly relevant to cargo liner services. A résumé of market pricing is contained in Chapter 11.

THE RELATIVE IMPORTANCE OF SPEED, FREQUENCY, RELIABILITY AND COST OF SEA TRANSPORT

There are four factors that influence the nature of a shipping service – speed, frequency, reliability and cost. Rapid and frequent services with a high degree of reliability will generally be found in the cargo liner trades, whereas cheap transport is usually the preserve of tramp vessels.

Speed and frequency of service are essential for the transportation of certain commodities, such as fresh fruit and vegetables. Manufacturers of consumer goods also value speed as it reduces the risk of obsolescence and the cost of having goods in transit. The need for speed is perhaps felt most keenly in the long-distance trades, where voyage time may be reduced appreciably and the shipper given the benefit of rapid delivery. Frequency of service can also be important where goods may be sold only in small quantities at frequent intervals. Reliability is an essential requirement for shippers who have to meet deadlines set by letters of credit and import licences. It also implies that the goods will arrive in good order and that the shipping company will provide adequate facilities at the docks and at its offices for the completion of the necessary documents and other formalities. These requirements are recognized and met by liner operators, who balance the need for speed against the additional capital and operating cost involved and phase their sailings to suit the rhythm of their customers' cargoes. Freight rates for such services are fairly stable and higher than those charged by tramp vessels; shipowners can hold rates at a reasonable level to yield a profit, although they have to liaise with shippers to ensure that they are not so high as to price the goods out of the market. There is some justification in the argument that those who ship goods by liner vessels should pay higher transportation charges for the service, which is expensive to provide.

Commodities of low value, on the other hand, have to be shipped as cheaply as possible, as the freight cost may have a direct bearing on their saleability. Many cargoes in this category, such as coal, mineral ores, timber, grain and other bulk commodities, are generally transported under programmed stockpile arrangements, so that speed and frequency of service are of minor significance. More important is the availability of tramp shipping space, the rates for which vary in accordance with supply and demand. If space is plentiful, rates will be only marginally above the operating cost of the vessel. When the market is tight rates will rise, but an upper limit will be set by the prospective price of the commodity at the point of sale.

Price remains a dominant factor in the shipper's choice of service, in spite of the fact that government trade policies and flag discrimination are exerting an increasing influence on international shipping. In broad terms distribution costs account for between 8 and 15 per cent of total product costs. It is therefore important that sea freight be set at a level that is reasonable but also generates the profits needed to sustain a modern fleet.

PORT OPERATION

An evaluation of ship operation would be incomplete if we failed to examine port operation and the points to bear in mind when assessing various port selection options. It is very important to attain maximum efficiency, above all in ship turnround time, and to ensure that port activities are carried out smoothly and do not constitute an impediment in the overall transit operation.

The following points are relevant to both port operation and the related formulation of ship schedules:

(a) Ship design should take account of flexible cargo transhipment arrangements to reduce ship turnround time. An example is the combi carrier (see Diagram X in Appendix B), which should help shipowners attain this objective.

(b) Close contacts should be maintained at all times with the port authority, shippers, agents, customs, trade associations and inland transport operators in order to facilitate rapid cargo transhipment.

(c) Particular attention should be paid to berth layout and back-up facilities, such as an adequate container stacking area, handling equipment, distribution network and customs clearance. It is essential that the short and long-term requirements for the incoming and outgoing consignments of each sailing be planned in advance; full use should be made of computers in this exercise.

(d) The port should be operational 24 hours a day and ideally should have a capital-intensive system of cargo transhipment to take advantage of modern technology. Access to the port should be continuous and its location should be such that cargo transhipment is not subject to disruption owing to bad weather.

(e) Good road, rail and canal communications should be available.

(f) Ideally, the port should be situated on a shipping lane. It should also be away from residential areas but be supported by a strong hinterland and should have room for expansion.

(g) Good industrial relations should prevail; the management should also be forward looking and keen to take advantage of modern technology in port operation and thereby maintain optimum efficiency.

(h) The berths should be designed for ease of transhipment to and from road, rail and inland waterway transport. There may be multi-purpose berths dealing with general cargo, container berths, a ramp for vehicular cargo, bulk cargo berths for particular cargoes such as oil, ore or grain which involve specialized cargo handling equipment and lay-up berths for vessels with no current employment or ships on standby. Berths may be leased by the shipping line from the port authority; in this case the company will provide its own cargo handling equipment and labour. Alternatively, the berths may be available to a number of shipowners in accordance with a berth occupancy programme negotiated annually between the port authority and the various ship operators.

(i) More efficient port operation and cargo transhipment can improve ship turnround time and thereby lessen the pressure for faster voyages, which can prove costly in an age of rising fuel costs. This should be borne in mind when examining ways of improving the overall cargo transit time.

Over the long term the role of ports will increase in importance in the development of economic ship operation. Closer liaison among all the parties involved, in particular shipowners, shippers and port authorities, will be essential if this objective is to be realized.

CHAPTER 6

The Freight Market

Tramp and liner freight rates. International road haulage freight rates.
Maritime container rates. International train ferry rates. Inland waterway
freight rates. Short sea and estuarial passenger trades. The constituents of
freight rates. Factors influencing the level of freight rates.

TRAMP AND LINER FREIGHT RATES

Freight is the reward payable to a carrier for the carriage and arrival
of goods in a recognized condition. The pricing of a cargo ship's
services is dependent on the forces of supply and demand, but the
factors underlying them are perhaps more complicated than is the
case with most other industries. As with all forms of transport,
the demand for shipping is derived from the demand for the commodities carried, which is itself affected by the competition of
substitute goods. Ships on any particular route are competing
against other carriers on the same route, vessels serving alternative
supply areas, air transport and, in coastal services, inland transport.

The cost of transport in relation to the market price of the goods
carried has an important effect on the demand for shipping services;
total distribution costs generally account for between 8 and 15 per
cent of the market price of commodities. The freight eventually
fixed depends largely on the relationship between buyers and
sellers. Where both groups are large and have equal bargaining
power, prices are set by the 'haggling of the market' and are known
as contract prices. The market for tramp charters operates under
such conditions; tramp companies are usually medium-sized concerns and the merchants who use their services usually possess equal
bargaining power.

Charter parties may be for a single voyage at a rate per ton of the
commodity carried (a voyage charter) or for a period at a stipulated
rate of hire, usually based on the ship's deadweight carrying
capacity (a time charter). The rates for the two kinds of contract
generally move in the same direction, although time charter rates
tend to fluctuate more widely than voyage rates as they reflect
market expectations. The factors determining fixture rates are
explained in Chapter 7.

The rate structure for tramps is therefore very simple, being the result of the competitive interplay of supply and demand. Rates in the liner trades are determined differently. Here the shipowners control fairly large concerns, and the bulk of their traffic comes from a host of small shippers. It is therefore more convenient for shipowners to estimate how much their customers are prepared to pay and to fix their rates accordingly. These are known as tariff prices, which are issued by the liner conferences. As liner rates are relatively stable, merchants can quote prices (including freight) before the goods have been shipped.

Liner rates are based partly on cost and partly on value. Commodities of very high value are charged at *ad valorem* rates. Many freight rates are quoted on the basis of weight or measurement, that is to say that they are applied either per tonne of 1000 kg (2205 lb) or per tonne of 1.133 m³, whichever produces the greater revenue. The reason for this method of charging is that heavy cargo will immerse a vessel to her loadline before her holds are full, while light cargo will fill her space without bringing her down to her maximum draught. To produce the highest revenue a vessel must be loaded to her full internal capacity and immersed to her maximum permitted depth. In most trades cargo measuring less than 1.133 m³ per tonne is charged by weight, while items measuring 1.133 m³ per tonne or more are charged by volume. Additional charges are usually made for heavy lifts, great length, dangerous classified cargoes and livestock requiring the provision of special facilities.

In general, liner and tramp rates move parallel to one another, although liner rates are more stable. Tramp rates provide liners with only limited competition, but liner operators will feel obliged to reduce their tariffs if tramp rates fall. However, the link is likely to be loosened by the increasing specialization of liners, which may eliminate competition from tramps entirely in some commodities.

A fuller treatment of tramp and liner freight rates will be found in *Elements of Shipping*.

INTERNATIONAL ROAD HAULAGE FREIGHT RATES

The growth of the international road haulage routes from the United Kingdom to Europe, the Middle East and Asia has been outstanding in recent years, particularly between the United Kingdom and the continent of Europe under CMR conditions. Britain's entry into the European Communities has undoubtedly facilitated this development.

Rates charged to freight forwarders and shippers for the carriage of vehicles or trailers on vehicular ferries are based on trailer/vehicle length and whether it is empty or loaded, accompanied or unaccompanied. They do not include items such as customs clearance charges. Additional charges are levied for excessive width or height and special rates usually apply to cargoes declared as valuable. Operators grant rebates to hauliers or agents who send a substantial volume of traffic by a particular route or service. Competition among operators is keen, not only with regard to rates but also in the fringe benefits offered, such as free passage and free cabins or meals for drivers. An increasing number of large and medium-sized exporters now undertake their own international distribution by road, a practice that has many advantages, particularly if the flow of goods in the two directions can be balanced.

Shippers using the services of international road freight forwarders – much of whose work involves groupage traffic – pay a rate based on the cubic measurement or weight of the cargo, the commodity classification and the origin and destination of the cargo. A volume of 1.133 m³ is the equivalent of 1 tonne. Rates are very competitive, particularly in relation to air freight and train ferry rates over distances up to 900–1000 km. An increasing number of the larger road haulage operators despatch their vehicles unaccompanied on vehicular ferries. By having drivers deposit the trailers at the ferry terminal and collect others that have returned they can avoid incurring driver lodging allowances, achieve better vehicle control and generally improve vehicle crew productivity.

MARITIME CONTAINER RATES

Rates for full container loads (FCL) are generally determined by the container type, its capacity and the origin and destination of the merchandise. The through rate will include the inland transportation cost, which comprises collection and terminal handling expenses but excludes items such as customs clearance charges and demurrage. Some containers are packed and unpacked at container bases, which may be situated at inland clearance depots. A number of large multinational companies have their own containers, which are usually of a specialized type offering a two-way traffic flow and subject to individually negotiated contract rates.

A very substantial volume of the cargo conveyed in containers is less than container load traffic (LCL). The goods are assembled and packed into containers at a container base or inland clearance depot, with each individual consignment attracting a separate rate calculated on the basis of weight or cubic measurement, the origin and destination of the merchandise and any likely disbursements such as handling or customs clearance charges.

Additional charges are levied on consignments requiring special facilities, such as livestock or indivisible loads needing heavy lifting gear.

Maritime container rates are very competitive over distances of more than 900 km and this mode of transport now accounts for a substantial proportion of deep sea general merchandise cargo.

INTERNATIONAL TRAIN FERRY RATES

Freight rail services throughout Europe are operated by British Rail and its European counterparts under CIM arrangements. Rates are based on the origin and destination of the consignment and include a charge per wagon to encourage full loads. Special rates apply to particular streams of traffic and to privately owned train ferry wagons.

A substantial volume of cargo is also consolidated into wagon loads by forwarding agents, who pay a tariff based on the wagon unit and charge shippers according to the weight or cubic measurement of the consignments.

Overall, the rates are very competitive over distances in excess of 900 km and the popularity of the service is increasing as new types of wagon are introduced by private operators.

INLAND WATERWAY FREIGHT RATES

Tariffs for sections of international transits undertaken by inland waterway are based on distance, the weight or volume of the consignment and the commodity type; they include transhipment costs, handling charges and any other miscellaneous expenses but exclude customs clearance charges. Reduced rates usually apply to containers and palletized cargoes and contract tariffs are available for regular shipments.

In some trades the lighter aboard ship (LASH) concept has been developed. This type of ship enables lighters to be carried from one port to another, thus combining inland waterway and oceanic transportation. Each ship can carry about 73 barges of 400 tons capacity. Rates are usually charged on a port-to-port basis.

The distribution of international trade by inland waterways reaching out from the major European ports is very extensive, for a variety of reasons. Here too, rates are based on weight or cubic measurement and vary by commodity and trade. It is a very competitive method of distribution for certain commodities and one that is continuing to expand as the system is further developed.

SHORT SEA AND ESTUARIAL PASSENGER TRADES

Since the 1960s the passenger market in the short sea and estuarial trades has substantially increased in many countries. Much of this growth can be attributed to the accompanied car market as, for example, in the passenger routes across the Irish Sea and the English Channel. The voyage time varies greatly from one route to another, ranging from 10 to 45 minutes in estuarial services and from $1\frac{1}{2}$ to 36 hours in the short sea trades. The bulk of the traffic in the latter falls within the 3–8 hour voyage band. Modern vessels are capable of carrying road haulage vehicles (see above), foot passengers, accompanied cars and occasionally caravans. The foot passenger market is vulnerable to competition from airlines, but this is not a threat in the case of accompanied cars as air ferry services have a fairly limited capacity.

The following factors determine fares:

(a) Length of voyage

(b) Competition from airlines and other shipping lines

(c) Port dues for passengers and vehicles

(d) Fuel and crew costs and other direct and indirect voyage expenses

(e) Agreements with other operators

(f) The season, the day of the week and the time of travel (day or night). On some routes concessionary fares are available for mid-week travel or in the off-peak season

(g) Class of travel, adult or child, type of cabin, if any. Concessionary fares are sometimes available to students, old-age pensioners or for travel to special events such as trade fairs

(h) Party travel. Concessionary fares are usually available to parties of ten persons or more; this is very much in evidence with the inclusive rail and sea holidays being offered by travel agents

(i) Length of car and number of accompanying passengers

(j) Any government statutory control over fares

(k) Revenue accruing from catering, entertainment facilities on board ship, advertising and shop sales of goods such as tobacco, spirits and gifts

Operators will set their tariffs to maximize revenue and ensure that capacity is utilized to the full during the off-peak season. They will also have regard to the needs of their regular clientele; regular road hauliers will thus be given preference over ordinary motorists in the allocation of deck space.

Further information on passenger fares in general will be found in *Elements of Shipping*.

THE CONSTITUENTS OF FREIGHT RATES

The tariff charged for a consignment may comprise not only the sea and inland transport freights but also a number of other elements. The extent to which they are included will depend on the custom of the trade and the shipowner. The constituents are therefore as follows:

1. Cargo tariff rate. In the case of maritime transport, this will be a port-to-port rate for containers, Ro/Ro vehicles and general cargo.

2. The customs clearance charge is usually based on the local port authority tariff. There are separate scales for imports and exports and charges vary according to commodity type, quantity and the degree of physical customs examination of the consignment, the latter usually attracting a separate charge that includes presentation of the requisite documents to the customs office. HM Customs have the legal authority to examine all imported consignments, but in reality only random inspection is made at the discretion of the customs officer. Customs clearance may be undertaken at an inland clearance depot, with the goods travelling under bond to or from the port. The presentation of the goods to customs and their ultimate clearance will be undertaken on behalf of the shipper by the port authority or the freight forwarder.

3. Freight forwarder's commission. Many small exporters engage the services of a freight forwarder to attend to the distribution of the

consignment. The commission charged usually amounts to 5 per cent of the total freight account. The role of freight forwarders is explained in Chapter 2.

4. Customs duty and value added tax – or its equivalent in other countries – are charged on imported consignments at rates varying according to the commodity specification.

5. Disbursements. These comprise a variety of items including freight services, telephone calls, telex messages, currency surcharges, fuel surcharges, feed for livestock and the protection of valuable consignments.

6. Cargo insurance. The premium depends on the trade and the method of forwarding (e.g. container, train ferry, Ro/Ro or general freight in a 'tween deck vessel). A surcharge applies to exceptional risks such as hostilities, fragile cargoes or art treasures.

7. Charges for the collection and delivery of the cargo if the shipper does not attend to this himself. The rate is normally determined on the basis of distance and the weight or cubic measurement of the consignment. In some circumstances these charges may be included in the through rate.

8. Transhipment costs, arising when the cargo is transhipped *en route* to continue its transit in another vessel or by air. The charge may be included in the through rate, depending on circumstance. Higher rates may apply to cargoes of awkward shape, excessive weight or size and to certain types of load such as livestock.

9. Documentation charge. In certain circumstances it is necessary to present a certificate of origin to the customs of the importing country in order to establish the place of manufacture of the goods. This document is obtained by the exporter from the local chamber of commerce or, if a consular invoice is required, from the consulate of the importing country. The consulate's charge for this service may be as much as £30.

10. Demurrage. Cargo detained at a seaport or inland clearance depot for longer than a prescribed period is subject to a daily demurrage charge. The delay may be caused by the wrong presentation of customs documents, the lack of export or import licences, the non-payment of customs duty or delay in collection by the consignee.

11. The cost of handling the cargo at the terminal. This is sometimes included in the through rate. In the case of containers, it is usually based on a tariff per container lift, varying according to

container type and whether it is empty or loaded. Extra charges are levied for special lifts, such as indivisible loads.

12. Wharfage charge, levied by the port authority for the transhipment of cargo.

13. Cargo dues, imposed by the port authority for goods passing over the quay.

14. Rebates. Exporters who generate substantial traffic are granted a rebate providing they adhere to the conditions laid down by the shipowner or liner conference. The level of rebate is usually negotiated between the parties concerned. Some companies offer immediate rebates on the published tariff while others give a deferred rebate payable six months in arrears. The latter is essentially a device to ensure that shippers will continue to use a conference or shipping line, as rebates of this kind can be lost if they turn to other carriers. Rebates are very prevalent in liner conference trades and Ro/Ro services between the United Kingdom and continental Europe, where they have amounted to as much as 37.5 per cent in exceptional cases.

FACTORS INFLUENCING THE LEVEL OF FREIGHT RATES

We shall now examine the main factors that influence the level of freight rates:

1. Competition in its many forms. Members of liner conferences charge uniform rates but compete fiercely with one another in service quality and ancillary services. They are also competing against non-members providing regular services and speculative shipowners offering irregular sailings when cargoes are plentiful. Moreover, airlines and overland routes, such as the Trans-Siberian Railway between Europe and the Far East, are competitors in some areas, as are certain multinational industrial companies that operate their own fleets to carry their raw materials or finished products. Ships serving similar routes will also be competing for the available traffic. Competition undoubtedly has a profound effect on rates and can result in manipulation of the rebate level. Shipowners must constantly bear in mind all aspects of competition to ensure that they can maximize their market shares.

2. The nature of the commodity, its quantity, overall cubic measurements, dimensions, value and the period of shipment(s). A

number of shipowners set their tariffs by commodity classification, with valuable, awkwardly shaped, heavy or dangerous cargoes and livestock attracting rather higher rates, while palletized cargoes are awarded concessions by some port authorities. In broad terms, large shipments conveyed regularly over a period of perhaps a year or longer attract favourable rate concessions; this usually takes the form of a negotiated contract rate, which generally does not qualify for rebates. Shipowners should take care not to obtain the bulk of their traffic from a few major shippers able to command large rate concessions and practically monopolize the service. It is better to have a mixture of large, medium-size and small clients with a wide range of commodities in order to maintain a reasonably high average rate and lessen the impact of the withdrawal of any one client from the service owing to recession, a rates war or some other cause.

3. The origin and destination of the cargo. Break bulk tariffs are based on distance from port to port, while in the case of combined transport a through rate is charged to cover sea freight and transportation by road, rail or canal between the ports and the inland points of departure and destination. Rates based on distance may be adjusted to keep a service competitive in relation to a shorter route serving the same market.

4. The overall transit cost. It is most important that traffic flows and particular commodities be costed to ensure that the rate is adequate. Costing a shipping service is a difficult task, as a break bulk cargo liner can convey up to 10 000 consignments on a single voyage. The unit load concept inherent in containerization and Ro/Ro operation has eased the situation, as one need only compute the cost for the units, which generally vary only in length and weight. The costing of bulk shipments is less complex, but requires careful evaluation nonetheless. The load factor at which the vessel will be profitable must also be determined; in liner trades this tends to be between 60 and 70 per cent.

5. The need for additional facilities to accommodate the cargo, such as heavy lifting gear, a strong room or stalls for livestock. Such facilities usually command a higher rate to offset the additional expense.

6. The mode(s) of transport. This will influence costs and hence the rate structure. Container vessels, Ro/Ro ships, break bulk carriers and train ferries each apply different tariffs.

7. Expected exchange rate variations. It may be necessary to introduce a currency surcharge scale in the event of violent exchange rate fluctuations.

8. Agreements with other operators. This is particularly applicable to liner conference trades, where uniform rates are charged by all members.

9. Any statutory controls. An increasing number of governments are tending to control or influence the level of rates on services to their ports. They require evidence to justify rate increases and do not usually favour cartels.

10. Relations with shippers' councils and trade associations established to safeguard their members' interests. Such bodies are active in most cargo liner trades and would not recommend their members to accept unjustifiably large rate increases.

11. Bunkering costs. In view of the rising cost of fuel, operators tend to impose a bunker or fuel surcharge to cater for unpredictable increases in fuel costs.

12. Operating subsidies paid by some countries tend to depress rates; for example, low wage scales and other financial advantages in Eastern bloc countries permit their fleets to offer rates 40 per cent below those of established cargo liner operators from Western countries. (See also Chapter 14).

Governments and shippers are both showing increasing interest in the level of freight rates. Shippers are having a more forceful influence on the formulation of rates through the shippers' councils that have emerged in recent years, while trade associations often reflect national government policies. International entities such as the EEC are also turning their attention to rates throughout the world. The combined pressure from these sources is likely to increase, thus keeping rates down to a level which many consider uneconomic.

In ship management terms the level of rates must keep pace with the increase in service costs and, at the same time, permit the maintenance of service standards to facilitate an expansion in trade. Shippers should therefore be sympathetic towards reasonable tariffs so that shipowners can afford to invest in new tonnage. A properly compiled tariff structure for all classes of cargo should ensure the best balance between revenue production and the full, economical utilization of vessels.

CHAPTER 7

Economics of Chartering

The determination of fixture rates. The charterer's requirements. The Baltic Mercantile and Shipping Exchange. The Baltic and International Maritime Conference (BIMCO). Worldscale.

Chartering is a complex and expanding part of the business of ship management. This chapter deals primarily with the economics of chartering rather than with technicalities or charter party clauses, which are examined in *Elements of Shipping*. Opportunity is also taken to describe the role of the Baltic Mercantile and Shipping Exchange, and the Baltic and International Maritime Conference.

THE DETERMINATION OF FIXTURE RATES

The fixture or rate of hire of a vessel depends on the following factors:

(a) The state of the market for chartered tonnage. When vessels are scarce fixture rates tend to be high, and vice versa. The extent of the fluctuations depends on other factors examined below, in particular the type and terms of the charter party and the vessel's specification.

(b) The world economic outlook. If events suggest an upturn in trade, rates will tend to increase; for example, a poor grain harvest in the USSR will give rise to large imports of wheat from the USA and other countries. Conversely, when the price of oil rose sharply in 1973 many countries were obliged to reduce their merchandise imports in order to fund their oil import bill.

(c) The type of vessel sought. The fixture rates for vessels of a common specification will tend to fluctuate more widely than those for specialized or purpose-built ships.

(d) The duration of the charter party. The fixture rates for voyage charters tend to be more volatile than those for time charters, primarily owing to the shorter duration of the former. Time charters can extend up to seven years, during which period the economy may pass through the entire trade cycle of depression and recovery, so that time charter rates tend to be influenced less by economic

87

variations than by financial factors such as those outlined in item (e) below.

(e) The overall cost of providing the vessel, a factor of particular relevance to time charters. Fixed costs comprise such items as survey expenses, insurance, depreciation, administration and, where applicable, mortgage payments. Non-demise charter parties, whereby the shipowner provides the crew, will also entail variable costs, such as crew wages and expenditure on fuel. Charter parties may provide for rates to be index linked, particularly if the fuel and crew costs are to be borne by the shipowner. Fixture rates for tankers would be linked to the Worldscale index. A similar costing exercise would be undertaken before a shipowner negotiated a voyage charter.

(f) Ship specification, comprising especially the vessel's capacity, speed, draught, age, classification society, type of propulsion and crewing level. On the basis of this the charterer will be able to evaluate the economics of the charter in terms of both revenue production and expenses. For example, the vessel may have a high capacity but be slow and too deep a draught for optimum operation on a service. As a compromise, the vessel may be used partly laden and chartered on an interim basis.

(g) Any scale guidelines that apply, such as the Worldscale index.

THE CHARTERER'S REQUIREMENTS

A prospective charterer, whether he be a merchant with a quantity of cargo available for shipment or a shipowner wishing to augment his fleet, must state his requirements to the shipbroker acting on his behalf. In so doing he should consider the following specifications:

(a) The desired capacity. This is a primary consideration, particularly if a voyage charter is required for shipment of a given quantity of cargo. Ship capacity involves not only cubic capacity, but also deadweight tonnage. The stowage factor is also a useful criterion. If a charterer is engaging tonnage to augment an existing fleet, it is desirable that the capacity specification be similar to that of other vessels on the service to ensure flexibility of operation.

(b) The ship's speed. Another critical factor is the speed of the chartered vessel must match that of an existing fleet in a particular trade. The type of propulsion and its cost are particularly relevant.

(c) The general layout of the vessel, including cargo handling equipment and crew accommodation. The adequacy of equipment, such as having both bow and stern loading in Ro/Ro vessels, could have a bearing on ship turnround time.

(d) The trade and the ports of call. The trade will determine the type of vessel required while the ports of call and the route will influence its draught, length and beam; some ports and maritime canals will impose constraints in this regard.

(e) The date and place of commencement of the charter and its duration. In many cases a charterer would be wise to include an option to extend the charter.

(f) Type of charter, i.e. demise or non-demise, voyage or time charter party. This will have a fundamental effect on the fixture rate. Furthermore, if a demise charter party is to be concluded, other considerations will arise, such as the appointment of the crew, manning levels and questions of industrial relations.

(g) Type of cargo to be carried. Certain dangerous cargoes may be subject to limitations.

(h) Classification and registration of the vessel. These will have an impact on cost, particularly maintenance and survey expenditure and manning levels.

(i) The range of fixture rates the charterer considers viable. This requires careful evaluation and consultation with the shipbroker, particularly in relation to the terms of the charter party.

Charterers who are accustomed to engaging tonnage will have established good relations with their brokers, who will be aware of their clients' needs. Detailed costing should be carried out to ensure that the operation will be viable and preferable to alternative methods, such as the use of cargo liners or air freight or the purchase of a vessel. Full use should be made of brokers' professional services. The code of practice under which brokers operate is set out on pp. 92–95.

THE BALTIC MERCANTILE AND SHIPPING EXCHANGE

The Baltic Mercantile and Shipping Exchange, or the Baltic Exchange as it is more commonly known, has its origins in the coffee houses of seventeenth-century London. It was here that ships' captains and merchants would meet to discuss terms and contracts for the shipment of cargo.

In 1891 the London Shipping Exchange was founded to meet the needs of liner shipping. As its activities overlapped with those of the Baltic Exchange, the two institutions merged shortly afterwards and began to look for a suitable site for new premises. The present building in St Mary Axe, London, was the outcome; in 1903 it became the Baltic Mercantile and Shipping Exchange as we know it today.

In simple terms, the Baltic Exchange is a market-place where shipowners with space available can meet merchants seeking space for their cargo. Many different cargoes are involved – practically always bulk cargo – and it has been said that the Baltic Exchange can 'shift anything anywhere'. Its work falls into four main classes:

1. Purchase and sale of oil seeds and vegetable oils
2. Purchase and sale of grains
3. Chartering of ships or space in ships for the carriage of all types of cargo, to and from all parts of the world
4. Chartering of aircraft or space in aircraft for cargo or passengers.

Grain is one of the main cargoes carried by ships chartered on the 'Floor'; many of the other cargoes, such as ores, coal and oil, could be classified as 'minerals'. More than 700 companies are members of the Exchange; their 2500 representatives are entitled to conduct business on the Floor of the Exchange every working day between 10 a.m. and 4.30 p.m. Despite one of the worst slumps the shipping world has seen for many years, membership of the Baltic Exchange has increased annually for the last ten years.

The Baltic Exchange is also a major source of 'invisible' earnings for Britain, netting about £150 million annually. It has been estimated that three-quarters of the world's open market bulk cargo is at some stage handled by members of the Baltic Exchange in London. Similar but less important centres operate elsewhere, such as in New York and Tokyo.

THE BALTIC AND INTERNATIONAL MARITIME CONFERENCE

The Baltic and International Maritime Conference (BIMCO) was founded in 1905 by a group of shipowners principally engaged in

the Baltic and White Sea trades and was initially known as the Baltic
and White Sea Conference. Over the years its membership and
activities became worldwide and the name was changed in 1927. It
is now the largest private association in the maritime industry.

BIMCO serves as a forum in which shipowners and other persons
and organizations connected with the shipping industry can consider action on all matters affecting the industry and can establish
contacts with charterers, shippers, merchants, receivers or other
interested parties. It has three categories of member – owner
members (those owning or managing ships), broker members
(shipbrokers, ship agents and chartering agents) and club members
(protection and indemnity associations, freight, demurrage and
defence associations, shipping federations, shipowners' associations and other combinations of shipowners). There are members
in 95 countries. The owner members include companies engaged in
all kinds of shipping activity, such as dry cargo tramp trades, regular
liner business, combined transport, oil and chemical tanker trades,
liquid gas trades, reefers, towage and salvage, offshore supply
vessels and drilling vessels. In 1979 the tonnage of owner members
totalled 169 million grt (about 286 million dwt). There were also
more than 1680 broker members and 50 club members.

Every two years BIMCO holds a general meeting, which is
normally attended by 1100–1200 representatives from all parts of
the world. A number of committees are also active. In addition,
special working sessions are arranged for members and lectures are
given on subjects of topical interest to members of the shipping
community by persons experienced in their own field. BIMCO also
provides an information service on a wide range of subjects,
including unfair practices, the interpretation of charter terms,
advice in the event of a dispute, dues and charges, taxation, stowage
coefficients, the current situation in ports and information on
navigation and ice.

One of the most important parts of the organization's work
relates to the negotiation and approval of charter parties and bills of
lading. The various documents that have been approved are listed in
Elements of Shipping (pp. 303–306) whilst Sundry other forms are
given in Table 7.1.

BIMCO has also established principles for the use of parties
engaged in chartering and ship's agency procedures. They are
reproduced below.

Table 7.1   BIMCO approved sundry other forms

Conlinebooking	Liner booking note to be used with Conlinebill liner bill of lading
Visconbooking	Liner booking note to be used with Visconbill liner bill of lading
Saleform	Memorandum of agreement (revised 1966, layout 1974)
	Standard statement of facts (both short and long forms)
	Standard time sheet (both short and long forms)
	Standard statement of facts (oil and chemical tank vessels); both short and long forms
	Standard disbursements account
Combidoc	Combined transport document (edition of 1st July, 1977) issued subject to ICC rules; available in English and French editions
Bimcosale	Recommended standard bill of sale

Recommended principles for the use of parties engaged in chartering and ship's agency procedures (as supported by the executive committee of BIMCO at its meeting held in Munich in May 1969)

1. In the conduct of his profession a broker shall exercise great care to avoid misrepresentation and shall be guided by the principles of honesty and fair dealing.

2. Under no circumstances may a broker avail himself of, or make use of an authority, if he does not actually hold it, neither can he alter the terms of an authority without the approval of principals concerned.

3. A broker, when requested to do so, must make it quite clear to others who wish to make him an offer than he has already received one or several firm offers for the particular order or vessel concerned.

4. No broker has authority to quote a vessel or a cargo, unless duly authorized by principals or their brokers.

5. Each party has to respect the channel through which a vessel or a cargo has been quoted to the broker in reply to a request from the party concerned.

6. An unsolicited offer or proposal does not in any way bind the party which receives it, unless this party takes such unsolicited offer or proposal.

7. Each party must describe honestly the conditions of availability of a vessel or cargo, namely in specifying whether, according to his knowledge, some reservations are attached to the vessel or the

cargo. In such cases reservations should be made quite clear.

8. The commissions due to the brokers are to be paid in accordance with the terms of the charter party and must not be retained by either party pending final settlement of accounts or eventually of a dispute in which the brokers have no liability.

9. Restrictions:

(a) The restriction 'subject stem' can only apply to shippers' and/or suppliers' agreement to make a cargo available for specified dates, to the exclusion of any other meaning. In case of stem not granted as required, no other ship can be fixed by charterers before the one initially fixed 'subject stem' has received the first refusal to accept the amended dated and/or quantity, provided they are reasonably near.

(b) The restriction 'subject open' or 'subject unfixed' can only apply when a vessel or a cargo is already under offer, once only, for a limited time, and the 'subject open' offer must be made with the same time limit. No extension can be granted, and no further negotiation can take place until the time limit has expired or until both offers have been answered.

(c) Any other 'subject . . .' to be clearly stipulated and limited and to be eventually properly justified.

10. The chartering conditions are hereunder described:

(a) *Dry Cargo*
   Names and domicile of contracting parties.
   Name of the vessel, flag, class and specifications.
   Ports and berths of loading and discharging.
   Laydays/cancelling dates.
   Accurate description of the cargo.
   Rates and conditions of loading and discharging.
   Rate of demurrage and despatch, if any.
   Rate of freight, basis of payment.
   Commissions.
   Type of the charter party with main amendments.
   Clauses of calculation of time, winch clause, etc.
   Special clauses for the trade concerned.

(b) *Oil charter party*
   Same as for dry cargo except:
   Laytime allowance all purposes.
   Rate of freight (plus or minus Intascale or any other internationally recognized scale).

(c) *Time Charter*

Names and domicile of contracting parties.
Name of vessel, flag, class and main specifications.
Places of delivery and re-delivery.
Date of re-delivery or period.
Intended trade and trading limits including exclusions.
Quantity and type of bunkers on board on delivery and re-delivery.
Price of bunkers.
Rate of hire, basis of payment.
Commissions.
Type of charter party with main amendments.

The details of a fixture consist of all items which are not described above, and in some cases can refer to a considerable number of typewritten clauses attached to printed charter party, or to alterations in the printed text of charter party.

If a fixture is confirmed, or an offer made or confirmed 'subject approval of details' or 'subject details' or 'subject arranging details' such negotiations can only be suspended if one party cannot agree and other party maintains one or more of such 'details' . . . and the above proviso cannot be taken as an excuse to break off negotiations for some other reason.

A broker shall not negotiate for or fix any vessel or any cargo on behalf of shipowners or charterers while he is interested directly or indirectly as charterer or shipowner or otherwise as principal, without the fact of such interest being previously disclosed to the shipowners or charterers.

Where a broker acts as a ship's agent

11. Duties. The protection of the vessel's interests at all times should be the aim and duty of a ship's agent, especially with regard to the quickest turnround of a ship in port at lowest possible expense.

12. Attendance to time chartered vessels. The agents appointed by the time charterers must perform all the normal services to the ship and her master as would have been performed if the vessel called under a voyage charter and the agent was appointed by the owners. All normal agency fees for ordinary agency services shall be charged against the time charterers.

13. Attendance as agents appointed by charterers. If a vessel

by the charter party is consigned to agents nominated by the charterers, the agents so appointed must perform all the normal services to the ship and her master as if the agent had been appointed direct by the owners, the agent charging the normal fees for his work, such fees not exceeding what would have been charged under a direct appointment by the owners.

14. Agency fees. The broker's agency fee should be clearly advised to shipowner and should be according to the scale of agency fees customarily applying in respective ports and countries. Such agency fee should represent the basis of all ship's agency negotiations.

15. Ship's disbursements. A ship's agent should not retain more freight than actually required for ship's disbursements, and should remit any balance promptly to owners.

Should the agent not collect any freight he should advise owners in good time the approximate amount required for ship's disbursements and owners should remit such funds to the agent in advance of ship's arrival in port.

The Institute of Chartered Shipbrokers works in close liaison with BIMCO.

Readers are particularly recommended to study BIMCO's very informative annual reports, which exemplify the importance of the organization in international shipping practice.

WORLDSCALE

The Worldscale is essentially an index of tanker freights calculated by the International Tanker Nominal Freight Scale Association Ltd, London, and the Association of Shipbrokers and Agents, New York. Worldscale 100 (WS 100) is a base rate calculation for a full cargo of crude or oil products transported on a round voyage from loading port or ports and back to the first loading port on the basis of the following factors:

1. The standard vessel:

   Summer deadweight – 19 500 long tons
   Summer draught – 30ft 6in laden in salt water
   Average speed – 14 knots
   Bunker consumption at sea – 28 tons/day, high viscosity fuel oil (h.v.f.o)

Bunker consumption in port – 5 ton/day, h.v.f.o.
Port time allowance – 96 hours (± 3 hours)
Fixed hire element – $1800/day (purely nominal value fixed)
Brokerage – 2.5 per cent

2. Port charges and weighted average contract bunker prices, as up-to-date as possible for the period under calculation.

3. Additional periods of 12 hours allowed for each additional loading and discharging port used; similarly, additional allowances of 36 hours for each transit of the Suez Canal and 24 hours for each transit of the Panama Canal.

Table 7.2 Monthly weighted average Worldscale rates for spot market dirty fixtures Arabian Gulf to North Europe, with corresponding average costs in US dollars per cargo ton (based on voyage Mena Al Ahmadi/Rotterdam via Cape/Cape

Month		1973	1974	1975	1976	1977	1978	1979
January	WS	116.70	95.60	24.70	25.80	26.001	19.70	34.40
	$	11.59	9.91	3.63	4.21	4.39	3.54	6.32
February	WS	119.90	87.00	23.40	27.00	26.10	22.80	26.20
	$	11.91	9.02	3.44	4.41	4.41	4.10	4.81
March	WS	120.20	86.80	26.10	25.10	28.80	20.70	41.30
	$	11.94	9.00	3.84	4.10	4.86	3.72	7.58
April	WS	108.60	64.50	18.40	31.90	24.30	20.80	39.90
	$	10.78	6.69	2.71	5.23	4.10	3.74	7.33
May	WS	158.80	64.90	18.10	29.50	20.80	19.80	40.70
	$	15.77	6.73	2.66	4.84	3.51	3.56	7.47
June	WS	239.00	76.20	24.80	27.00	20.90	19.40	44.80
	$	23.73	7.91	3.65	4.43	3.53	3.48	8.23
July	WS	183.60	48.30	30.40	29.80	23.20	25.70	66.6
	$	18.23	5.01	4.47	4.90	3.93	4.63	12.23
August	WS	282.60	47.00	29.40	30.60	24.20	30.70	49.90
	$	28.06	4.87	4.32	5.03	4.10	5.53	9.36
September	WS	313.30	51.20	33.40	27.00	22.40	33.90	–
	$	31.11	5.31	4.91	4.44	3.79	6.11	–
October	WS	284.80	71.90	20.10	30.30	24.30	44.90	–
	$	28.28	7.46	2.96	4.98	4.11	8.90	–
November	WS	102.90	42.30	18.80	33.10	27.60	49.40	–
	$	10.22	4.39	2.76	5.45	4.67	8.90	–
December	WS	88.20	41.40	19.40	32.10	32.70	44.00	–
	$	8.76	4.29	2.85	5.28	5.54	7.93	–

The dollar equivalents have been calculated at the banker prices current at the time of fixture.

Hence, irrespective of vessel size and route, the Worldscale freight index expresses tanker rates as a percentage of the costing of a standard vessel; for example, WS 175 = 75 per cent more than the cost of running the standard vessel. In all, there are Worldscale rates for seven categories of tanker, including general purpose, medium range, large range 1, large range 2, VLCC Worldscale and ULCC Worldscale.

Table 7.2 shows Worldscale rates for the period 1973–79.

CHAPTER 8

Finance of International Trade

Export and import prices. Payments on 'open account'. Bills of exchange.
Documentary credits and allied documents. Transferable credits. Back to
back credits. Revolving credits. Red clause credits. Acceptance credits.
Factoring. Bank finance for exports. Finance guaranteed by the ECGD. Less
common forms of trade. Changing methods of payment.

In the days when the United Kingdom had extensive overseas
investments and a dominant position in world trade, business was
fairly straightforward for British exporters. They encountered few
foreign exchange problems, as most transactions were conducted in
sterling, and the seller's market that prevailed allowed them to
dictate terms and to grant or refuse credit as they wished.

Today the picture is entirely different. Britain's overseas investments have been dispersed to pay for two wars, her products have
to compete with those of equally efficient and sometimes more
efficient producers in a buyer's market and sterling is no longer the
dominant currency but, like other currencies, is subject to considerable exchange rate fluctuations. Moreover, the ability to sell goods
abroad no longer depends solely on quality, delivery and price; a
new factor of growing importance is the ability and willingness to
grant credit. The granting of credit terms, which are lengthening as
the dominance of buyers increases, means that the exporter must
wait longer for payment. This automatically reduces cash flow and
sooner or later forces the exporter to seek assistance from his bank.
Hence the financial aspects of selling goods abroad are likely to
assume increasing importance and, as a consequence, influence the
fortunes of the shipping industry.

EXPORT AND IMPORT PRICES

In the periods when rates of exchange remained stable for many
years, import and export prices tended to find their own level; they
probably owed little to serious research and careful consideration
but just emerged naturally. However, in the present period of
exchange rate instability, which may be said to have begun with the
devaluation of the pound sterling in November 1967, the setting
and adjustment of prices has become a serious problem.

In 1967 few traders had a pricing policy to content with a devaluation. Some held their sterling prices level, thus passing the 'full benefit of devaluation' on to their overseas dealers and customers. In consequence, they were flooded with orders that they were unable to fulfil, finance or deliver on time, with the result that they lost many orders and customers. Others kept their overseas prices unchanged and thus upset their customers, who thought they were entitled to a price reduction.

It should be borne in mind that a 10 per cent devaluation does not lead to a 10 per cent change in the local price of a commodity, as the export price is only one element in the final cost to the consumer. Customs duty, import and distribution costs and local mark-ups, which are expressed in local currency, account for about half the retail price of many goods. Hence a 10 per cent devaluation may at best lead to a change of about 5 per cent in local price.

In establishing prices, firms must decide whether to charge 'what the market will bear' in each case or to set prices that cover costs and give a reasonable return on the capital employed. It may be argued that if a manufacturer does not charge as much as the market will bear, other operators in that market will add the difference and make an easy profit; according to this view, it is unlikely that the final consumer will be charged any less. On the other hand, there is little point in charging what the market will bear if this fails to show a return.

Hence the question of pricing will revolve around:

1. The extent to which costs and returns on capital can be related to the price that the market will pay. This will involve a close study of the size and potential of the market, the strength of competitors and the elasticity of demand for the product.
2. The extent to which exchange rate changes can be used to advantage.
3. The credit terms that are usual in the market and whether the cost of the credit is borne by the buyer.
4. Sources of raw materials and possible price changes.

The practice of expressing export prices in the customer's currency is a marketing principle that has much to recommend it; from the buyer's point of view the price is clear and relatively stable and there are no problems with exchange rates. By selling in foreign currency, the exporter has assumed the exchange risk himself, but he can protect himself against any exchange rate fluctuations by selling the currency in the forward market (see Chapter 2).

PAYMENTS ON 'OPEN ACCOUNT'

Credit terms and the method of payment are agreed when the sales contract is concluded. If relations between the buyer and seller are good, they may agree to trade on 'open account' terms. This means simply that the seller will despatch the goods directly to the buyer, send him an invoice and await payment, as in domestic trading.

The debtor may use a number of means to pay his supplier:

1. Personal cheque. This is not very satisfactory from the creditor's point of view. Apart from the usual risk that the cheque may be dishonoured, it has to be sent through banking channels to the buyer's country for collection, thus incurring additional expense.

2. Banker's draft. This would be a draft drawn by the buyer's bank on its correspondent bank in the exporter's country. As such it is a good means of payment, but there is always the danger that the draft may be lost in the post; a new draft could be issued only against indemnity, as bank drafts cannot be 'stopped'.

3. Mail transfer (MT). This is the most common method of payment. The debtor instructs his bank to request its correspondent bank in the exporter's country to pay the specific amount to the exporter. The whole procedure is effected by accounting entries; the buyer's bank debits his account and credits the account of the correspondent bank which, on receipt of the payment instructions, passes a reciprocal entry over its account with the remitting bank and pays the money to the exporter. The instructions between the banks may be sent by ordinary mail or air mail.

4. Telegraphic transfer (TT). The procedure is essentially the same as for mail transfers except that the instructions are sent by cable, thus ensuring that payment is affected more quickly.

BILLS OF EXCHANGE

If 'open account' terms have not been agreed, the exporter has to arrange for collection of the amount due. One way in which this can be done is by drawing a bill of exchange, the traditional instrument for claiming that which is due from a debtor. Bills of exchange can be used in international trade involving practically all countries of the world. Indeed, in some countries a trader would be unwise to forgo the protection a bill can provide.

The use of bills of exchange presents several advantages:

1. The bill of exchange is an instrument long recognized by trade custom and by the law, so that it is governed by an established code of practice.
2. A bill is a specific demand on the debtor, which the latter refuses at his peril.
3. The bill is a useful instrument of finance.
4. The bill provides a useful mechanism for granting a pre-arranged period of credit to an overseas buyer. Thus if an exporter has to offer his client a period of credit of 90 days, the bill can be drawn at 90 days after sight.
5. The bill permits the exporter to maintain a degree of control over the shipping documents by making their release subject to payment or acceptance of the bill. Nevertheless, it should be noted that the drawing of a bill of exchange does not guarantee payment; bills too can be dishonoured.

In normal circumstances the exporter draws a bill of exchange, attaches the shipping documents to it and lodges the whole with his bank, giving very precise and complete instructions as to the action to be taken in certain circumstances: whether to forward the bill by air mail and ask for the proceeds to be remitted by cable or air mail; whether the documents are to be released against payment or acceptance of the bill; whether the bill is to be 'protested' if dishonoured; whether the goods should be stored and insured if not taken up by the buyer; whether rebate may be given for early payment; the party to whom the collecting bank may refer in case of dispute.

The exporter's bank will forward the bill and documents to its correspondent bank in the buyer's country, passing on exactly the instructions received from the exporter. Acting as collecting bank the correspondent will present the bill to the buyer and release the documents in accordance with the instructions received. If the arrangement called for payment to be made immediately, then the bill of exchange will be drawn at 'sight' and the instructions will be to release the documents against payment (D/P). If a period of credit has been agreed, then the bill will be drawn at, say, '90 days sight' and the instructions will be for the documents to be released against acceptance of the bill by the buyer (D/A). In this case, the buyer signs his acceptance across the face of the bill, which now becomes due for payment in 90 days, and he receives the documents of title to the goods. The collecting bank will advise the remitting bank of the date of acceptance and hold the bill until maturity, when it will present it to the buyer for payment. In the event of dishonour, the collecting bank will arrange 'protest' by a notary if it has been instructed to do so. This procedure provides legal proof that the bill was presented to the drawee and was dishonoured, and enables action to be taken in the courts without further preliminaries.

The procedures and responsibilities of the banks and other parties are laid down in the *Uniform Rules for the Collection of Commercial Paper* issued by the International Chamber of Commerce and accepted by major banks throughout the world.

The method of collecting payment described above is based on the documentary bill, but in certain circumstances use may be made of a 'clean' bill, that is, a bill to which no documents are attached. Such bills may be drawn for the collection of monies due for services or for any debt which does not relate to goods. A clean bill may also be used to obtain payment for goods sent on 'open account', especially where payment is overdue.

DOCUMENTARY CREDITS AND ALLIED DOCUMENTS

Apart from requiring 'cash with order', the most satisfactory method of obtaining payment is by means of a documentary credit. It provides security of payment to the exporter and enables the buyer to ensure that he receives the goods as ordered and delivered in the way he requires. It is an arrangement whereby the buyer requests his bank to establish a credit in favour of the seller. The buyer's bank (the issuing bank) undertakes, or authorizes its correspondent bank in the exporter's country, to pay the exporter a sum of money (normally the invoice price of the goods) against presentation of specified shipping documents. It is a mandatory contract and completely independent of the sales contract. It is concerned only with documents and not the goods to which the documents refer. Liability for payment now rests with the issuing bank and not the buyer. Such credits are usually 'irrevocable', which means that they cannot be cancelled or amended without the agreement of the beneficiary (the exporter) and all other parties. The exporter can thus rely on payment being made as soon as he has shipped the goods and produced the necessary documents. The security provided by an irrevocable credit may be further enhanced if the bank in the exporter's country (the advising bank) is requested by the issuing bank to add its 'confirmation'. The exporter then has a 'confirmed irrevocable credit' and he need look no further than his own local bank for payment. If a credit is not 'confirmed', liability for payment rests with the issuing bank abroad, although the advising bank would usually be prepared to negotiate with recourse.

A documentary credit contains a detailed description of the goods: price per unit and packing; name and address of the beneficiary; the voyage, that is, port of shipment and port of destination; whether the price is FOB, C & F or CIF; and whether part shipments and transhipment are allowed. In some cases, the ship will be named. Details of insurance (if CIF) and the risks to be covered will also be shown. The credit will specify a latest date for shipment and an expiry date, which is the latest date for the presentation of documents. It will also stipulate a time limit for presentation measured from the issue date of the bills of lading; in the absence of such a stipulation, banks refuse to accept documents presented later than 21 days after issuance of the bills.

The basic documents usually required are the following:

1. Invoice. The amount must not exceed the credit amount. If terms such as 'about' or 'circa' are used, a tolerance of 10 per cent is allowed (in respect of quantity the tolerance is 3 per cent). The description of the goods on the invoice and the packing must be precise and agree with the credit. An essential part of the description is the marks and numbers on the packages. These must appear on the invoice, which should be in the name of the buyer.

2. Bills of lading. These are the document of title to the goods, without which the buyer will not be able to obtain delivery from the shipping company. The credit will call for a full set; they are usually issued in sets of three. They must be clean, that is to say bear no superimposed clauses derogatory to the condition of the goods such as 'inadequate packing', 'used drums' or 'on deck'. Unless the credit has specifically permitted the circumstances contained in the clause, the negotiating bank will request an indemnity. The bills of lading must show the goods to be 'on board'. Bills marked 'received for shipment' are not acceptable unless they bear a subsequent

notation, dated and signed, stating that the goods are 'on board'. Under the new regulations set out in the *Uniform Customs and Practice for Documentary Credits* the following bills of lading will be accepted:

(a) Through bills issued by shipping companies or their agents, even though they cover several modes of transport.
(b) Short form bills of lading which indicate some or all of the conditions of carriage by reference to a source or document other than the bill of lading.
(c) Bills covering unitized cargoes such as those on pallets or in containers.

Unless specifically authorized in the credit, bills of the following type will not be accepted:

(a) Bills of lading issued by forwarding agents.
(b) Bills which are issued under and are subject to a charter party.
(c) Bills covering shipments by sailing vessels.

The bills must be made out to the order of the shipper and endorsed in blank. If the sales contract is CIF or C & F, then the bills must be marked 'freight paid'. The general description of the goods including marks and numbers must match the details given in the invoice. The voyage and ship, if named, must be stated in the credit. Unless transhipment is expressly prohibited in the credit, bills indicating transhipment will be accepted provided the entire voyage is covered by the same bill. Part shipments are permitted unless the credit states otherwise.

3. Insurance. The policy or certificate must be as stated in the credit and must have been issued by an insurance company or its agent. Cover notes issued by brokers are not acceptable. The details on the policy must match those on the bills of lading – it must also be in the same currency as the credit and endorsed in blank. The amount covered should be at least the invoice amount – credits usually call for invoice value plus 10 per cent. The policy must be dated not later than the date of shipment as evidenced by the bill of lading. The risks covered should be those detailed in the credit, usually Institute cargo clauses W & SRCC. If cover against 'all risks' is called for but is unobtainable, a policy covering all insurable risks will be acceptable.

According to circumstances, the credit may call for other documents, such as consumer certificates, certificate of origin, quality, analysis or health certificates (which assure the buyer that the goods are as ordered), air waybills, railway (CIM) or road (CMR) consignment notes or post office receipts.

The credit may stipulate a last shipment date and the bill of lading must show shipment by that date. Extension of the shipment date automatically extends the expiry date, but not vice versa.

It is very important that exporters immediately check the details of credits established in their favour to see that the goods and terms agree with the sales contract and that all the necessary documents are at hand. If any amendment is required, they can approach the advising bank in good time for action to be taken before expiry.

Besides the basic irrevocable credit there are revocable credits which, as the name implies, can be cancelled or amended at any time without notice to the beneficiary. They do not constitute a legally binding undertaking by the banks concerned. Once transmitted and made available at the advising bank, however, their cancellation or modification are only effective when that bank has received notice thereof and any payment made before receipt of such notice is reimbursable by the issuing bank. The value of these credits as security for payment is plainly doubtful. They are used mainly between parent and subsidiaries companies, where a continuing series of shipments is concerned, or as an indication of good intent.

Where a buyer wishes to provide his supplier with the security of payment afforded by a documentary credit, but at the same time requires a period of credit, he may instruct his bank to issue a credit calling for a bill of exchange drawn at so many days after sight instead of the usual sight draft – this would, of course, be an irrevocable credit. In this case the beneficiary would not receive immediate payment upon presentation of the documents as under a sight credit, but his term bill would be accepted by the bank. It could then be discounted in the money market at the finest rates. Thus the beneficiary would still receive payment, but the buyer would not be called upon to pay until the bill matured.

TRANSFERABLE CREDITS

These arise where the exporter is obtaining the goods from a third party, say the actual manufacturer, and as middleman does not have the resources to buy outright and await payment from his overseas customer. The credit is established in favour of the middleman (the prime beneficiary) and authorizes the advising bank to accept instructions from the prime beneficiary to make the credit available, in whole or in part, to one or more third parties (the second beneficiaries). The second beneficiary is then notified of the credit on the original terms and conditions, except that the amount and unit price are reduced and the shipment and expiry dates shortened. The original credit relates to the price the buyer is paying to the prime beneficiary, but the latter will be obtaining the goods at a lower price, hence the reduction in amount. When the second beneficiary presents the shipping documents, he obtains payment for his invoice price, and the prime beneficiary is called upon to substitute his own invoice and receive the difference (his profit). The negotiating bank then has documents in accordance with the original credit.

Where more than one second beneficiary is involved the credit must permit part shipments. If the prime beneficiary does not wish his buyer and supplier to be aware of each other, he may request that his name be substituted for that of the opener on the transfer credit, and that shipping documents be in the name of a third party blank endorsed.

BACK TO BACK CREDITS

Back to back credits arise in circumstances similar to those of the transferable credit and particularly where both the supplier and the buyer are overseas. In this case, the middleman receives a credit in his favour from the buyer and asks his bank to establish a credit in favour of his supplier against the security of the credit in his own favour. Hence there are two separate credits instead of one as in the case of a transferable credit, and this can create problems in the matching of documents and credit terms.

REVOLVING CREDITS

Revolving credits are used where a series of shipments are made at intervals and the parties wish the programme to proceed without interruption. A credit is established for a certain sum and quantity of goods with a provision that, when a shipment has been made and documents presented and paid, the credit is automatically renewed in its original form so that another shipment can be made.

RED CLAUSE CREDITS

Red clause credits are sometimes called packing credits. These are mainly encountered in connection with shipments of wool from Australia, New Zealand or South Africa. A clause (in red) inserted into the credit authorizes the negotiating bank to make an advance by way of loan or overdraft to the beneficiary to enable him to purchase the wool, collect and warehouse it and prepare it for shipment. The loan is repaid out of the amount due upon presentation of the shipping documents.

ACCEPTANCE CREDITS

Acceptance credits were originally provided by merchant banks but they are now also available through clearing banks. The bank opens a line of credit in favour of the exporter, who is then able to draw bills on the bank, which are accepted by the latter and can then be discounted in the money market at the finest rates. Such credits usually run parallel with the bills drawn by the exporter on his overseas buyer and are drawn on the same terms as the latter. In due course the payment received for the commercial bills will meet the amount due to the bank on its acceptances. This facility is a means of obtaining export finance and can occasionally be cheaper than ordinary bank accommodation.

FACTORING

Although 'factoring' had its origins in the conduct of sales and collection of payments by the representatives sent to North America by English textile manufacturers, in its present form it is regarded as an American idea that has been introduced to the United Kingdom in recent years. The main function of a factoring service is the maintenance of suppliers' sales ledgers on the basis of copy invoices received from the suppliers themselves. Factors neither make sales nor issue invoices at the time of delivery of the goods; these functions are performed by the suppliers against the background of the factors' credit approval. The willingness of

factors to make advance payments in respect of outstanding receivables increases suppliers' cash flow; usually 70 per cent of
amounts awaiting collection can be drawn in this manner. The
factoring of export sales, which is a relatively recent development,
provides a comprehensive package of export services to exporters
requiring short-term finance. The collection of payments overseas is
handled either by the British factor's own offices or by correspondent factors. This network provides factors with a broad
knowledge of payment patterns for credit control purposes and
enables them to deal with overseas buyers in their own language and
handle sales expressed in foreign currency. Credit cover of 100 per
cent is provided for approved buyers.

BANK FINANCE FOR EXPORTS

Theoretically, a company should be able to finance all its operations
from the resources available to it, that is, its capital and any funds it
is able to borrow from the bank. Its capital will depend on the
amount that the members of the company are prepared to invest in
the enterprise, and its borrowing from the bank will depend on such
factors as balance sheet figures, the profit and loss account, turn-
over or the security it can offer by way of mortgages, life polices and
stocks. Both these sources are subject to strict limitations and, for
reasons already mentioned above, they are bound to prove inadequate for a company expanding its export trade. To meet the
cash flow problems engendered by long credit terms, extra sources
of finance must be tapped over and above the basic sources of
capital and bank lending. This finance can best be found in ways
related to the export transactions themselves and, in particular, to
the method of payment. Let us examine the various methods by
which payment is made and the types of finance associated with
them:

1. Sales on open account. The exporter is entirely dependent on
the goodwill of the buyer to remit payment when due. Admittedly,
the outstanding debts will increase the receivables item in the
company's balance sheet and may therefore enable it to obtain
additional overdraft facilities from the bank. However, the best
answer to the problem of finance in this case would be use of the
services of a factoring company (see above).

2. Collection by means of a bill of exchange drawn on the buyer.

Finance may be obtained by discounting the bills with the bank or obtaining loan accommodation against bills outstanding for collection. The bank has some element of security in the documents pertaining to the goods, which are attached to the bills. The possibility of obtaining bank finance in this way is enhanced if the export sale is covered by a policy issued by the Export Credits Guarantee Department (ECGD), as the rights under the policy may be assigned to the bank.

3. Documentary credits. An irrevocable credit assures the exporter of payment immediately he has shipped the goods and presents correct documents to the bank, so that his need for finance is reduced. He may, however, be able to obtain some extra help from his bank to produce and ship the goods on the strength of the payment assured under the credit.

FINANCE GUARANTEED BY THE ECGD

As the various sources of export finance mentioned above have proved insufficient and costly and have not always been readily available, special arrangements for short, medium and long-term finance have been concluded between the banks and the Export Credits Guarantee Department.

The short-term finance arrangement is designed to provide finance for exporters of consumer or consumer durable goods where the credit terms will not normally exceed two years. There are in fact two separate schemes, both subject to interest $\frac{1}{2}$ percentage point above the lending bank's base rate:

(a) Bills and notes. Where there is an instrument, that is, where the exporter draws a bill of exchange on the buyer or receives a promissory note from him, the bank will advance the full face value of the bills. In the case of sight bills and unaccepted term bills, the bank retains recourse to the exporter if the bills are not met. Once the bills are accepted the bank has recourse to the ECGD alone. If an accepted bill is dishonoured, the bank recovers the amount from the ECGD, which has recourse to the exporter for the difference between the amount paid to the bank and that which is due to the customer under the ECGD policy. Original shipping documents must be attached to the bill.

(b) Open account scheme. This applies where there is no instrument such as a bill of exchange and the sales terms do not exceed

180 days from receipt of the goods. The exporter makes a promissory note in favour of the bank for the invoice value of the goods exported and maturing on the last day of the month in which settlement is due. The bank advances the face value of the promissory note at once and the note must be paid at maturity whether or not the proceeds of the invoice have been received. The bank only has recourse to the ECGD if the customer fails to honour his note. Copies of shipping documents must be submitted.

The medium-term arrangement is designed to assist exporters or producers of capital goods, where credit terms may be as long as five years. In this field exporters are faced not only with a longer wait for payment but also the extra cost of financing the credit period and the greater possibility of changes in interest rates. Accordingly, the ECGD provides a specific unconditional guarantee for post-shipment finance granted by banks for terms ranging from two to five years from the date of shipment. Interest is charged at a fixed rate of 7 per cent for periods up to five years and 7.5 per cent for longer periods. The ECGD guarantees normally apply from the date of shipment; any finance required at an earlier stage must be obtained within the customer's normal banking arrangements.

The ECGD has laid down certain conditions for the medium-term arrangement:

1. The goods must be deemed to be capital goods or of a category acceptable to the Department.

2. The period of credit is limited to five years, although in certain exceptional cases six- or even seven-year terms have been agreed.

3. Generally the purchaser must pay a deposit upon confirmation of the order and a further sum upon shipment; these deposits average 10 per cent each.

4. The cover provided under the guarantee is 100 per cent.

5. The exporter will be expected to arrange to draw bills of exchange for acceptance or obtain from the buyer promissory notes covering the instalments of principal and interest spread over the period of credit. These are usually drawn in series, payable at six-monthly intervals, and bear an interest clause. When negotiations have taken place between the exporter, the bank and the ECGD, the bank draws up a facility letter addressed to the exporter setting out the terms and conditions under which it will make funds available to him on a non-recourse basis. Agreement in principle for

finance under this scheme is usually given for three months to enable the customer to complete his negotiations with the buyer. If at the expiry of this period the negotiations are incomplete, a new approach by the customer must be made.

The ECGD has introduced a 'finance guarantee' for exports of heavy equipment and ships, which require credit on longer terms than the five years provided under the medium-term arrangement. In this instance credit takes the form of buyer finance, as opposed to supplier finance granted under the schemes described above. The ECGD thus provides full cover for the principal and interest of the direct loans made by banks to overseas purchasers to enable them to pay their suppliers on cash terms. Purchasers are generally expected to provide 20 per cent of the purchase price from their own resources, the remaining 80 per cent being paid to the exporters out of the loan. The minimum amount considered is normally £250 000. Interest is charged at the same rates as under the medium-term arrangement.

The bank providing the finance purchases the buyer's promissory notes covering repayments of principal and interest. The exporter is paid irrevocably out of the proceeds of the purchase of the notes after presenting to the bank the documents set out in the supply contract and the financial agreement. The buyer has full responsibility for repayment of the loan irrespective of the supply contract.

This arrangement is ideally suited to cases where several suppliers are parties to a single contract. If the amount involved is considerable and the credit terms correspondingly long, the loan may be provided by a consortium of banks, often with a merchant bank acting as manager. Banks may also arrange Euro-currency loans outside the guarantee arrangement to finance the portion of the total price that purchasers must themselves provide.

Within the context of buyer credit the ECGD also provides cover for financing contracts under lines of credit. Loans made available by British banks to overseas borrowers to facilitate the purchase of a wide range of capital goods from British suppliers are guaranteed under an overall financing scheme available for sums as small as £5000. Some lines are allocated to particular projects, in which case the borrowers are often governments or government agencies. Other lines are 'general purpose', in which case the borrower is usually a bank and the line may be used by any buyer approved by that bank. The interest rate applicable is the same as for other buyer credit. The ECGD actively encourages the financing of buyer credits in foreign currency.

LESS COMMON FORMS OF TRADE

1. Consignment trade: goods sent by an exporter to a nominal importer in another country, that nominal importer being in fact, a nominee or agent of the exporter. The intention is that the merchandise shall come into the physical possession of the agent, whose duty it is to sell it on the exporter's behalf and remit to his principal the proceeds of the sale, less all expenses of handling, storing and transport, customs duties, fees and his commission.

2. Participation. Joint venture in which a British manufacturer and a foreign concern co-operate in marketing the exporter's product, assembling it or manufacturing it abroad.

3. Licensing. A licence may be granted to an overseas company to manufacture products on a royalty basis under either the UK manufacturer's brand name or the name of the licensee.

4. Barter or compensation trade. Arising from the restrictive effects of exchange control and the shortage of foreign exchange in some countries. For instance, an importer may be unable to obtain an allocation of sterling or other acceptable currency, so that he offers goods in payment of those he wishes to buy. This has been quite a common practice in trade with some countries in the Eastern bloc, South America and Africa, but it is fraught with problems: the goods offered may not be required by the other party or may not be easy to sell, the trader may find himself involved in trades with which he is not acquainted and it may be difficult to agree the quantities to be exchanged. Some of the merchants and merchant banks in London have set up a type of 'clearing' system for exchanging goods and finding outlets for the goods received in settlement.

CHANGING METHODS OF PAYMENT

Transfers of funds from one centre to another arise from a variety of transactions in international trade, such as the collection of bills of exchange, payments for goods received on 'open account', payments under documentary credits, transfers of funds to subsidiaries and the settlement of balances within multinational companies. The ways in which such transfers are made have not changed in principle, but improvements in banking arrangements and technology have enabled the banks to expedite them. For example, the Society for Worldwide Interbank Financial Telecommunication (SWIFT) has set up a highly sophisticated communications network which enables its members to send authenticated messages to one another automatically. The system caters for international payment instructions in a variety of currencies, funding advices, account statements, debit and credit confirmations and a range of foreign exchange transactions. It is cheaper than telex and has two levels of priority – normal and urgent. A normal message is expected to take ten minutes for transmission and an urgent message one minute. Systems such as this and the general improvement in the methods of interbank transfers should go some way towards meeting traders' demands for the more rapid execution of payments.

Other developments also have an effect on the way in which payments for goods are made. The increased speed of modern transport has meant that on shorter sea voyages bills of lading have to be sent in the ship's bag to avoid demurrage at the port of destination. As there is therefore no document of title to support a documentary bill, banks will regard such a bill lodged for collection as tantamount to a clean bill and be less prepared to provide finance. The development of container transport and groupage has created a problem in that individual consignments are the subject of a forwarding agent's certificate referring to the bill of lading covering the container. Certificates issued by forwarding agents of repute are accepted, but in the case of documentary credits banks are unable to pay against such certificates unless the credit authorizes them to do so. Payment delays may therefore result pending confirmation from the buyer that the documents are acceptable.

CHAPTER 9

Combined Transport Operation

Combined transport concept. Containerization. International road haulage.
Piggy back operation. Train ferries. Inland waterways.

COMBINED TRANSPORT CONCEPT

In international trade a multi-modal or combined transport service entails the use of more than one mode of transport on a particular journey offered by a single operator acting as principal for the entire journey. It is thus a through transport service from door to door or warehouse to warehouse; it is orientated to the needs of the user in that it caters for the entire consignment journey required, in contrast to a traditional single-mode service covering only the leg of the journey performed by the one mode. Operators may attempt to offer a combined service by subcontracting to operators in other modes, but they cannot be called multi-modal transport operators until they accept the responsibility of acting as principal. Any mode of transport – road, rail, inland waterway, sea or air – may be involved in a multi-modal transport operation.

In 1977 the International Chamber of Commerce and other organizations approved a combined transport document. By the 1980s consideration was being given to multi-modal transport arrangements based on a new convention sponsored by UNCTAD. The development of a smooth and efficient multi-modal transport service that meets the requirements of trade will accelerate under the stimulus of a favourable political and economic climate; on the one hand governments are fostering improvements in services in order to encourage growth in exports and, on the other, transport operators are continuously examining ways of reducing costs, including the development of alternative transportation arrangements.

The combined transport concept presents a number of advantages over rival services:

(a) Governments are continuously examining ways of reducing energy consumption, especially in the transport field. Rail and inland waterway systems offer high capacity transport units with substantially lower fuel consumption than that of alternative means

114

of transport, particularly road haulage. As most rail and inland waterway systems are in state ownership, governments can directly influence the extension of these modes of transport internationally.

(b) A through service involving containers, train ferry wagons and road haulage units permits rapid transhipment at ports, thereby eliminating the long delays often encountered in the main alternative method of conveying break bulk consignments on 'tween deck vessels. Lack of transhipment also reduces the risk of damage or pilferage, reduces the packing required, permits lower cargo premiums than those obtainable for shipment by conventional means and brings considerable savings in labour costs.

(c) It offers the best prospect of attaining good utilization of transport units and their infrastructure in the face of escalating labour and capital costs. It also encourages the development of a capital intensive system.

(d) Documentation is simplified by the use of through consignment notes, through rates and the unified code of liability; this in turn brings benefits when arranging finance and insurance for export consignments.

(e) The more rapid transits facilitate earlier payment, particularly where delivery terms are CIF. Furthermore, rapid transits enable the importer to keep warehouse stocks to the minimum and thus avoid immobilizing an excessive amount of working capital. The combined transport concept exploits the benefits of the transport distribution analysis technique, which is explained in *The Elements of Export Practice*.

(f) The low relative cost of the system offers the best prospects of exploiting world resources.

(g) The concept encourages the elaboration of common codes of practices on an international scale, such as the common specification for containers to aid their ubiquitous use, the common code of liability and the common layout of documentation. Progress in these fields fosters understanding and confidence among trading nations.

(h) The rationalization and efficiency inherent in the use of common facilities such as ISO containers and equipment permits optimum use to be made of the available capital.

(i) The reliability of combined transport services enhance shippers' prospects of maintaining and expanding their export markets.

(j) Goods conveyed by combined means of transport generally

arrive in better condition than those shipped in the conventional way.

In the sections that follow we shall examine various forms of combined transport operation.

CONTAINERIZATION

Containerization is a method of distributing merchandise in a unitized form suitable for transportation by rail, road, canal and sea. The system is long established, having been in existence at the turn of the century in a less advanced form. It came into wider use in the North American coastal trade in the 1930s, when the vessels were called van ships. The fourth generation of container ships has now evolved and the benefits of containerization are recognized in a large number of countries. Some 85 per cent of liner cargo is now containerized.

Container services usually operate from a container base, where break bulk cargoes destined for a particular area or country are consolidated into full container loads. Such a service is of particular value to small exporters and importers. The container base may be under the management of a port authority, a consortium of container ship operators, a container operator or operators engaged in the freight forwarding business or a consortium comprising freight forwarders, road hauliers and other members of the freight industry. It may be situated in the port itself (often the case in developing countries), in the environs of the port or in an inland industrial area that generates sufficient containerized traffic. In the last instance the base may be an inland clearance depot with customs facilities for incoming and outgoing cargoes, thus alleviating port congestion caused by containers awaiting clearance. The number of container bases will undoubtedly increase as the container trade continues to expand.

A variety of company structures are encountered in the container business. They generally fall into the following categories:

(a) New companies formed by the amalgamation of existing companies (e.g. the formation of Hapag-Lloyd from the amalgamation of Hamburg-Amerikanische Packetfahrt-AG and Norddeutscher Lloyd) or the establishment of separate subsidiaries (e.g. Overseas Containers Ltd set up by four well-known British shipping companies). In the first instance the former companies cease trading as separate entities, but in the second the parent companies continue to operate independently in other fields.

(b) Joint subsidiaries created by a number of shipping companies to operate in a specific trade or group of trades, such as the Atlantic Container Line in the Northern Atlantic trade or Scan-Dutch in the Europe–Far East trade. The parent companies vest their interest in the trade entirely in the joint subsidiary but remain free to compete with each other elsewhere.

(c) Fleet operating arrangements between various kinds of transport operator. They answer more accurately to the description of consortium than do the first two types. Examples of this category include five lines of three nationalities in the Europe–Far East trade, five lines of different nationalities in the Australia Europe Container Service (AECS) and the ACE group operating between Europe and the Far East. The prime object of this category is to provide a sufficient number of ships to offer traders a regular service and yet achieve the economies of scale that stem from the use of large vessels. By definition, these fleet agreements are limited to a trade or closely identified geographical group of trades. They are not profit centres or centres of decision on commercial strategy; these attributes remain with the individual lines. It may also be noted that any trade rights which parties to fleet operating agreements enjoy on particular routes and the rates of freight they charge are likely to derive from membership of a shipping conference rather than adherence to the fleet operating arrangements *per se*.

Established container routes include the following: US East Coast (USEC)/Canadian East Coast (excluding Gulf)–North Europe; US Gulf Coast–North Europe; US West Coast (USWC)/Canadian West Coast–North Europe; USEC/Canadian East Coast–Mediterranean; USWC/Canadian West Coast–Mediterranean; USEC/ Canadian East Coast–Far East/South East Asia; USWC/Canadian West Coast–Far East/South East Asia; USEC/Canadian East Coast–Australasia; East Coast North America–West Africa; East Coast North America–Caribbean/South America; Far East/South East Asia–North Europe; Far East/South East Asia–Mediter-ranean; Australasia–North Europe; Australasia–Caribbean; Japan–Australia; Japan–New Zealand; South East Asia–Australia; North Europe–Caribbean; North Europe–South Africa; North

Europe–Mediterranean; Mediterranean–South Africa; Europe–Middle East; North America–Middle East; Far East/South East Asia–Middle East; North America–South Africa; Japan/South East Asia–South Africa; and Europe–West Africa.

In conclusion, we shall briefly review the advantages and disadvantages of containerization over and above those of combined transport operations in general.

Advantages of containerization

(a) Less packing is required. For instance, tea chests have been replaced by cardboard cartons for packing tea for shipment by container and tobacco no longer needs to be packed in expensive hogs heads. Where cargoes continue to be bagged, lighter bags can be used for many products when loaded into containers and yet the protection is still greater than in a ship's hold. The reduction in packing can bring substantial savings in costs.

(b) As containerization is a capital intensive system, rates are less vulnerable to inflation than those of labour intensive services and are thus likely to remain more competitive, provided that the available resources are put to optimum use.

(c) Transits are much quicker than those of conventional cargo shipments owing to a combination of faster vessels, the rationalization of ports of call and substantially faster cargo handling. For example, the round voyage between the United Kingdom and Australia now takes container vessels approximately six weeks, compared with the twenty required by conventional services a few years ago.

(d) Containerization has permitted fleet rationalization. On average, each container vessel – usually of much increased capacity and speed – has displaced six 'tween deck vessels on deep sea services. With regard to the infrastructure of the container transhipment system (see *Elements of Shipping*).

(e) Container vessels attain higher utilization rates than 'tween deck tonnage. This in turn makes for a viable service, thereby ensuring the finance of modern vessels.

(f) Some delicate cargoes, such as avocado pears, that do not normally travel well can be successfully shipped by container, thanks to temperature control and protection from damage.

(g) Containers save dockers having to handle dirty cargoes such as wet hides or bones. Containers fitted with disposable linings are packed and unpacked by staff suitably equipped to handle the cargo.

(h) The general reduction in costs brought about by containerization makes it possible for liner services to continue to carry cargoes of low value and acts as a stimulus to world trade.

(i) The use of containers to the ISO specification facilitates optimum utilization of the transport resources employed.

Disadvantages of containerization

(a) The high capital cost of containerization, which entails not only specialized cellular vessels but also at least three sets of containers per ship, is beyond the financial reach of many shipowners. The burden can be reduced somewhat by leasing containers. The port infrastructure involving berths, specialized lifting equipment, straddle carriers and stacking areas also require considerable capital resources, as does the inland distribution system, which is usually based on rail or road. Land-based facilities are generally provided by the authority controlling them, that is to say the port authority, railway company or road haulage operator.

(b) Not all merchandise is suitable for carriage by container, although the percentage of such traffic is steadily declining as new types of container are introduced (see *Elements of Shipping*) and more manufacturers adapt their production processes, premises and packaging to meet the constraints imposed by containers. A very small range of cargoes, such as livestock, are physically incapable of containerization.

(c) Exporters with limited cargo are unable to fill containers to capacity, so that they cannot take full advantage of the economical through rates offered. This disadvantage has been largely overcome, however, by the consolidation of consignments at container bases.

(d) The use of containers has exacerbated traffic imbalances in certain trades (see pp. 71–73).

(e) Ensuring full utilization of containers spread around a number of countries and ports is a complex exercise. Most major shipowners use computers to monitor and control their inventory of containers, an essential but costly task.

(f) In some countries restrictions prevent the transportation by road of loads exceeding certain dimensions or weight. This has tended to hinder the full development of the largest containers –

particularly those measuring 40 ft (12.20 m) – but in the long term this constraint is likely to disappear.

(g) The maritime operating cost of container shipment tends to be low, but terminal costs tend to be high. Hence the longer the overall voyage distance the greater the economic advantage of container-ized distribution. In the short sea trades Ro/Ro units offer a cheaper service for journeys totalling less than 900–1000 km.

There can be no doubt that in the next few years containerization will further expand in many deep sea services, primarily under the aegis of liner conferences. An annual growth rate of 10 per cent seems likely for the remainder of the decade; developing countries in South East Asia and the Far East – Malaysia, Singapore, Hong Kong, Taiwan and South Korea – will account for much of this expansion. Services will also be stepped up in the Caribbean and West African trades and in the Middle East. The rate of growth in the developing countries will depend largely on the availability of capital. The construction of port facilities is likely to be financed by international organizations such as the International Bank for Reconstruction and Development. In some countries the container operation will terminate at the port until the inland distribution network is adequate.

Another use of containers that is likely to intensify is based on the land bridge concept, which involves the block movement of con-tainer trains or bulk freight railway wagons for cargoes such as grain to interconnect with shipping services at maritime terminals. Examples of such a development are to be found in the UK land bridge between Ireland and continental Europe, enabling a through road haulage transit by a combination of road, sea and possibly piggy back rail transport, and the Canadian Pacific Railway service that has been opened for traffic in transit between the Far East and Europe. The Trans-Siberian Railway is also providing a land bridge for the movement of ISO containers between Europe and the Far East by rail and sea. It is very sensitive to rates and transit times offered by alternative shipping services, such as the Far Eastern Freight Conference. The Trans-Siberian land bridge will become more attractive to shippers after completion of the BAM line and the installation of computer systems to speed up the handling of block trains. Shipowners do not regard the TSR as a strictly com-mercial operation as it undercuts liner conference rates by an average of 20 per cent and by as much as 50 per cent in the case of some high value cargoes. In 1980 some 10 per cent of the liner trade between the Far East and Europe was conveyed on the TSR, most of the consignments coming from Japan, Hong Kong and South Korea.

INTERNATIONAL ROAD HAULAGE

The last decade has seen a rapid expansion in international road haulage. This has been greatly facilitated by the use of the TIR carnet, which permits simplified customs treatment of goods carried by road; a fuller description is to be found in *The Elements of Export Practice*. In the years to come the boom in the construction of Ro/Ro tonnage will continue, perhaps at a slower rate as escalating fuel prices begin to have an adverse effect on the international road haulage sector, but multi-purpose vessels with ramp facilities capable of conveying both vehicular units and containers, such as the one illustrated on p. 235, are likely to become more popular in view of the ease of transhipment they permit and the increasing emphasis on rapid ship turnround.

Advantages of road haulage

We shall now examine the merits of international road haulage over and above those mentioned earlier in connection with the combined transport concept in general:

(a) The service is reliable, owing partly to the route flexibility inherent in road transport and the availability of facilities to remedy breakdowns quickly.

(b) The exporter or importer can use his own vehicle and crew, thus maintaining complete control over schedules and costs. Such an arrangement may prove less expensive than employing a professional road haulier, but much will depend on whether a return load is available; owner operators are not permitted to convey goods for other parties. By 1980 owner operators accounted for about 10 per cent of the Ro/Ro traffic between the United Kingdom and continental Europe and the proportion was growing annually.

(c) The system is flexible, even as regards ferry crossings. Reservations on Ro/Ro vessels are still desirable but by no means essential except in the case of dangerous cargo; with regard to the latter (see *The Elements of Export Practice*).

(d) No customs examination arises in transit countries, provided that the goods are carried under TIR bond or, within the EEC, are covered by the appropriate Community transit documentation.

(e) Documentation is simple, as under CMR a through consignment note is issued on the basis of common liability conditions.

(f) The capital investment in a vehicle 12 or 15 metres in length with an overall capacity of 40 tonnes is small in comparison with that in a railway wagon or freight aircraft.

(g) It is ideal for general merchandise and selected bulk cargo conveyed in small quantities. Freight groupage by freight forwarders accounts for a considerable volume of traffic.

(h) Road haulage tariffs and transit times compare favourably with those of air freight over distances of less than about 800 km.

(i) Delays at customs are reduced, as the goods are usually accompanied. This contributes towards efficient port operation and prompt financial settlement of the export invoice.

Disadvantages of road haulage

(a) It is essentially a labour intensive operation. A vehicle with a capacity of up to 40 tonnes – depending on national regulations governing gross axle weights – has one or two drivers; by contrast, a train of 2000 tonnes' capacity has a crew of three or less.

(b) Fuel consumption per tonne-mile is heavy in comparison with that of trains. This is a very relevant point for countries dependent on imported oil, such as the Federal Republic of Germany, which is discouraging international road haulage in favour of rail as exemplified in the Kombiverkehr operation explained on pp. 123–124.

(c) The limited capacity of road haulage units restricts their application to the groupage and general merchandise markets.

(d) International road haulage is subject to increasingly severe regulations on the construction and use of vehicles, pressure from environmental lobbies in some countries to prevent an increase in the size of vehicles, route restrictions, motorway tolls and, in countries such as France, the Netherlands and the Federal Republic of Germany, rigid restrictions on the passage of road haulage vehicles at weekends and on public holidays. A system of quotas based on bilateral road agreements among various countries also operates (see *The Elements of Export Practice*).

(e) Regulations governing drivers' working hours are being strengthened in order to improve driving standards, road safety and the observance of rest periods. This will necessitate two-driver crews on long transits and thus substantially increase costs. As a countermeasure, an increasing number of major operators in the UK/Continental trade are shipping their trailers unaccompanied.

International road haulage thus presents considerable advantages in terms of convenience, but its further expansion may be jeopardized by rising costs and government restriction on road transport, particularly in countries with a heavy fuel import bill.

PIGGY BACK OPERATION

Piggy back services involving the use of road, rail and vehicular ferries are a recent development of the combined transport concept. Such a service is operated between the United Kingdom and the Federal Republic of Germany by a company called Kombiverkehr, which is sponsored jointly by the German Federal Railways and the German road haulage industry. Road trailers are conveyed by vehicular ferry from Harwich to Hook of Holland or from Dover to Ostend, whereupon they are loaded onto railway wagons for carriage by scheduled rail services to selected industrial centres in the Federal Republic. They then continue their journey by road to the consignee's premises.

The piggy back scheme offers the following advantages in addition to those inherent in the combined transport concept:

(a) Fast transit times through the provision of scheduled road, sea and rail services

(b) No inordinate delays at ports owing to customs or transhipment arrangements

(c) No need for the permits required by international road hauliers operating between the United Kingdom and the Federal Republic

(d) Quality service at competitive rates

(e) Less wear and tear on trailer equipment

(f) Exemption from the restriction on the movement of goods at weekends or during holiday periods to which normal international road hauliers are subject.

(g) Drivers' hours can be arranged more easily to comply with EEC regulations.

(h) By discouraging through journeys by road haulage, the system saves fuel.

(i) It combines the best features of road and rail and thereby provides an optimum service; it is a good example of transport integration.

Similar services operate throughout the world and it is likely that the concept will spread, particularly as the continuous rise in the cost of fuel creates an urgent need to conserve oil in a number of countries.

TRAIN FERRIES

During the next decade many governments are likely to favour the development of the international railway wagon services in preference to international road haulage wherever practicable on the grounds of fuel economy and, to a lesser extent, for environmental reasons. This is particularly relevant to countries that are anxious to reduce their high oil import bills. Existing vehicular ferry services for Ro/Ro traffic are therefore being examined in detail with a view to developing train ferries and larger vessels are being built with two or three decks for wagons instead of one.

At the same time, economies of scale are being realized by the introduction of the latest generation of bogie bolster wagons with a larger capacity. They are owned by railway companies or shippers or are available on hire from wagon hire companies. The range of types available includes the following:

(a) Covered wagons with a 25.5 tonne payload, internal width of 2.069 m, length of 12.376 m and centre height of 2.258 m; ideal for palletized traffic.

(b) Covered wagons with a payload of 53.7 tonnes, internal width of 2.43 m, length of 19.854 m and centre height of 2.22 m. They have a two-door access with a 6.55 m door width and are intended for general cargo in unitized or break bulk form.

(c) Covered wagons with a payload of 54 tonnes, internal width of 2.47 m, length of 17.638 m and centre height of 2.55 m. Three doors give a combined access width of 9.239 m, facilitating loading. Designed for general cargo.

(d) Polybulk hopper wagons with a payload of 58 tonnes and a capacity of 70 m³ for carrying a wide range of bulk dry cargoes.

(e) Liquid tank wagons with an overall length of 16.916 m, a payload of 46.4 tonnes and a capacity of 91 300 litres. Wagons of this type, which are usually privately owned, are used for transporting liquid chemicals and oil.

The major advantage of these wagons is their low tare weight/payload ratio, which increases the payload of the train ferry in relation to the ship's deadweight capacity. As their capacity is substantially larger than that of road haulage units, they should also help tip the scales in favour of rail transport, provided that the infrastructure is adequate.

The optimum application of the train ferry concept occurs in the movement of complete train loads by integrated shipping and rail services, ideally between private sidings. This permits rapid transits with unimpeded transhipment at the ports and no lengthy delays on account of customs procedures. Where trains use inland clearance depots, customs formalities at the frontier are reduced to a minimum.

The following are some of the train ferry services in operation today; all convey freight wagons, but those marked with an asterisk also carry passengers:

Harwich (England) to Zeebrugge (Belgium)
*Dover (England) to Dunkerque (France)
*Sassnitz (German Democratic Republic) to Trelleborg (Sweden)
*Nyborg (Denmark) to Korsør (Denmark)
*Rødby (Denmark) to Puttgarden (Federal Republic of Germany)
*Helsingør (Denmark) to Helsingborg (Sweden)
*Gedser (Denmark) to Warnemünde (German Democratic Republic)
Villa San Giovanni (mainland Italy) to Messina (Sicily)
Swinoujscie (Poland) to Ystad (Sweden)
Ilichevsk, near Odessa (USSR) to Varna (Bulgaria)
Istanbul (European Turkey) to Haydarapasa (Asian Turkey)
Wellington (North Island of New Zealand) to Picton (South Island of New Zealand)

The longest route, involving a distance of 370 km, is that between Ilichevsk and Varna, which avoids the land route through Romania. Each of the four ships on the route has three decks and conveys 108 freight railway wagons, giving a total payload of 12 000 dwt per sailing.

Advantages of train ferry operations

(a) Simplified documentation involving the through consignment note between rail depots; the CIM consignment notes used in Europe is explained in *The Elements of Export Practice*.

(b) Flexible payment arrangements are available; the sender or the consignee may pay all the charges or each may pay a portion of the cost.

(c) A railway wagon has a greater payload than a road haulage unit and is thus suitable for larger items.

(d) No permit quotas apply, in contrast to international road haulage.

(e) There is no need to have balanced working loads in the two directions as wagons are provided on the common user principle.

(f) There is every prospect that international rail tariffs will increase more slowly than road haulage rates in view of the differing incidence of fuel costs.

(g) A train with a capacity of up to 2000 tonnes in the charge of two or three railwaymen is more economical in terms of fuel consumption and direct labour costs than a road haulage vehicle with a maximum capacity of 40 tonnes requiring two drivers.

(h) For environmental reasons rail tends to be preferred to road as the means of transporting dangerous cargoes.

Disadvantages of train ferry operations

(a) The operation tends to be inflexible owing to the small number of shipping routes available. Hence serious delays could occur in the event of a service disruption.

(b) A serious drawback in terms of cost and time can be the need to use road transport for the collection or delivery of goods from or to the rail freight terminal. However, the longer the overall transit, the less significant the cost of this element becomes. For example, collection and delivery by road might account for 5 per cent of the cost of a transit of 1500 km, compared with 15 per cent in the case of a transit of 300 km.

(c) Rail is competing against the highly developed road transport system that has tended to dominate the distribution of freight in many industrial countries over the last decade. This trend is likely to be reversed in the years ahead owing to the need to conserve oil, but progress may be slow in some countries.

(d) The cost of building private sidings, which major shippers wishing to use rail services economically will need, can be high. In some countries, such as the United Kingdom, the government helps finance such projects.

INLAND WATERWAYS

Shipping is becoming more closely integrated with inland waterways as the concept of the combined transport system develops. The LASH, BACO and SEABEE liner services, which employ ocean-going barge carriers for voyages between ports with inland waterway connections, are encouraging this trend (see *Elements of Shipping*). Other types of vessel based on the unit load concept have to rely greatly on feeder transport by road or rail.

The increasing acuteness of the energy situation, which is forcing countries to reduce their consumption of imported energy, will strongly favour the development of inland waterways where suitable conditions obtain. In Western Europe this situation is particularly evident in the Netherlands, the Federal Republic of Germany and France. In 1980 the proportion of freight conveyed by inland waterway came to 40 per cent in the Netherlands, 25 per cent in the Federal Republic and 8 per cent in France. Modernization of the canal system in these countries will soon permit an increase in the capacity of barges using the network and lead to an extension in services. For example, the widening of the 229 km canal between the Saône and the Rhine, due for completion in 1990, will connect Fos (Marseilles) with Rotterdam and the opening of the Rhine–Main–Danube canal in 1985 will link Rotterdam to the Black Sea. Another scheme under consideration is a connection between the Seine and the Moselle in north-eastern France. Hamburg, Rotterdam, Paris and Strasbourg are among the ports that rely on inland waterways to an appreciable degree.

The viability of inland waterways depends upon the size of the barges. The Canal du Nord between Paris and Lille can take barges of up to 600 tonnes' capacity, whereas the Canal du Midi between Bordeaux and Sète, which saves a passage of 5000 km around the Iberian peninsular, can accommodate only vessels up to 150 tonnes. Craft of up to 5000 tonnes can navigate the Rhine, and when the pusher technique is used the tonnage rises to 10 000 tonnes. In broad economic terms, the transportation of 5000 tonnes by road requires 48 000 horsepower and 25 000 litres of fuel per 100 km; by rail the figures are 7000 hp and 7500 litres, but inland waterways return results of 1800 hp and 5000 litres.

Aspects of the inland waterway system that make it suitable for the distribution of international trade include the following:

(a) It is cheap, subject to certain conditions, namely relative absence of locks, reasonable distances and an average lighter capacity in excess of 500 tonnes.

(b) It can be fully integrated with ocean shipping services such as LASH and BACO.

(c) Transhipment can take place in open roadsteads, thereby avoiding costly port transhipment and easing the pressure on port facilities.

(d) Although it is slow compared with rail or road, the overall transit time of other means of transport may be affected by factors such as delays in obtaining a berth, a slow discharge rate owing to the inadequacy of dock labour and equipment or delays in receiving customs clearance.

(e) Inland waterways transport can accelerate ship turnround, particularly if the situations mentioned in item (d) obtain in some ports.

(f) Cargo can be conveyed under bond direct to and from the consignee's premises or agent's warehouse if they are situated on a canal network.

(g) The canal system tends to be reliable and free of congestion.

(h) Fuel consumption and manpower requirements are low; as canals are widened and the number of locks reduced, the economics of transportation by lighter can be exploited through quicker transits and larger shipments.

(i) The system is suitable for an increasing range of consumer goods and bulk cargoes; it is expanding rapidly in Europe and many developing countries, especially in Africa.

CHAPTER 10

Ship Management

The shipping company. Shipping company consortia. Ship management companies. Planning. Revenue, expenditure and investment budgets. Marketing. Market pricing. Computerization.

Ship management is a many-faceted exercise designed to produce the best results from the resources invested and to take advantage of the opportunities that present themselves. Many of the elements have already been described, such as the operational aspects treated in Chapters 4 to 7. This chapter will therefore deal with other sides of the question, particularly the organization of management tasks.

THE SHIPPING COMPANY

The structure of a shipping company is determined primarily by the nature of the trade in which it operates and by the scale of its activities; the structure of a tramp operator will generally be different from that of a much larger liner company. Irrespective of the size of the company, its structure should be designed to permit swift decision-making. A cumbersome organization tends to lead to procrastination, which does not contribute to general competitiveness. Furthermore, the line of responsibility should be precise and self evident, with each person having a well-defined job specification. It is also important to ensure that responsibility is delegated wherever possible. As a centralized organization tends to frustrate initiative and discourage an *esprit de corps*, liner companies have tended to set up separate divisions or subsidiaries corresponding to individual trades or services. These operate as self-contained units under their own management board with extensive autonomous powers. The major advantages come in the shape of prompt decision-making, reduced administrative cost and a more precise orientation towards specific targets. The greater delegation of responsibility also simplifies the task of measuring the competence of employees.

The organization of a typical liner company is shown in Diagram I.

SHIPPING COMPANY CONSORTIA

The development of containerization in recent years has stimulated

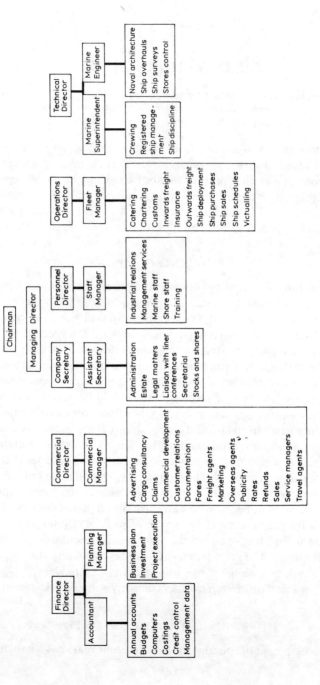

Diagram I   A liner company organization

the creation of shipping consortia by the companies formally operating 'tween deck vessels on the routes involved. By pooling resources and expertise they are able to provide the considerable capital required and operate a service of a high standard. A recent example of such a development is the container service between Europe and South Africa, which involved an investment of £520 million. It would have been impracticable for a single shipowner to raise capital on this scale and to bear the risk involved.

This is not the only advantage of such consortia, however. Relations with the governments of the countries served are likely to be improved by having a resident shipping company as a member of the consortium. As politics seem to play an increasingly important role in international trade and shipping practice, it is evident that countries with registered tonnage in particular trades are more likely to take an interest in developing those trades and to show greater understanding towards other operators within the consortium, which tends to reinforce the economic links between the countries involved and hence to stimulate trade. For this reason, a consortium constitutes the best defence against unfair competition and infiltration by Eastern bloc fleets, as consortium members are in a better position to press for concerted action by their governments than individual operators would be.

It is not only for reasons of increased influence that the consortium approach has gained ground. It also produces cost savings through the bulk purchase of supplies and the employment of fewer agents. It encourages the use of common services, particularly where ports provide common berths, and strengthens the group's marketing resources, as each shipowner is usually responsible for developing the business in his own country within the framework of the consortium's corporate policy.

In view of these advantages, it is likely that consortia will become more common in the years to come.

SHIP MANAGEMENT COMPANIES

The poor investment return on shipping in recent years has caused an increasing number of large shipping companies to diversify their business activities so that they would be less vulnerable to a downturn in the shipping industry proper. Some of them now have subsidiary companies engaged in the fields of real estate, road haulage, oil exploration, brokerage, shipbuilding, freight forwarding, port operation and ship management. It is the last of these, ship management, that has aroused the interest of many shipowners.

Ship management companies are often the subsidiaries of established liner companies and are thus able to draw upon a wealth of experience and expertise. In return for a management fee, they operate vessels to a high standard of service and economy for their owners. They also attend to maintenance, find charterers for vessels under their management, recruit and train crews and shore-based staff and advise on questions of purchase, registration, manning and trading. Moreover, they are able to secure lower insurance premiums by including vessels on their main own-fleet policy and to obtain reductions in price by purchasing stores and spares in bulk.

A large number of the clients of ship management companies are to be found among the many multinational manufacturing companies that have build up their own fleets in the last decade to carry their raw materials or manufactured products. Fleet ownership enables the companies to integrate distribution with their manufacturing programmes and to transport their goods at a cost below the normal tariffs charged on cargo liner services. Having the fleet operated by experienced professionals makes equally good economic sense. The major oil companies recognized long ago the tremendous advantage of placing their heterogeneous fleet of owned, time-chartered and spot-chartered vessels in the hands of ship management companies rather than incurring the expense of setting up their own operations' department.

PLANNING

Planning is essential to modern ship management in that it maximizes profitability over the long term and permits management to harness the resources of the business in the most effective way possible in the pursuit of its chosen objectives.

The basic purpose of planning in the shipping industry, as elsewhere, is to identify commercial opportunities and to exploit them by providing the necessary resources in the right place at the right time. As the major assets of shipping companies are moveable, the firms have a real choice as to their most effective utilization; this may involve both the transfer of ships from one route to another and the allocation of new vessels to the most profitable sectors.

An increasing number of shipping companies, particularly those in the liner field, are now operating within the context of a company business plan, which forms the basis of a strict system of budgetary control. The company business plan sets out the aims of the company over a period of five or ten years, depending on the nature of the business. It generally comprises the following:

(a) Introduction, outlining the company's objectives over the period, traffic forecasts on an annual basis and the related revenue and expenditure so that a cash flow forecast can be made.

(b) Prospects and strategies on each route. A typical entry may read as follows:

Route X	1981	1982	1983	1984	1985
			(in thousands)		
Ro/Ro (units conveyed)	100	103	105	108	110
Containers	45	50	55	100	110
Trade cars	10	11	12	13	14

Competition will intensify in the Ro/Ro market but the volume of trade will grow. A modest annual increase of 3 per cent is predicted, but the average yield of £100 per unit (based on 1980 prices) will fall by 1 per cent annually from 1983 onwards owing to increased competition and the need to offer higher rebates to help retain the traffic.

The container market will grow dramatically from 1984 onwards to coincide with the arrival of new tonnage. The new container ship will displace two 'tween deck vessels and virtually eliminate the carriage of break bulk cargoes on the route. This latest vessel completes the six-year programme of introducing container vessels in place of the life expired 'tween deck tonnage, and from 1983 onwards should reduce ship costs by £2 million annually (on the basis of 1981 prices). Further investment in the service will be reviewed in the mid-1980s in the light of market developments. Opportunity will also be taken in 1983 to rationalize the service by reducing the number of ports of call from ten to eight, resulting in substantially better ship utilization and cargo transit times.

A modest increase in trade car carryings of around 10 per cent annually is forecast, but this traffic flow is very vulnerable to import restrictions and industrial action in the car industry. It is confidently expected that the net yield per car will increase in real terms, following talks now under way to improve handling and particularly stowage of this traffic. It is not expected that additional streams of trade car traffic will be secured on the route in the next five years unless import tariffs are reduced, a development that seems unlikely in the foreseeable future.

(c) Company organization: this deals with variations in manpower needs and organizational changes. For example, a new service may be introduced in 1983 which requires the appointment of personnel to manage the service.

(d) Planning issues: this will highlight increases in the price of fuel oil, the labour costs of crew and shore-based staff, the level of investment within the company, the incidence of car ownership, exchange rates, real disposable income, gross national product and interest rates. Much of the data would be obtained from consultants or gleaned from the reports of commercial and government agencies. The company's investment might be set out as shown below, reflecting higher investment in the early years of the plan:

Services	1981	1982	1983	1984	1985
		(in millions of pounds sterling)			
X	2.0	12.0	12.5	2.0	nil
Y	0.5	0.7	0.1	0.4	1.0
Z	0.5	0.7	0.1	0.4	1.0
Total	3.0	13.4	12.7	2.8	2.0

The means of financing the investments would also be indicated.

(e) Competition: a broad appraisal of existing competition and likely future developments.

(f) Political factors: attitudes of governments towards the trade in which the company is engaged.

(g) Statutory requirements: the effects of current and foreseeable legislation governing ship construction and consumer protection.

(h) Manpower and productivity: this will reflect staff requirements to meet projected changes in services and improvements in crew productivity due to the acquisition of new vessels.

(i) Agreements: information on the conclusion of new agreements and the revision of existing ones as they fall due for renewal.

(j) Forecast trading results for each service on an annual basis.

(k) Balance sheet and cash flow, outlining forecast dividends and the cash flow for each year.

(l) Risk areas: certain elements of the plan, such as bunkering prices, trade restrictions and competition, are subject to sharp variations and are not capable of accurate prediction over a five-year period. The plan therefore has to be based on certain assumptions and must be adjusted promptly if any serious divergence occurs. For example, a substantial rise in the price of bunker oil would encourage slower schedules and would lead to a downturn in world trade.

(m) Ship disposition, that is to say the allocation of ships to particular routes.

(n) Chartered tonnage: details will be given of fixtures likely to be secured during the currency of the plan.

(o) Investment programme and rates of return, comprising details of all projects, their time scales, methods of funding, the return on investment and the impact on ship disposition.

(p) Subsidiaries: under this heading the business plans of any subsidiaries of the company engaged in activities such as shipbroking, freight forwarding, ship management or stevedoring would be set out.

(q) Taxation: any likely changes in taxation levels should be taken into consideration.

The company business plan should be reviewed periodically in order to take account of any sharp variations in circumstances, such as a downturn in trade or the eruption of hostilities. The net revenue, punctuality and load factors of individual services should also be examined at regular intervals to ascertain whether the vessels employed are best suited to the prevailing conditions.

REVENUE, EXPENDITURE AND INVESTMENT BUDGETS

Effective budgeting is the key to maximum profitability, w¹
turn helps attract the investment that is vital to the long-te′
of the company. There are several ways in which the e·
budget can be advantageous:

(a) The forecasts of revenue and expenditure expressed in the budget enable management to predict the cash flow during the year and hence to make the best use of monthly cash surpluses or to meet any expected deficits. Knowledge about the pattern of income makes it possible to finance the company's investment programme efficiently and to make optimum use of the company's resources. The budget should also reveal the profit centres within the firm's activities and thus help avoid non-productive expenditure.

(b) The budget acts as a yardstick against which to judge performance at regular intervals and hence allows management to adapt their policies to changing events. For instance, a fall in revenue below the forecast level may give early warning of the need to reduce expenditure in the face of a decline in business. The achievements of management and staff may also be gauged objectively against the budget.

(c) The targets that a budget necessarily implies encourage the development of an *esprit de corps* among managers, who are then better able to win the support of their staff. Having such targets also encourages cost consciousness, especially among senior and middle managers, who are most deeply committed to realization of the budget.

(d) The budget facilitates the formulation of tariff increases in line with predicted rises in expenditure and ensures that the company's profitability remains adequate.

Budgets are generally compiled for one year and the income and expenditure are then spread over the period, usually on a monthly or four-weekly basis, so that the results can be assessed at regular intervals. Tables 10.1 and 10.2 show the budget for January 1981 of a fictitious shipping company operating multi-purpose vessels; subsequently monthly tables would probably also show the cumulative results for the year to that date alongside the month's figures. The budget headings, layout and contents of the tables will vary according to the particular service or trade to which they refer.

Revenue budget
The revenue budget is drawn up by the company's traffic officers and represents their commitment to fulfil the predictions. Failure to achieve the expected revenue results would cause serious cash-flow problems, which in turn would affect not only profits but also future investment and development of the services. The projections are

Table 10.1 XYZ Service Group, Eastern Division: budgeted trading results for January 1981

Revenue	Physical facts			Average receipt			Gross receipts			Explanations			
	Actual	Budget	Discrepancy	Actual (£)	Budget (£)	Discrepancy (£)	Actual (£)	Budget (£)	Discrepancy (£)	Pricing	Schemes	Traffic volume	Other
Passengers (foot)	11 000	10 000	+1 000	9.50	10.00	−0.50	104 500	100 000	+ 4 500				
Motorists	5 500	6 000	− 500	12.75	12.00	+0.75	70 125	72 000	− 1 875				
Accompanied cars (units)	2 100	2 000	+ 100	16.50	16.00	+0.50	34 650	32 000	+ 2 650				
General freight (tons)	1 100	1 000	+ 100	16.00	15.00	+1.00	17 600	15 000	+ 2 600				
Container freight (units)	1 900	2 000	− 100	95.00	90.00	+5.00	180 500	180 000	+ 500				
Trade cars (units)	600	500	+ 100	12.50	12.00	+0.50	7 500	6 000	+ 1 500				
Parcel post (bags)	10 000	11 000	−1 000	00.75	00.70	+0.05	7 500	7 700	− 200				
Letter mails (bags)	6 000	5 000	+1 000	00.50	00.60	−0.10	3 000	3 000	nil				
Ro/Ro vehicles (units)	500	450	+ 50	105.00	100.00	+5.00	52 500	45 000	+ 7 500				
Catering – Restaurant sales	–	–	–	–	–	–	21 000	20 000	+ 1 000				
Ship shop sales	–	–	–	–	–	–	30 000	25 000	+ 5 000				
Total revenue							528 875	505 700	23 125				

Table 10.2 XYZ Service Group, Eastern Division: budgeted trading results for January 1981

Expenditure	Actual	Budget	Discrepancy	Explanations					
				Staff cost	Fuel stores cost	Foreign exchange variation	Traffic volume	Number of voyages	Other price variations
Ship provision and maintenance									
Depreciation									
Repairs and overhauls									
Staff expenses									
Officers and crews									
Other cost									
Fuel and power									
Other operating expenses									
Shore terminal expenses									
Home ports: Staff expenses									
Harbour dues and pilotage									
Other expenses									
Overseas ports: Staff expenses									
Harbour dues and pilotage									
Other expenses									
Booking and consignment of traffic									
Staff expenses									
Commission paid to agencies									
Other expenses									
Miscellaneous									
Administration									
Publicity									
Compensation for accidents									
Chartering									
Insurance									
Catering expenses									
Total expenditure									
Net trading surplus or loss									

usually formulated in September and October for the following year
on the basis of the circumstances expected to prevail. These include
the following:

(a) Competition. If competition is intense, companies tend to
hold down their 'average' tariff rate in an effort to sustain or
generate traffic.

(b) The international economic situation. The relaxation of trade
barriers could increase trade, but a rise in oil prices might cloud the
prospects of an expansion in trade as developing countries restrict
certain types of imports in order to meet the cost of imported crude
oil.

(c) The political situation worldwide. Any escalation in flag discrimination or the risk of hostilities may have a bearing on trade
prospects.

(d) The fiscal policies of the countries served. Stringent credit and
taxation measures have a marked impact on passenger and car ferry
services through their effect on disposable incomes.

(e) Any conference agreements or government controls on
tariffs.

(f) Additional revenue expected to accrue from the provision of
new tonnage, new services, improvements in schedules, publicity or
tariff changes.

(g) Fluctuations in exchange rates. Countries with a depreciating
currency tend to attract an increasing number of overseas visitors
and to boost their exports provided that the goods are competitive.
Conversely, the appreciation of a currency may deter overseas
visitors and have an adverse effect on exports. Tariff levels are also
affected by currency fluctuations, as explained on pp. 26–30 with
regard to the currency adjustment factor (CAF).

The draft budget is considered collectively by the chief officers
and ultimately by the board of directors. Each revenue area is
scrutinized objectively with a view to improvement and the basis of
the figures is examined, particularly where there are significant
variations from the previous year's results.

The revenue budget consists of three main elements: the physical
facts (i.e. the number of units carried), the average receipt and gross
receipts, each expressed in terms of actual results in the particular
period, the budget forecast and any discrepancy between the two
(see Table 10.1). A further column is provided to explain such

variations in terms of pricing (e.g. changes in tariff levels), schemes (e.g. new tonnage or additional services), traffic volume (e.g. extra traffic secured by virtue of a new contract) and miscellaneous causes.

The figures for the various items in the revenue budget are largely self-explanatory. For example, foot passengers were expected to total 10 000 in January, but 11 000 were actually carried. The average yield per passenger was £9.50 against £10 in the budget. Overall income in the period was thus £4500 higher than expected. Similarly, freight containers totalled 1900, which was 100 units below the forecast. However, the average yield was £5 higher than expected owing to the negotiation of a better rate with major shippers than had been anticipated; gross receipts therefore improved by £500.

Trade cars involves the shipment of newly manufactured cars and lorries for sale in the importing country. Some 600 units were shipped in January, 100 above budget, and total revenue came to £7500. As the rate is based on vehicle length, the average receipt was 50p higher than the budget figure owing to the shipment of a greater proportion of longer vehicles.

The currency adjustment factor contributed to the improvement in average receipts from containers, trade cars and Ro/Ro vehicles.

Overall revenue totalled £528 875, which was £23 125 (4.5 per cent) above budget.

Revenue budget results such as these can be regarded as reasonably satisfactory. Items showing a variation in excess of 2.5 per cent will require particular scrutiny when the following year's budget is compiled in order to ascertain whether any further refinements are necessary.

Expenditure budget
The expenditure budget is compiled at the same time as the revenue budget by all the departmental officers, each of whom thus becomes committed to achieving the predicted results. A shipping company has direct control over expenditure but less influence over income, so that much thought must be given to the type and level of expenditure to ensure that the principle of 'value for money' is applied. Close liaison must be maintained with the traffic departments, particularly as regards survey dates and sailing schedules, to ensure the optimum use of resources. The fleet manager plays a decisive

role in ensuring that the fleet is economically deployed and that adequate cost consciousness permeates all levels of management. Companies usually issue guidelines to assist in the formulation of departmental budgets.

The layout of an expenditure budget will obviously depend on the needs of the individual company. The example given in Table 10.2 relates to the month of January 1981. As in the case of revenue, there are columns for actual and projected expenditure, variations and explanations of the latter under various headings. Hence, if the wages of officers and crew exceed the budget by £10 000 in the period under review, £2000 may be due to increased bunkering expenses, recorded under 'Fuel stores cost', and £8000 may be attributable to additional voyages, recorded under 'Number of voyages', to cater for increased traffic.

Let us examine individually the various items recorded in the expenditure budget:

(a) Ship depreciation, repairs and overhauls are major areas of expenditure. The annual depreciation may represent a fixed absolute amount or a constant percentage of the remaining value of the asset, so that the absolute amount of depreciation diminishes each year. For example, if assets of £1000 with an estimated residual value of £50 are to be depreciated at a rate of 10 per cent per annum, the amount of depreciation will be £95 in the first year, £85.50 in the second, £76.95 in the third and so on. If the straight-line method were used the amount of depreciation would remain the same throughout the estimated life of the asset. Another aspect of depreciation relates to the change in values over time. Ideally, depreciation should be based on the current replacement cost of the asset rather than on the original or historical cost. Very tight control should be kept on ship survey and overhaul costs. Some companies enter survey costs in the period or periods in which they occur, whereas others spread them equally over the twelve months. The latter method probably gives a fairer picture, particularly when reviewing the overall profit and loss result for a particular month.

(b) Staff expenses, another area of high expenditure to be monitored closely, comprise crew costs such as wages, overtime and travel expenses. As explained in Chapter 11, shipboard management techniques that commit the ship's master to his ship's expenditure budget have tended to have highly beneficial effects on financial control.

(c) Fuel and power are now formidable items of expenditure. Ways of reducing fuel consumption, making up for lost time and taking advantage of differences in the cost of bunkering have been described in Chapter 5.

(d) Other operating expenses include the cost of meeting contingencies such as a service disruption.

(e) Shore terminal expenses at home and overseas ports can be kept under control by eliminating overtime and bonus payments wherever possible, avoiding ports with a poor record of industrial relations, encouraging masters to obtain a pilot exemption certificate to obviate the need for a pilot on entering and leaving port and ensuring that port agents obtain competitive port tariffs.

(f) The booking and consignment of traffic is a broad item covering staff expenses, commission paid to agencies and other costs. Many cargo liner companies rely to an equal extent on their own sales force and agents to secure traffic.

(g) Administrative expenditure can be kept down by employing the methods of shipboard management.

(h) Publicity expenses should be related to the level of revenue production. A contingency element should be included in the budget to cater for unforeseen promotions. For example, should competition intensify, it may be wise to increase publicity to sustain traffic volume.

(i) Compensation for accidents arises where no cover is provided under insurance policies; it may cover certain areas for which the P & I clubs normally provide.

(j) Chartering involves the fixture of vessels. It is not usually possible to predict fixture rates several months before commencement of the charter as the rate depends on market conditions at the time of negotiation.

(k) Insurance cover relates to marine insurance on the hull, machinery and freight and the provision of P & I clubs. With replacement costs high, it is now rare to find shipowners carrying their own insurance risk; they usually seek coverage through an insurance broker and/or P & I clubs. Moreover, ship mortgage agreements are conditional on the conclusion of an insurance policy.

(l) Catering expenses relate to victualling provisions.

The results of the period relating income to expenditure will reveal a trading profit or loss, which must be compared with the budget forecast. Experience has shown that it is easier to effect expenditure cuts quickly than to generate additional income at short notice, but both courses must be pursued vigorously in the event of a serious shortfall.

The budget results should be reviewed monthly by a meeting of departmental officers as soon as the data are available, ideally two weeks after the period to which they relate. Departmental officers should be aware much earlier of the results achieved by their own department and be able to take remedial action where necessary. It is usual to conduct a major budget review in the sixteenth and thirty-second weeks of the year, or in April and August, in order to ascertain whether adjustments are required in the light of changed circumstances. It may be necessary to amend traffic forecasts and hence to modify the sailing schedule. In this way the management ensures that its objectives are up to date and that financial control of the company remains tight, particularly with regard to cash flow.

Investment budget
The investment budget is formulated along similar lines and is regularly reviewed as an integral part of the financial management of the company. If the revenue and expenditure predictions are not fulfilled, the investment budget is usually subjected to more critical scrutiny, as failure to realize an adequate trading surplus will affect cash flow and the arrangements for financing the investment programme.

MARKETING

Marketing is an extensive and rather specialized subject that cannot be examined in depth within the scope of this book. Nevertheless, it is appropriate to touch upon the major elements of marketing strategy that are relevant to shipping practice.

The promotion of a shipowner's business involves four basic elements:

1. Advertisement of the product or service;
2. Pricing policy with regard to passenger fares or freight tariffs;
3. Publicity, embracing press releases and general relations with the press; and
4. Direct selling of the company's services by travel agents or by salesmen negotiating contracts with exporters.

The marketing policy pursued by any shipowner has a profound influence on the overall annual results of the company. Accordingly, an annual marketing plan should be adopted at the same time as the budget and should match the aspirations expressed therein; it is, after all, a key instrument in securing the traffic predicted in the budget itself. The object of such a plan is to identify the products that the shipping company wishes to convey and to win the maximum market share consistent with adequate profitability.

The details of the marketing plan will depend upon the type of ship operator and the trades in which he is engaged, but the general features will be as follows:

(a) The plan is usually drawn up for a particular service or trade.

(b) Details are given of the traffic forecast and analysis shown in the budget. The breakdown may be by commodity type, by country of origin and destination, by cargo classification or by type of vehicle conveyed in each direction.

(c) A brief description of the ports, ships and schedules involved in the service.

(d) Details of significant changes in the service since the previous year or planned in the future.

(e) The pricing policy. The subject of market pricing is discussed in the final section of this chapter.

(f) Great stress should be laid on the advantages of the service over its competitors, thereby helping salesmen and agents to persuade clients to use the route. These should also be given prominence in advertising and other forms of promotion.

(g) Details will be given of sales conferences and any promotional campaigns in the press and trade journals, on commercial radio and television and at trade fairs and similar events. Large shipping companies, particularly those in passenger trades, engage advertising agencies to devise their advertising and promotion plans; separate agents are generally employed in each country in order to reflect different advertising customs and techniques. Market research should be carried out before an advertising campaign is launched to assess market potential and determine the factors that cause shippers or passengers to use the service. Close liaison between advertising agency and shipping company is essential throughout an advertising campaign so that the response can be monitored and the campaign modified if necessary.

(h) The plan will include details of the year's marketing budget broken down according to country, commodity and medium: newspapers, trade journals, commercial radio, television, brochures, sales conferences, trade fairs, promotions, etc. In general, only large shipping companies engaged in the travel trade advertise on television and radio. The marketing budget should be in proportion to the budgeted gross revenue derived from the service or commodity in question; amounts between ½ and 3 per cent are generally considered reasonable, although the figure will be higher for the promotion of a new service. Ship operators are collaborating increasingly with tourist boards, hoteliers' associations and local ship operators in the joint promotion of inclusive tours. Cargo liner services may involve promotions with chambers of commerce and trade associations.

(i) The plan should include a timetable of sales conferences and promotions in the press and trade journals. Timing plays an important role in achieving the maximum impact, so that note should be taken of competitors' programmes. An attempt should be made to keep the company in the public eye throughout the year.

(j) Agents and personnel responsible for executing the plan should be allotted realizable revenue targets; incentives may be offered in the form of annual awards for outstanding results. Reports on achievements in individual countries or services should be prepared at regular intervals wherever practicable.

We have already touched briefly upon the need for market research to establish the characteristics of a market that the shipowner is already serving or may wish to enter if it proves economically viable. Market research can be used to ascertain market shares and other aspects of the business. In a progressive shipping company the individual commercial, operating and technical departments should request the market research department to undertake specific projects in order to maximize the profitable development of the company. Relatively simple surveys may be carried out to discover, for instance, where motorists learned of a particular ferry service, while at the other end of the scale specialist consultants may conduct research that will result in far-reaching developments, as in the case of the market research used to determine service patterns and tonnage requirements for deep-sea container services when that sector was being established.

Simple market surveys may be carried out in a number of ways:

1. By questionnaire distributed by mail or to all passengers on a cruise; questions may relate to the reasons for taking the cruise, good and bad points about the cruise, age, income bracket and profession.

2. By desk research, in other words by extracting statistics and other information from trade journals, newspapers, government reports and publications of chambers of commerce and the like.

3. By direct personal interview in a field survey; this is the most expensive but most reliable method of obtaining data from individual prospective customers.

MARKET PRICING

An increasing number of shipowners in cargo liner and passenger trades are now using the techniques of market pricing, which is essentially the practice of correlating passenger and freight tariffs to potential market demand and sensitivity in order primarily to maximize cash flow, attain high load factors, counter competition, stimulate market growth and improve profitability. We have already seen examples of market pricing elsewhere in this book; for instance, rather than shipping containers empty in one direction, a company may reduce tariffs for the return trip in order to attract new custom that would otherwise find shipment uneconomic. The different fares charged on short sea passenger services at various times of the year are another application of market pricing.

In adopting a market pricing policy care must be taken to ensure that full-rate traffic is not diverted to the lower rate in endeavouring to generate a higher volume of business. Moreover, whereas the basic tariff must cover direct costs and make a major contribution to indirect costs, the reduced tariff should at least cover direct costs if possible. The formulation of graduated tariffs requires careful evaluation of existing tariff levels, costs, competition, agreements with other operators and, above all, market sensitivity. For example, there is nothing to be gained by offering a 40 per cent 'off season' discount for particular traffic if the market is insensitive to price; the slightly higher load factor that would ensue, say 5 per cent higher, would produce less revenue overall, so that in accordance with the principle of profit maximization the tariff should remain unchanged. Finally, market pricing policies that lead to a tariff war should be avoided. They may generate additional traffic, but the average rate will fall and there may be little prospect of increasing revenue.

COMPUTERIZATION

In the years to come the increasing use of computers in the shipping industry will contribute towards greater efficiency and profitability by facilitating the optimum use of available resources.

The introduction of computers is not to be undertaken lightly, however. A feasibility study should first be made by systems analysts to ascertain whether the work in question is suitable for computerization and to compare the costs of the existing methods with those of the proposed computer application. All departments likely to use the computer should be consulted to ensure that any scheme ultimately adopted contains the necessary data. Scope should also be provided for future development.

In the shipping industry computers can be used in the following fields:

(a) Stores control. By recording in the computer details of stores in stock, their value and consumption, statements of consumption over a given period and an inventory of stocks by quantity and value can be produced at regular intervals, thus keeping consumption and stocks down to an economic minimum and facilitating ordering.

(b) Wage bills. Staff salaries including national insurance contributions, overtime, productivity bonuses, pension contributions and tax deductions can be calculated by the computer.

(c) Reservations. The use of computers to record vehicle deck space, cabins and seats booked on passenger vessels and space allocated for road haulage units, trade cars and trade caravans on Ro/Ro carriers improves traffic control and avoids outshipments due to overbooking.

(d) Ship design and specification. A number of classification societies use computers to provide a basic ship profile in response to a specification of traffic needs, such as capacity, length, beam, draught and speed.

(e) An increasing number of modern ships are equipped with a computer to regulate their optimum speed and fuel consumption. Computer navigation aids are also available.

(f) Preparation of bills. Large shipowners now bill their customers at regular intervals with the aid of a computer, thereby ensuring prompt despatch, automatically reminding late payers and identifying potential bad debts.

(g) Formulation of sailing programme schedules.

(h) Documentation. The design and transmission of shipping documents has been transformed in recent years. The cargo shipment details found on shipping documents can now be sent to the destination port and the consignee electronically thereby facilitating speedy customs clearance and prompt settlement.

(i) Containers. Computers are used extensively in the control, stowage and overall shipment arrangements, greatly facilitating the optimum use of the container units and infrastructure.

(j) Ship maintenance. The use of computers facilitates the formulation of maintenance and survey programmes for individual vessels and provides data on costs and future requirements.

(k) Customs clearance. Computers now play a large part in the customs clearance procedures at many UK ports.

(l) Management information. Statistical data on the many subjects mentioned above (e.g. staff numbers, number of sailings, carryings, load factors, etc.) can be obtained from the computer whenever required and used to generate further information, such as the average fuel consumption and cost per nautical mile of a specified vessel in particular years, or the average tariff yield per container on specified services. Such general data availability is very useful when a choice has to be made between various options.

The use of computers within the industry is likely to grow, particularly as financial management techniques improve and routine clerical work is automated. Companies should examine their procedures continuously to determine whether management areas that hitherto have used traditional methods would benefit from computerization. Close attention should be paid to the cost and benefits to be derived from the use of computers, particularly any financial savings.

CHAPTER 11

Shipboard Management

Essentials of shipboard management. Organization of shipboard management. Operation of shipboard management. Advantages of shipboard management.

Over the past decade there has been a substantial increase in the cost of labour, fuel, maintenance and ship survey. At the same time, the capital cost of providing new tonnage has risen sharply. Tariffs and fixture rates have not kept pace, however, so that the discrepancy between expenditure and revenue has progressively widened. Shipowners are therefore obliged to reduce costs if they are to operate profitably. Throughout this book stress has been laid on various ways of achieving this objective by improving the design and utilization of vessels, exploiting economies of scale, increasing crew productivity, reducing fuel consumption and cutting the cost of maintenance. Another avenue open to them is that of shipboard management.

ESSENTIALS OF SHIPBOARD MANAGEMENT

Shipboard management constitutes a new approach to ship operation pioneered in recent years by the Danish shipping company DFDS A/S. Its objective is simply to entrust the entire economic running of the vessel to the officers on board, with the shore-based organization providing only back-up services. In effect, the ship becomes a 'floating' subsidiary company with the master as managing director. He and his team are authorized to operate within fixed budgetary limits and are responsible for generating an agreed amount of revenue. The approach can be used on mercantile vessels of any kind and will doubtless find increasing application throughout the world, but especially in those countries where crew salaries and/or manning levels are high.

The following requirements must be met if a system of shipboard management is to operate efficiently:

(a) The vessel must have a permanent crew; multi-crew operation is unacceptable. When an officer is absent on leave his place is taken by the officer next in rank, so that a relief officer comes in at the

149

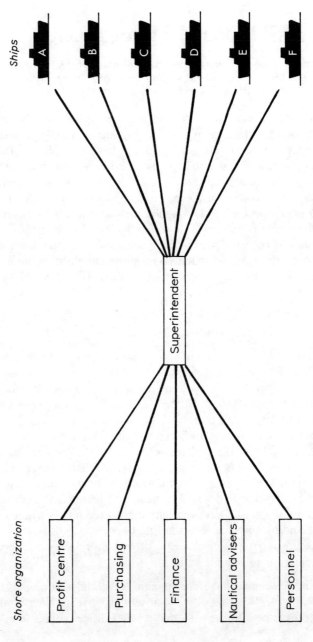

Shore organization

Ships

Profit centre

Purchasing

Finance

Nautical advisers

Personnel

Superintendent

A

B

C

D

E

F

Diagram II Shipboard management – shore organization

bottom of the scale. This ensures that officers are involved in the management of the same vessel for as long as possible and gives junior officers occasional experience of added responsibility. As the ship's crew gains an intimate knowledge of the ship and learns how best to manage her at minimum cost, an *esprit de corps* develops that brings greater job satisfaction and in the long term raises productivity.

(b) A system of shipboard preventive maintenance is required to take the place of sporadic maintenance.

(c) A fixed standard of maintenance and service should be laid down. Such a shipboard work load is defined in the engineer's schedule and reflected in his budget.

(d) An effective system of budgetary control should be instituted.

A major obstacle to the introduction of shipboard management in some companies would be the need to revise manning agreements, as nowadays many ships are run on the basis of multi-crew operation. However, the potential benefits are so outstanding as to warrant close evaluation and the possible consideration of a pilot scheme.

ORGANIZATION OF SHIPBOARD MANAGEMENT

The organization of shipboard management will naturally depend on the needs of individual shipping companies, but the sole objective of such schemes will be to attain the highest level of efficiency practicable. The following description of the structure should therefore be regarded as the essential framework of any scheme devised.

As stated above, each vessel has a management team responsible for the management of the vessel within its defined authority. The master presides as managing director, with the other officer-directors responsible for their own domains – the chief engineer for ship's machinery, the chief officer for technical matters including deck personnel and the purser for catering. As shown in Diagram II, the shipboard management team is itself responsible to a shore-based superintendent, who may have charge of six cargo vessels or rather fewer passenger ships. He might be a former marine engineer or marine superintendent; the most suitable person would have wide experience in the technical, commercial, operational and administrative fields. His role is essentially to provide liaison between the ships and the organization ashore.

The shore-based organization shown in Diagram II has a number of profit centres (also called result centres) plus certain service divisions, such as purchasing, finance, nautical advisers and personnel. Some companies may also have other specialist departments to advise the ships' masters on such matters as long- and short-term planning and marketing. The more important shore-based departments call for the following comments:

(a) The profit centres are responsible for ensuring that their own divisions, which may comprise up to five vessels, operate according to the budget. This involves devising feedback systems. Failure to realize the budget objectives causes the profit centre to institute remedial action with the approval of the ship's master.

(b) The role of the purchasing department primarily consists in formulating company policy and routines with regard to ship's stores, victualling and bunkering and preparing a list of approved suppliers among whom the ships' masters can choose.

(c) The financial department attends to the settlement of accounts, devises accounting procedures, supervises credit and records the overall financial results of the company.

(d) Nautical advisers are involved in matters affecting the technical aspects of ship management, such as surveys, life-saving provisions, navigational equipment, relevant Merchant Shipping Acts, manning levels, maintenance systems and the provision of spare parts.

(e) The personnel department attends to crew matters, primarily pay, training, service conditions and industrial relations.

It must be stressed that the above-mentioned divisions are flexible and would be modified to suit individual companies. The various departments act primarily in an advisory capacity and disseminate company policy to the ships' masters.

OPERATION OF SHIPBOARD MANAGEMENT

The budget for the year is drawn up by the master on the basis of the collective experience of the ship's officers and information provided by the shore-based departments on such matters as traffic forecasts, predicted exchange rates, wage awards, bunker prices, port charges, shipyard and survey costs, prices of stores from accredited suppliers and – in the case of passenger vessels – fares, cabin charges and catering tariffs. The process of advice and consultation is not a one-way affair, as the shipboard management team can assist the marketing department with the formulation of the marketing plan. It will also play a public relations role towards agents and potential shippers at its various ports of call.

The predicted financial result for the year is discussed and ultimately approved by the company and the master; at this point the forecast becomes an objective to which the entire ship's complement is committed. It comprises the following main items:

(a) Maintenance and lubrication programmes
(b) Spare parts programme
(c) Condition control programmes
(d) Status procedures
(e) Budget routines
(f) Routines for paperwork and reporting
(g) Purchasing routines

During the year the master would usually confer with the superintendent once a fortnight, depending on circumstance, and submit written reports on the ship's performance only once a month; indeed, nil returns could be made unless the budget forecast had been subject to a major upset that could not be remedied effectively by the shipboard personnel, such as damage requiring the vessel's withdrawal from service for a few days. The budget control and reporting procedures must be adequate so that serious deviations from the budget are notified to the profit centre promptly and measures taken by the superintendent and the master.

Under the system of preventive maintenance, components should be checked at regular intervals according to a set programme of work, which forms the basis of an accurate budget for spare parts and repairs. File cards are kept to show the dates on which major items of machinery have been inspected and to record any problems. Where possible, repairs are carried out by the ship's own personnel. The extent of any work to be carried out in a shipyard and the yard to be employed are decided by the master and chief engineer in consultation with the superintendent. Competitive tenders are invited and a detailed list is prepared showing the repairs that can be done before docking and those that require checking. In this way some companies have been able to reduce the period a vessel is out of service from four weeks to ten days; in some cases ships are now being dry-docked in alternate years instead of annually, largely as a result of the much improved standard of shipboard maintenance. While the vessel is in dry dock the chief engineer and his officers are responsible for ensuring that all the work is carried out in a satisfactory manner; no shore-based superintendent marine engineer is present as in a traditional management structure. The chief engineer also checks the invoices and passes them to the purchasing department for payment.

ADVANTAGES OF SHIPBOARD MANAGEMENT

The advantages of shipboard management will obviously depend ultimately on the shipowner's needs and the trade in which his vessels are engaged. However, the following benefits should accrue:

(a) The size of the shore-based organization is reduced by the delegation of many tasks to the shipboard management team and the introduction of a common code of integrated planned maintenance, spare parts organization and purchasing procedures. Certain shore-based departments, such as the catering department and the marine engineer's department, may be abolished entirely. As a result, administrative costs have been reduced by about 50 per cent in some companies.

(b) A substantial improvement in crew productivity can be achieved as a result of a large increase in the work load.

(c) The system of planned preventive maintenance, spare parts organization and purchasing procedures shortens the time a vessel spends in dry dock on survey – in many cases by more than half – and consequently reduces the cost of obtaining a relief vessel.

(d) The commitment of officers and crew to budgetary targets encourages cost-consciousness and leads to financial savings in all fields of the ship's expenditure.

(e) The increased responsibility entrusted to the ship's personnel and the employment of a permanent crew generate an *esprit de corps*, strengthens the crew's commitment to the targets and makes for swift decision-making, as the master can settle many matters within his clearly defined field of competence without referring to the shore-based departments.

(f) The standard of shipboard maintenance and service tends to be much higher as the permanent crew has an intimate knowledge of the ship and takes a pride in achieving the objectives, whether they relate to economical maintenance or maximum revenue production in the ship's bars, restaurants and shops.

(g) Greater job satisfaction creates better industrial relations. The master would settle any disputes in the light of the circumstances of the case, its financial implications and the company's policy guidelines.

(h) The improved profitability of the ship greatly facilitates the long-term planning of investment and enables the company to go forward with confidence.

(i) The general economical operation of the vessel helps keep rates competitive and this maximizes market share and revenue.

There is no doubt that shipboard management will be introduced more widely in the years to come; the development of modern telecommunications systems, the relentless increase in crew costs and the need to keep administrative expenditure within bounds make its adoption almost inevitable in certain trades.

CHAPTER 12

Role of British and International Shipping Organizations

Council of European and Japanese National Shipowners' Associations (CENSA). General Council of British Shipping (GCBS). Inter-Governmental Maritime Consultative Organization (IMCO). International Association of Independent Tanker Owners (INTERTANKO). International Cargo Handling Co-ordination Association (ICHCA).

Our study of the economics of shipping practice would be incomplete without an examination of the role and increasing influence of some of the numerous national and international organizations in the fields of shipping and trade. Many of them work in close association with governments and they are undoubtedly making an increasing contribution towards the facilitation and development of international trade. In this chapter we examine those organizations that relate solely to the shipping industry. Chapter 13 describes a number of other organizations whose scope is far wider but nevertheless affects shipping or trade.

COUNCIL OF EUROPEAN AND JAPANESE NATIONAL SHIPOWNERS' ASSOCIATIONS (CENSA)

During the late 1950s doubt was cast upon the legality of dual rate contracts used in the American trades. A group of continental European lines felt that the implications were so serious that they established the Committee of European Shipowners (CES) with headquarters in Bremen. The ensuing discussion about the whole scope of the US Shipping Act of 1916, including the extent of anti-trust immunity it afforded, soon aroused the interest of European governments. Accordingly, an *ad hoc* group of European conference lines was formed that subsequently became known as the Committee of European National Shipowners' Associations (CENSA). For some time this Committee operated alongside the CES, which was enlarged by the inclusion of British lines. In 1966 an international secretariat was established in London to serve the two bodies, which were merged in 1974 to form the Council of

European and Japanese National Shipowners' Associations. Today its membership comprises the national shipowners' associations of twelve major maritime nations, namely the Union des Armateurs Belges (Belgium), Danmarks Rederiforening (Denmark), Suomen Varnstamoyhdists r.y. (Finland), Comité Central des Armateurs de France (France), Verband Deutscher Reeder (Federal Republic of Germany), Union of Greek Shipowners (Greece), Confederazione Italiana Armatori Liberi and Società Finanziaria Marittima (FINMARE) (Italy), Japanese Shipowners' Association (Japan), Koninklijke Nederlandse Redersvereniging (the Netherlands), Norges Rederforbund (Norway), Sveriges Redareforening (Sweden), and the General Council of British Shipping (United Kingdom). It also has individual line members (including consortia) that trade to or from the United States. The shipowners of the CENSA countries own almost 55 per cent of the world's merchant fleet in terms of numbers.

CENSA aims to promote and protect sound shipping policies in all sectors of shipping, to co-ordinate and present the views of its members and to exchange views with other groups of shipowners. The organization has four sections responsible for monitoring (1) the work of the United Nations on shipping policy, (2) shipping policy developments in the United States, (3) legislation and policies in other areas of the world and (4) the practice and development of consultation between liner conferences in Europe and European shippers' councils.

The Council acts as adviser to the governments of its members countries, which constitute the Consultative Shipping Group. It also enjoys consultative status with the United Nations Conference on Trade and Development (UNCTAD) and maintains links with European shippers' councils and European-based liner conferences.

GENERAL COUNCIL OF BRITISH SHIPPING (GCBS)

The General Council of British Shipping (GCBS) is the representative body of the British shipping industry, at both national and international levels, on all aspects of corporate policy affecting it. The scope of its activities is wide and varied, encompassing such matters as consultations with government departments on policies affecting the interests of its members, negotiations with seafarers' unions on industrial relations and manpower questions and the provision of services to its members in the recruitment and training of seafarers and the provision of crews. The GCBS came into being on 1st March 1975, when it took over the roles of the Chamber of Shipping of the United Kingdom and the British Shipping Federation, which had both been established for nearly a century. It is an incorporated company limited by guarantee and has no share capital.

There are three classes of member, namely:

1. Members, who are persons resident in the United Kingdom or corporate bodies registered in the United Kingdom and owning or managing ships registered there.

2. Associate members, comprising associations of shipowners established in the United Kingdom protection and indemnity associations or similar bodies to which UK shipowners belong.

3. Honorary members, who may be admitted at the discretion of the General Council.

The primary object of the GCBS is to promote and protect the interests of the owners and managers of British ships and to take appropriate action, nationally and internationally, to achieve that end. The comprehensive nature of its membership permits it to speak for the industry as a whole. It is not directly involved in the commercial affairs of individual companies but endeavours to create a climate in which shipping can best serve trade and operate as a competitive industry according to the principles of free enterprise. It monitors legislative proposals that affect or could affect shipping and, while maintaining a position of strict political neutrality, advises, consults, negotiates and, where necessary, takes issue with the government of the day on policies which could impinge directly or indirectly on the interests of the shipping industry.

Where sea-going personnel are concerned, the GCBS represents British shipowners and managers on bodies such as the National Maritime Board, the Merchant Navy Training Board, the Seafarers' Pension Funds and the Merchant Navy Welfare Board. It provides an advisory service to its members on the development of industrial relations policies. The Council is responsible for the recruitment and shore training of most of the rating personnel employed in the merchant navy and it administers the Merchant Navy Established Service Scheme. It also plays an important role in the recruitment of deck and engineer cadets and in the formulation of policy on the training of officers.

As shipping is an international business, the GCBS maintains close working relations with a great number of organizations concerned with trade and shipping throughout the world. It also provides the secretariat for the International Chamber of Shipping (ICS) and the International Shipping Federation (ISF).

The governing body of the GCBS is the General Council, which comprises all members and meets at least once a year. The conduct of the business of the GCBS is vested in a General Policy Committee (GPC) of not more than forty persons, some of whom are elected – including the President and Vice-President – and others co-opted. The GPC, which meets at regular intervals, is in effect the organization's 'board of directors'. It is supported by a carefully integrated structure of Sections (each representing a different category of shipping), Districts and Functional Committees composed of senior managers and staff of member companies who voluntarily give their time, knowledge and experience for the benefit of the industry.

Further details of the work of the GCBS are to be found in *Elements of Shipping*.

INTER-GOVERNMENTAL MARITIME CONSULTATIVE ORGANIZATION (IMCO)

Undoubtedly one of the most important organizations active in the field of shipping today is the Inter-Governmental Maritime Consultative Organization (IMCO), the specialized agency of the United Nations concerned with maritime affairs. It is primarily concerned with shipping engaged in international trade. The organization has 118 member states and one associate member.

The convention establishing IMCO was drafted by the United Nations Maritime Conference at Geneva in 1948, and reflected the desire of maritime nations to consolidate the diverse forms of international co-operation that had evolved over the years in the world of shipping. The convention came into force in 1958 and the first IMCO Assembly met in London in January 1959.

In the meantime, the maritime nations had made considerable progress in improving and enlarging the existing body of international maritime law. In 1948 a new International Convention for the Safety of Life at Sea was adopted, followed by the International Convention for the Prevention of Pollution of the Sea by Oil in 1954.

One of the main advantages of a permanent international body concerned with shipping is that it provides a forum in which representatives of all member countries can meet regularly to discuss matters of mutual interest. It also provides accepted machinery through which action can be taken to introduce, amend and implement legislation and other agreed international regulations and standards.

IMCO's main objective is to facilitate co-operation among governments on technical matters affecting international shipping in order to achieve the highest practicable standards of maritime safety and efficiency of navigation. The Organization has a special responsibility for safety at sea and for the protection of the marine environment through the prevention of pollution of the sea caused by ships and other craft. It also deals with legal matters connected with international shipping, promotes the easier flow of international maritime traffic and provides developing countries with technical assistance in maritime matters.

IMCO co-operates with other international bodies on shipping matters and co-ordinates its activities with those of other specialized agencies of the United Nations. The Organization is responsible for convening international shipping conferences and drafting international conventions or agreements in this field. At present the main organs of IMCO are the Assembly, the Council and the Maritime Safety Committee. There are also four subsidiary bodies: the Legal Committee, the Committee on Technical Co-operation, the Marine Environment Protection Committee and the Facilitation Committee. Important amendments to the IMCO Convention adopted by the Assembly in 1975 and 1977, under which the Organization will be renamed the International Maritime Organization, will formalize the status of the first three of these committees and place them on the same footing as the Maritime Safety Committee.

The Assembly, IMCO's supreme governing body, consists of representatives from all member states; it lays down the work programme, approves recommendations made by IMCO, votes the budget to which all member states contribute on an agreed scale of assessments, approves financial regulations, elects the IMCO

Council and approves the appointment of the Secretary-General. The Assembly normally meets in London, regular sessions having been held every two years since 1959.

The Council, which is IMCO's governing body between Assembly sessions, consists of representatives of 24 member states elected by the Assembly for a term of two years; it normally meets twice a year. The Council at present comprises representatives of Algeria, Argentina, Brazil, Canada, China, Egypt, France, the Federal Republic of Germany, India, Indonesia, Japan, Kenya, Kuwait, Liberia, Malta, Mexico, Nigeria, Norway, Pakistan, Peru, Romania, the USSR, the United Kingdom and the USA.

The Maritime Safety Committee consists of representatives of all member states. It normally meets twice a year and deals with such matters as the safety of navigation in general, safety regulations for fishing vessels, aids to navigation, the construction and equipment of ships, rules for preventing collisions at sea, bulk cargoes (including grain, ores and chemicals), dangerous cargoes, life-saving appliances, marine radio communications, the standardization of training, watchkeeping and qualifications of officers and crew and search and rescue. The Committee has established a number of technical sub-committees to consider specific subjects and report their findings; the power to initiate action normally rests with the Assembly.

The Legal Committee, the Marine Environment Protection Committee and the Committee on Technical Co-operation are open to all member states; the Facilitation Committee is open to member states that are parties to the Convention on Facilitation of International Maritime Traffic.

The role of IMCO in the field of international shipping is growing continuously. The conventions formulated by the Organization are listed in *Elements of Shipping*, pages 116–117.

The adoption of a convention marks the conclusion of the first stage in the process by which it becomes international law. It will not come into force, however, until it has been formally ratified in accordance with the conditions laid down in the convention itself. The more important and more complex the convention, the more stringent are the conditions. For example, the International Convention on Tonnage Measurement of Ships, 1969, must be accepted by 25 states owning not less than 65 per cent of the world's gross merchant shipping tonnage. Such rigorous conditions are required in order to ensure that the major technical conventions apply to a large section of the shipping community immediately upon their entry into force; if they did not, they would tend to confuse shipping practice rather than clarify it. In the case of some conventions that affect a small number of states or deal with less complex matters, the requirements may be less stringent. For example, the Convention Relating to Civil Liability in the Field of Maritime Carriage of Nuclear Material, 1971, came into force 90 days after ratification by five states; the Special Trade Passenger Ships Agreement, 1971, came into force six months after its acceptance by three states, including two with ships or nationals involved in special trades.

When the appropriate conditions have been fulfilled, the convention enters into force for the states which have accepted it – generally after a period of grace to enable the states to take the necessary implementation measures. Acceptance of a convention does not merely entail the deposit of a formal instrument; it imposes an obligation on the government to take measures required by the convention. National law often has to be amended to enforce the provisions of a convention. In some cases special facilities may have to be constructed, such as the reception facilities outlined in the 1973 International Convention for the Prevention of Pollution from Ships; an inspectorate may have to be appointed or trained to carry out functions under the convention, and adequate notice must be given to shipowners, shipbuilders and other interested parties in order to ensure that they take account of the provisions of the convention in their future acts and plans.

On average, IMCO conventions come into force within five years of their adoption. Although this compares favourably with the record of other organizations, member governments are not satisfied with such a performance and have been considering measures to accelerate the process wherever possible.

IMCO also co-operates closely with the United Nations, its subsidiary bodies and commissions. A full report on the Organization's work is submitted annually to the UN Economic and Social Council, details of IMCO's work programmes are sent to the UN Secretariat for submission to appropriate bodies within the system and IMCO participates in the various bodies established to promote co-ordination. The Organization's links with the Economic Commissions have been strengthened in recent years, particularly in view of IMCO's increasing activities in the field of technical co-operation. Most of the projects carried out under IMCO's technical assistance programme receive financial support from the United Nations Development Programme. Many other UN agencies have involvement with some aspects of shipping and the sea. For example, IMCO, the Food and Agriculture Organization (FAO) and the International Labour Organisation (ILO) have formed a group of experts to deal with the safety of fishing vessels. In 1976 IMCO and the United Nations Environment Programme, which has a particular interest in combating marine pollution, drew up a Memorandum of Understanding in order to strengthen the links between the two organizations in this area. The Regional Oil-Combating Centre for the Mediterranean Sea is one outcome of their close co-operation. Another joint initiative in the environmental field has been the creation of the Group of Experts on the Scientific Aspects of Marine Pollution (GESAMP), which is sponsored by IMCO, the United Nations, the FAO, the United Nations Educational, Scientific and Cultural Organization (UNESCO), the World Meteorological Organization (WMO), the World Health Organization (WHO) and the International Atomic Energy Authority (IAEA). Close relations have also been formed with the United Nations Conference on Trade and Development (UNCTAD), which has a particular interest in many aspects of shipping, and the United Nations Commission on International Trade Law (UNCITRAL). In addition, IMCO has contributed to several conferences organized by the United Nations, notably the Conference on the Human Environment, held in Stockholm in 1972, and the United Nations Conference on the Law of the Sea, which held its tenth session in 1981.

INTERNATIONAL ASSOCIATION OF INDEPENDENT TANKER OWNERS (INTERTANKO)

The membership of the International Association of Independent Tanker Owners, which has its headquarters in Oslo, comprises more than 300 tanker companies from all the major maritime nations controlling over 180 million dwt of tanker and combined tonnage. Oil companies and state-owned tanker operators are not eligible for membership.

INTERTANKO initially sprang from the tanker crisis of the 1930s, which promoted closer co-operation in an otherwise competitive industry. The successful tanker lay-up pool, commonly known as the Schierwater plan, was administered by the International Tanker Owners' Association Ltd (INTERTANKO), which was established in the spring of 1934. When the tanker market improved towards the end of the 1930s, however, the organization went into hibernation and was formally dissolved in 1954. Nonetheless, the successful experiment of the Schierwater plan fostered an atmosphere of international co-operation that led to the revival of INTERTANKO in London in the mid-1950s. However, the organization failed to gain the support and momentum necessary to effectively promote its members' interests, so that it subsequently went into decline.

In 1970 a group of independent tanker owners from ten countries met in Oslo and established the International Association of Independent Tanker Owners, again called INTERTANKO. The new organization began work in January 1971, with its secretariat and headquarters in the building of the Norwegian Shipowners' Association in Oslo.

The new INTERTANKO was given a broader mandate, but it was agreed that it should not participate in lay-up schemes. The association was to be a non-profit-making body whose objectives would be to promote internationally the interests of its members in matters of general policy, to co-operate with other technical, industrial or commercial interests or bodies on problems of mutual concern to its members and to take part in the deliberations of other international bodies as far as may be necessary for the attainment of its objectives.

The main features of the work of INTERTANKO are as follows:

(a) It operates a port information service giving members details of important changes in port costs and facilities, institutional requirements and other information relevant to tanker operations.

(b) It maintains close liaison with the Worldscale Association, particularly in up-dating the Worldscale freight schedule and the principles on which it is based. Currently the Worldscale system simplifies transactions in the charter market by serving as a standard reference and by providing standard charter party conditions (see also Chapter 7).

(c) The Documentary Committee deals primarily with bills of lading and charter parties and ensure that they adequately reflect members' wishes. To cite a recent example, INTERTANKO facilitated the introduction of the INTANKBILL 78, a bill of lading to be used with a charter party. It also studies the need to amend any existing documentation as a consequence of IMCO resolutions relating to tankers.

(d) It deals with the need to eliminate sea pollution by tankers as a result of spillage or collision and collaborates closely with IMCO in this regard.

(e) It acts as a forum for the exchange of views among members and presents the tanker owners' opinions to governments, the press and the general public. For example, during the period of surplus tanker tonnage there was need for close liaison between the shipbuilding and shipowning sectors in order to avoid the construction of unwanted vessels that would have aggravated the surplus and depressed freight rates.

INTERNATIONAL CARGO HANDLING CO-ORDINATION ASSOCIATION (ICHCA)

The International Cargo Handling Co-ordination Association was established in 1951 with the aim of facilitating improved handling techniques in the world transport system. It has its headquarters, the Central Office, in London.

The new Association expanded rapidly. In the first four years of its existence eight national committees were established in Western Europe by the strong local membership in the transport field. While maintaining their participation in matters of international scope through their close links with the Central Office, the national committees dealt primarily with problems peculiar to their own countries, organizing meetings and seminars which often attracted participation from beyond their frontiers. Today there are twenty-three national secretariats in all parts of the world.

The prime function of the ICHCA is co-ordination. This is achieved by including in its worldwide membership and activities the diverse disciplines that have an impact on cargo handling efficiency; by bringing together both ends in any transportation operation; by stimulating interest and cross-fertilization of ideas through technical meetings, seminars and technical publications; by gathering and disseminating pertinent technical, conceptual and procedural information; and by identifying trends and evolving concepts in the science of cargo handling, thus crystallizing ideas in this field.

The ICHCA has pursued this crystallizing function since its inception, as a brief survey of its major activities shows. In the mid-1950s the Association was discussing the packaging of timber and the handling of sugar in bulk, while Ro/Ro operations were first debated at the 1957 Biennial Conference in Hamburg. Containers were the subject of a conference in the same decade, and the ICHCA continued to monitor the development of this unit load device in the 1960s. Barge carriers and computer operations in cargo handling were examined in 1969 and 1970.

In 1973 the Technical Advisory Sub-Committee (TASC) was formed to monitor technical matters considered to be of particular concern to the Association's members; it is composed of representatives from national sections of the ICHCA, seventeen nations at present being represented. The TASC normally meets four times a year in different participating countries. The major part of its work, however, is conducted by correspondence, which is co-ordinated by the Technical Secretary of the ICHCA at the Central Office in London.

The studies undertaken by the TASC have resulted in the publication of four significant reports:

1. *Condensation in Containers* (1974) quickly came to be regarded as the standard work on this important topic. It won widespread approval throughout the industry and was recommended by the International Union of Marine Insurance as mandatory reading.

2. *Cargo Security in Transport Systems* (1976) was a project in two parts; the first dealt with pilferage and the second examined the incidence and prevention of major theft. The reports formed the basis of two conferences on cargo security that were held in London and Amsterdam.

3. *Pre-Slinging and Strapping of Cargo* (1977) examined simple, low-cost methods of unitizing cargo; it aroused considerable interest, particularly in developing countries.

4. *Ro/Ro Shore and Ship Ramp Characteristics* (1978) was the first collation of information on more than one thousand Ro/Ro ramps in ports and on ships throughout the world. The data were initially intended to assist the International Standards Organisation in harmonizing ship-to-shore connections for Ro/Ro vessels, but they proved to be of such value to ship operators, naval architects, equipment manufacturers, terminal managers and shippers that the ICHCA is to co-operate with the College of Nautical Studies,

Southampton, in placing the data on a computer so as to improve access to the information.

A survey conducted in 1977 to ascertain the research topics that corresponded most closely to the needs of members indicated that the TASC should undertake further work with regard to containers and Ro/Ro operations and revealed a great need for studies involving certain break bulk commodities. As a result, TASC is now examining the handling and packaging of steel products.

Besides crystallizing and stimulating views, the ICHCA acts as a catalyst for the cargo handling industry; the past two years have seen the emergence of a new aspect of the Association's work – the secondment of trainees. The Henri Kummerman Foundation offered to fund a research project in the 1979/80 biennium, the first six-month handling project being undertaken in conjunction with the Central Office in 1980. The advantages of this type of assistance are twofold: the general bank of cargo handling knowledge is improved and the experience of those undertaking the projects will be widened by exposure to an international environment. This is part of the training scene, which has been one of ICHCA's enduring interests over the years. Although the structure of the Association does not lend itself easily to the establishment of training courses, much has been done in the past to arrange projects in conjunction with educational bodies and other organizations in various parts of the world. The ICHCA will continue to take an active role in training at all levels.

The threads of the Association's activities are drawn together at the biennial Conference and General Assembly held in different countries at the invitation of the local national committee or section. The themes of the conferences epitomize the Association's work, and the differing venues provide a unique opportunity for members to meet and exchange views and expertise.

CHAPTER 13

Role of other National and International Organizations

International Chamber of Commerce (ICC). International Labour Organisation (ILO). International Monetary Fund (IMF). Organisation for Economic Co-operation and Development (OECD). Organization of the Petroleum Exporting Countries (OPEC). Simplification of International Trade Procedures Board (SITPRO). United Nations Conference on Trade and Development (UNCTAD). United Nations Commission on International Trade Law (UNCITRAL).

The preceding chapter described a number of organizations directly concerned with the shipping industry. Here we examine certain other institutions whose activities include matters relating to shipping or which are devoted to the furtherance of world trade.

INTERNATIONAL CHAMBER OF COMMERCE (ICC)

The fundamental role of the International Chamber of Commerce is to promote an expansion in international trade and investment by encouraging national economic growth. Its objective is the integration of the business community's approach to world economic progress and problems.

The ICC is represented in 101 countries, where it functions through national committees and councils. Its headquarters are in Paris.

At present the ICC has the following commissions and committees:

Commission on Multinational Enterprises
Commission on Environment
Commission on Social Issues
Special Committee on Information Questions
Commission on Asian and Pacific Affairs
International Bureau of Chambers of Commerce
East–West Committee with the Chambers of Commerce in Socialist Countries
ICC–United Nations, GATT Economic Consultative Committee
Commission on International Monetary Relations

168

Commission on International Trade, Industrial and Commercial Policy

Commission on International Investments and Economic Development

Commission on Energy

Commission on Insurance Problems

Commission on Law and Practices relating to Competition

Commission on Taxation

Commission on International Arbitration

Commission on Marketing – Advertising and Distribution

Commission on Industrial Property

Commission on International Commercial Practice

Commission on Banking Technique and Practice

Maritime Transport Studies

Air Transport Studies

The range of these activities demonstrates the breadth of influence of the ICC today in developing world trade on the sound basis of ethical, economic and financial codes of practice. Its importance will grow as a result of the increasing integration of the world economy in the years to come. The ICC will continue to play a foremost role in preparing codes of business practices, facilitating international trade and investment through the harmonization and standardization of trade practices, and finally in providing a central forum for the discussion of policy problems faced by businessmen in communities throughout the world.

INTERNATIONAL LABOUR ORGANISATION (ILO)

The International Labour Organisation was set up in 1919 to bring governments, employers and trade unions together for joint action in the cause of social justice and better living conditions. It is a tripartite organization, with the representatives of workers and employers taking part in its work on an equal footing with those of governments. The Organisation was awarded the Nobel Peace Prize in 1969, its fiftieth anniversary.

In 1964 the ILO became the first specialized agency associated with the United Nations. Since then, a system of close co-operation has grown up between international organizations attempting to eliminate the grave inequalities and imbalances among the world's various regions. In the field of social policy the ILO is playing an active part in one of the most striking changes since the Second World War: the large scale development of international technical co-operation. New problems continue to arise as a result of technological, economic and social change. While the improvement of working and living conditions and the promotion of full employment remain central aims of the ILO, it now also has to deal with such matters as migrant workers, multinational corporations, the working environment and the social consequences of monetary instability.

The ILO remains a standard-setting body, but today it also lays marked emphasis on operational programmes and educational work in the broadest sense. This led to the creation of the International Institute for Labour Studies (Geneva) in 1960 and the International Centre for Advanced Technical and Vocational Training (Turin) in 1965 and to the launching of the World Employment Programme. The operational programmes have also been largely responsible for the current effort to transfer responsibilities from headquarters in Geneva to the various regions of the world.

The ILO has 144 member states, compared with 42 in 1919 and 58 in 1948. Its regular budget has grown from $4.5 million in 1948 to $203 million in 1980–81. Growth has been accompanied by considerable changes in policy and geographical representation. The former preponderance of industrial countries with market economies has given way to a more varied mixture in which the centrally planned economies of Eastern Europe, the newly independent countries and the third world in general also play an important part.

The organs of the International Labour Organisation are the International Labour Conference, the Governing Body and the International Labour Office. It also works through subsidiary bodies such as regional conferences, industrial committees and panels of experts.

The International Labour Conference, which is an annual general assembly, elects the Governing Body, adopts the ILO's budget, sets international labour standards and provides a world forum for the discussion of social and labour questions. Each national delegation is composed of two government delegates, one employers' delegate and one workers' delegate accompanied by technical advisers if required.

The Governing Body normally holds three sessions a year in

Geneva to decide questions of policy and lay down the programme of work. It is at present composed of 28 government members, 14 employer members and 14 worker members. Ten states of chief industrial importance have permanent government representatives, the others being elected every three years by the Conference.

The International Labour Office, which is the Organisation's permanent secretariat, is headed by a Director-General appointed by the Governing Body. The staff comprises more than 100 nationalities. The number of officials has grown from 500 in 1948 to some 1500 in 1978, plus more than 660 experts serving on technical co-operation programmes around the world. In addition to its operational activities, the Office undertakes research and publishes documents on a wide range of labour and social matters.

At the outset the main task of the ILO was to improve conditions of life and work by building up a comprehensive code of law and practice. The Organisation's founders felt that standards laid down through the joint efforts of governments, management and labour would be realistic, solid and widely applicable. This standard-setting function is one that the ILO still performs. Since 1919 a total of 153 Conventions and 162 Recommendations have been adopted by the International Labour Conference. Conventions are legal instruments regulating a particular aspect of labour administration, social welfare or human rights. By ratifying a convention, a member state formally undertakes to apply its provisions and at the same time signifies its willingness to accept a measure of international supervision. Recommendations are similar to conventions but are not subject to ratification and provide more specific guidelines. Both conventions and recommendations define standards and provide a model for national legislation and practice in member countries.

ILO conventions cover a wide field of social problems, including basic human rights (such as the freedom of association, the abolition of forced labour and the elimination of discrimination in employment), minimum wages, labour administration, industrial relations, employment policy, working conditions, social security, occupational safety and health, and employment at sea.

It is the last of these that is of particular interest in the context of this book. The ILO has established an international code for seafarers and regularly holds special sessions of the International Labour Conference, prepared by its Joint Maritime Commission, to consider applications for additions and extensions to the code. The subjects covered by its brief include the establishment and updating of international minimum standards for various maritime questions such as recruitment (including minimum age, medical examinations and articles of agreement), repatriation, vocational training, the decasualization of employment, occupational safety and health, crew accommodation, labour problems arising from technological change, wages, hours of work and manning, holidays, health and welfare facilities and maritime industrial relations. The ILO co-operates with IMCO on the training and certification of merchant seafarers in the standing Joint IMCO/ILO Committee on Training. Several ILO instruments have been adopted concerning maritime fishermen; a Committee on Conditions of Work in the Fishing Industry was convened in 1978 to set the future programme in this field. A revised convention dealing with the protection of dock-workers against accidents was scheduled for adoption in June 1979.

Through its technical co-operation programme the ILO helps countries in the process of establishing, developing or improving their maritime industries to apply the Organisation's maritime labour standards.

The ILO has also been involved in resolving problems encountered in the offshore petroleum industry, including related offshore construction and diving activities, within the framework of the Programme of Industrial Activities.

Recent ILO activities in the field of shipping include the adoption of the following international labour standards at the 62nd (Maritime) Session of the International Labour Conference held in Geneva in October 1976:

1. A convention concerning minimum standards in merchant ships, which gives ratifying countries the right to report on sub-standard working conditions on board ships calling at their ports and the right to have conditions rectified in ships which are 'clearly hazardous to safety and health'.

2. A convention concerning seafarers' annual leave with pay, which sets minimum annual leave with pay at 30 calendar days after one year of service.

3. A convention and a recommendation designed to promote national policies to encourage the provision of continuous or regular employment for qualified seafarers, as far as is practicable.

4. A recommendation for the protection of seafarers aged less

than 18 (excluding those in warships, fishing vessels or training vessels) in such matters as health, morals and safety and to promote their vocational guidance and training.

The traditional standard-setting activities of the ILO and its newer technical co-operation activities complement one another and are inseparable from its research and publishing work. Without the modernization of social structures and increasing economic development of production, ILO standards would be only a distant hope in many of the emerging countries rather than reasonable and immediately applicable measures.

INTERNATIONAL MONETARY FUND (IMF)

The International Monetary Fund was established in 1944 at the International Monetary and Financial Conference of the United and Associated Nations held in Bretton Woods, New Hampshire, USA.

Before the advent of the Fund, national economic policies had frequently involved restrictions on international trade and payments, which had led to economic conflict. The coming of the IMF, the International Bank for Reconstruction and Development (its sister organization for development finance) and, in 1948, the General Agreement on Tariffs and Trade (GATT) in the field of trade regulation, marked progress in international co-operation. These organizations were founded in a spirit of enlightened, long-term self-interest to function in domains where governments had previously exercised exclusive authority and where decisions had generally reflected narrow and immediate national interests. A detailed code of good conduct was drawn up calling for exchange stability, orderly exchange arrangements, avoidance of competitive exchange depreciation and a liberal regime of international payments. The international monetary system reflected in this code was commonly referred to as the 'Bretton Woods system', or the 'par value system', because a par value agreed with the Fund for each currency lay at the heart of the mechanism.

Adherence to a code of conduct, or to a particular international monetary system, was not an end in itself. It was assumed that good conduct in international financial relations would foster a high level of international trade and investment. Fixed exchange rates, freedom from exchange restrictions, the convertibility of currencies and multilateral trade and payments were believed to form the best basis for international monetary co-operation and the promotion of trade and investment. Expanding trade and investment were, in turn, regarded as essential for full employment and economic development – primary postwar goals.

It was also realized, however, that members would need assistance in following the new code of conduct. As the harmful exchange policies and restrictions of the 1930s had been adopted because countries were short of foreign exchange, the fund was provided with substantial resources which could be made available to members as 'drawings' or 'purchases' of currencies. From the beginning, therefore, the Fund has had complementary regulatory and financial functions. Although one or other may appear to have dominated at different periods, both continue to be essential to achievement of the Fund's objectives, namely:

(a) To promote international monetary co-operation through a permanent institution which provides the machinery for consultation and collaboration on international monetary problems.

(b) To facilitate the expansion and balanced growth of international trade and to contribute thereby to the promotion and maintenance of high levels of employment and real income and to the development of the productive resources of all members as primary objectives of economic policy.

(c) To promote exchange stability, to maintain orderly exchange arrangements among members and to avoid competitive exchange depreciation.

(d) To assist in the establishment of a multilateral system of payments in respect of current transactions between members and in the elimination of foreign exchange restrictions which hamper the growth of world trade.

(e) To give confidence to members by making the general resources of the Fund temporarily available to them under adequate safeguards, thus providing them with opportunity to correct maladjustments in their balance of payments without resorting to measures destructive of national or international prosperity.

(f) In accordance with the above, to shorten the duration and lessen the degree of disequilibrium in the international balances of payments of members.

The Fund has had to devise policies both to implement its code of conduct and to govern the use of its resources. Because circumstances in the world economy have changed with tremendous rapidity in the three and a half decades since Bretton Woods, the Fund has constantly faced new problems requiring it to adapt its policies and to introduce new ones.

When the Fund opened in 1946, with a membership of 40 countries, exchange and trade restrictions were prevalent and only the US dollar, the Canadian dollar and the currencies of some Central American countries were convertible. Furthermore, many members were suffering from the wartime destruction of their industries and were experiencing a chronic dollar shortage, as the productive capacities of the United States and the rest of the Western Hemisphere countries, which also required payment in dollars, greatly exceeded those of the rest of the world.

In these circumstances, the task of the Fund was clear but difficult, and the problems were exacerbated by the difficulties the Fund encountered in establishing its authority. Countries were understandably jealous of their sovereignty in the important fields of exchange rates and restrictions. Moreover, it quickly became apparent that a prerequisite for implementation of the Fund's objectives was the maintenance of internal financial stability. However, domestic monetary and fiscal policies had not been made a matter of international obligation under the Articles of Agreement. On the contrary, care had been taken to ensure that the obligations of members with respect to international transactions should not impede the use of domestic policies to achieve national goals. Nonetheless, inflation was a serious problem in most countries and achievement of the goals of the Fund would be frustrated unless governments took appropriate domestic measures. There was therefore need both to establish the Fund's authority in the fields where it had jurisdiction and to extend its influence over domestic financial policies. The Fund's operations were hampered further by the fact that the United States, which had launched the European Recovery Programme (the Marshall Plan), did not wish members to make drawings from the Fund as well. At that time members were under no obligation to repurchase drawings within a specified period. In 1948 the Executive Board took a decision under which countries participating in the European Recovery Programme were precluded from drawing on the Fund.

By 1952 economic recovery in the Western European countries

and Japan was beginning to take hold and the world dollar shortage was abating. In February of that year the Executive Board took a decision on the use of the Fund's resources that has been the basis of Fund policy ever since. Drawings were arranged into 'tranches' – a gold tranche under which drawings were virtually automatic and four credit tranches under which drawings were subject to progressively more stringent conditions. The conditions were related to a member's progress in liberalizing its exchange and trade restrictions and achieving convertibility of its currency. Thus the Fund linked its financial assistance with its regulatory functions. At this time the Fund also devised the stand-by arrangement, by which a member is assured that it can draw on the Fund's resources during an agreed period if it needs to do so. These policies, together with the expectation that members would repurchase currencies that they had purchased from the Fund within three to five years, in effect unlocked the Fund's resources.

Procedures for the comprehensive consultations that the Fund holds regularly with each member were also established in 1952. These consultations have become the principal vehicle by which the Fund and its members explore a wide range of topics of mutual interest, including exchange rates, multiple currency practices, exchange restrictions, internal financial policies, use of the Fund's resources and quotas. The consultation procedure has evolved over the years and is today, under the Second Amendment to the Articles of Agreement, at the centre of the Fund's obligation to exercise firm surveillance of members' exchange rate policies.

In the financial year 1956–57 use of the Fund's resources increased sharply. Drawings in that year amounted to $1.1 billion, which was more than the total of all previous drawings. In addition, stand-by arrangements agreed or extended totalled $1.2 billion, considerably more than the total of all such arrangements made in previous years. The main cause of this sudden surge of activity was the Suez Canal crisis; France and the United Kingdom, which had both been harmed by closure of the canal, requested substantial stand-by arrangements from the Fund. The reluctance of larger members to seek drawings from the Fund and their preference for raising loans from private banks or from other governments had thus been overcome, and thereafter more and more members began to turn to the Fund for financial help.

The most notable postwar achievement in the foreign exchange field was realized shortly afterwards. In December 1958, 15 western European countries made their currencies externally convertible, and in 1961 these members formally accepted their convertibility obligations under Article VIII of the Fund's Articles of Agreement.

Nearly all of the Fund's objectives in the fields of restrictions and convertibility of currencies had been achieved by 1965. Not only were all the major currencies convertible, but the introduction and successful maintenance of convertibility had brought a virtual end to discriminatory exchange restrictions. Many countries had gone even further than they were obliged to do in reducing restrictions on payments: although the Articles permitted controls on capital movements, even the restrictions on these were gradually eased, so that international financial transactions became freer than they had been for decades. Moreover, by the end of 1965 the great majority of the Fund's members, which now numbered 103, had agreed par values or fixed exchange rates. The use and complexity of multiple exchange rates, which had been widely adopted in the 1950s, especially by developing countries, had also greatly diminished.

The assumptions on which the Fund had been founded had proved correct. The expansion in trade and investment had brought a period of unparalleled economic growth, and unprecedented levels of prosperity and consumption had been attained. The Fund had also been instrumental in the achievement of harmonious international co-operation and consultation in the monetary and financial fields, which was in sharp contrast to the period before the Second World War, when countries pursued their financial policies with little understanding or regard for their negative effects on all countries.

Emergence of problems and collapse of the Bretton Woods system
Signs of serious trouble with the Bretton Woods system were also beginning to emerge by the mid-1960s, however, and most academic economists and monetary officials were concerned about the prospects for its continued smooth functioning. Three problems – liquidity, adjustment and confidence – were identified.

The problem of liquidity reflected the lack of adequate provision for enlarging the supply of world reserves to keep pace with the expansion in international trade and investment. The supply of gold was hardly increasing, if at all, and most of the increase in world reserves had been spawned by the growth in the dollar liabilities of the United States, which was running continuous payments deficits.

The problem of adjustment derived from the fact that by the mid-1960s industrial countries were finding it increasingly difficult to correct imbalances in their external payments positions, either deficits or surpluses, through the use of demand management policies and that they were unwilling to make changes in par values, even though the Articles of Agreement made provision for such changes. Payments imbalances were therefore becoming larger and more persistent, the counterpart of the large deficits of the United States being the large surpluses of other industrial countries, especially the Federal Republic of Germany and Japan.

The problem of confidence stemmed from the fact that, as the volume of dollars held by the central banks outside the United States began to exceed the value of US gold holdings, there was the chance of a run on the dollar that would force suspension of the convertibility of the dollar into gold, the basis of the par value system.

The IMF, national officials and monetary experts had focussed their attention on the liquidity problem as early as 1963 in the belief that it was fundamental to the solution of the other two problems. After six years of negotiation the First Amendment of the Articles of Agreement took effect on 28th July 1969, establishing a facility based on special drawings rights (SDRs) – the only reserve asset ever created by international agreement. The Fund was given authority to create SDRs in the expectation that eventually there would be international regulation of the supply of global liquidity.

Even before the first allocation of SDRs, however, the international monetary system was being subjected to stresses more severe than any experienced since the Second World War. The imbalance in international payments and the flows of short-term capital from one money centre to another that had emerged in the late 1950s and early 1960s became steadily greater, and the resulting problems became increasingly harder to solve, or even to alleviate. After the devaluation of sterling in November 1967, a series of exchange crises began which were to buffet the Fund for more than five years, from January 1968 until March 1973, by which time all elements of the par value system had collapsed.

In particular, on 15th August 1971 the United States suspended the convertibility into gold of officially held dollars, thus pulling out the linchpin of the Bretton Woods system. The Ministers and central bank Governors of the Group of Ten (Belgium, Canada,

France, the Federal Republic of Germany, Italy, Japan, the Netherlands, Sweden, the United Kingdom and the United States) then
convened at the Smithsonian Institution in Washington in December 1971 and reached agreement on a realignment of the currencies of their countries, including the first devaluation of the
dollar in more than 35 years. Shortly afterwards, the Fund adopted
a decision temporarily permitting central rates in lieu of par values
and allowing wider margins. This realignment was to last only 14
months, however. In February 1973 the dollar was devalued again,
and in March 1973 the members of the European Economic Community introduced a system whereby their currencies floated jointly
against the dollar. The end of the par value system established at
Bretton Woods was at hand. A new era was born, in which some
currencies floated jointly, some floated independently and some
were pegged. In the process, many countries had drawn on the
Fund's resources, especially in 1968 and 1969. After the collapse of
the Bretton Woods system, attempts were made to negotiate a
completely reformed international monetary system. The Committee of Twenty (the Committee on Reform of the International
Monetary System and Related Issues) was established for this
purpose and'held its first meeting in September 1972. In January
1974 the Committee recommended a shift to an evolutionary
approach to reform, in view of severe world economic problems. An
advisory Interim Committee of the Board of Governors was established in 1974 to continue the reform effort and in January 1976 it
reached agreement on a wide range of issues. This was the basis of
the Second Amendment of the Articles, which came into effect on
1st April 1978. In addition, the joint Ministerial Committee of the
Boards of Governors of the Bank and the Fund on the Transfer of
Real Resources to Developing Countries (the Development Committee) was formed to focus on the needs of developing members.

Over the past six years, possibly the most difficult in the history of
the Fund, there have been other problems as well: the sharp
increases in the price of oil and the resulting large imbalances
in international payments, intractable inflation co-existing with
extensive unemployment, rising protectionism and a greater use of
restrictions. These difficulties threatened the development efforts
of many member countries just as some of them had begun to
achieve notable progress.

To help resolve these economic problems, the Fund has introduced a number of new policies governing the use of its resources: an oil facility for 1974 and 1975; a Subsidy Account to reduce the burden of interest payable on drawings under the oil facility for 1975 by the most seriously affected members; an extended facility to help members correct structural imbalances; liberalizations in 1975 and 1979 of the compensatory financing facility to finance export shortfalls; extension of stand-by arrangements, when required, for two years rather than one; a Trust Fund to provide additional resources on concessional terms to developing countries; and a supplementary financing facility to assist members requiring balance of payments financing in a larger amount and for a longer period than is possible under regular credit tranches. Members' drawings on the Fund reached a record level in 1976. To expand its regular resources, the Fund implemented an SDR 9.8 billion quota increase under the Sixth General Review of Quotas, and reached agreement on a further increase under the Seventh General Review which, if accepted by all members, would raise the total of Fund quotas to SDR 58.6 billion.

To lay the operational basis of the new international monetary system, the Fund took important decisions to strengthen the SDR and to reduce the monetary role of gold gradually by abolishing the official price, eliminating the use of gold in Fund transactions and undertaking the sale of a third of the Fund's gold holdings. In 1978 new allocations of SDRs were agreed that will increase the total in existence to SDR 21.3 billion in 1981. Under the Second Amendment of the Articles the Fund has been assigned the difficult task of firm surveillance of members' exchange rate policies.

The structure of the Fund provides for a Board of Governors, an Executive Board, a Managing Director and a staff.

The highest authority of the Fund is the Board of Governors, in which each of the member countries – currently numbering 141 – is represented by a Governor and an Alternate Governor. In most cases the Fund's Governors are ministers of finance or central bank Governors in their countries, or hold comparable rank. The Board of Governors normally meets once a year, but it may vote by mail between meetings.

The Articles, as amended with effect from 1st April 1978, provide that the Board of Governors may decide to establish a new Council at ministerial level which would 'supervise the management and adaptation of the international monetary system, including the continuing operation of the adjustment process and developments in global liquidity, and in this connection (would) review developments in the transfer of real resources to developing countries'. The Council, which is intended to be a decision-making body, would also consider proposals to amend the Articles of Agreement.

Pending establishment of the Council, a 21-member Interim Committee on the International Monetary System, established by a resolution adopted at the 1974 Annual Meeting, advises the Board of Governors in the areas outlined above that would become the responsibility of the Council. In addition, the Interim Committee advises the Board of Governors 'in dealing with sudden disturbances that might threaten the international monetary system'.

The Board of Governors had delegated many of its powers to the Executive Board, which is responsible for conducting the business of the Fund and is therefore in permanent session at the Fund's headquarters in Washington. The Executive Board regularly deals with a wide variety of administrative and policy matters, issues annual reports to the Board of Governors, conducts discussions to complete the process of consultation with members and from time to time produces comprehensive studies on financial issues of particular relevance to the economies of Fund members.

There are now 22 executive directors: seven appointed by the United States, the United Kingdom, the Federal Republic of Germany, France, Japan, China and Saudi Arabia and fifteen elected by as many constituencies representing the remaining members of the Fund.

The Executive Board selects the Managing Director, who is Chairman of the Executive Board. In addition, he is chief of the operating staff of the Fund and conducts the ordinary business of the Fund under the direction of the Executive Board.

During these years of economic and monetary turmoil, the Fund has adapted and strengthened its role, and has again shown its ability to meet the challenge of continuing to serve the world community.

ORGANISATION FOR ECONOMIC CO-OPERATION AND DEVELOPMENT (OECD)

The Organisation for Economic Co-operation and Development was established in 1961 by the Convention on the Organisation for

Economic Co-operation and Development. It was the successor to the Organisation for European Economic Co-operation (OEEC), which had been established in 1948.

The aims of the OECD are to promote economic and social welfare throughout the OECD area by assisting member governments in the formulation and co-ordination of policies designed to this end and to stimulate and harmonize members' efforts in favour of developing countries. The twenty-four member countries are Australia, Austria, Belgium, Canada, Denmark, Finland, France, the Federal Republic of Germany, Greece, Iceland, Ireland, Italy, Japan, Luxembourg, the Netherlands, New Zealand, Norway, Portugal, Spain, Sweden, Switzerland, Turkey, the United Kingdom and the USA. Yugoslavia has a special status that allows it to participate in the work of the Organisation.

The governing body of the OECD is the Council, in which all member countries are equally represented. Its permanent representatives meet weekly under the chairmanship of the Secretary-General, and ministerial meetings are held annually. Decisions and recommendations are adopted by mutual agreement of all members of the Council.

The Council is assisted by an Executive Committee composed of 14 members of the Council designated annually by the latter. The major part of the Organisation's work, however, is prepared and carried out in numerous specialized committees and working parties, of which there are more than two hundred. Examples of these are the Committees for Economic Policy; Economic and Development Review; Development Assistance (DAC); Trade; Invisible Transactions; Financial Markets; Fiscal Affairs; Restrictive Business Practices; Consumer Policies; Tourism; Maritime Transport; International Investment and Multinational Enterprises; Energy Policy; Industry; Steel; Scientific and Technological Policy; Education; Manpower and Social Affairs; Environment; Agriculture; and Fisheries. There is also a High-Level Group on Commodities.

Several autonomous or semi-autonomous bodies have been set up within the framework of the Organisation, namely the Nuclear Energy Agency (NEA, 1958), the Development Centre (1962), the Centre for Educational Research and Innovation (CERI, 1968), and the International Energy Agency (IEA, 1974). Each of these bodies has its own governing committee.

The OECD's activities relating to the shipping industry are conducted through Council Working Party No. 6 on Shipbuilding and the Maritime Transport Committee.

Working Party No. 6 of the Council is the forum for discussions between governments on short- and long-term policies and problems affecting the shipbuilding industry. One of the short-term problems considered is that of the equitable distribution of orders, which is discussed in a spirit of international co-operation to avoid a concentration of the few new orders available in one country or group of countries. The long-term problems and policies relate to the necessary restructuring of the industry to take account of changes in the market and to avoid the burden of the crisis being shifted from one country or group of countries to another.

The Maritime Transport Committee is the oldest committee in the Organisation. It first met on 22nd July 1947 as one of the Technical Committees established in response to General Marshall's call to the countries of Europe 'to seek, with United States moral and financial support, a co-operative solution to their post-war reconstruction problems'. Since then it has continued to function without interruption, becoming first a part of the OEEC and then, in 1960, a committee of the OECD. Throughout its existence the Committee has consistently defended the thesis that 'the shipping practice of the participating countries is based on the free circulation of shipping in international trades, in free and fair competition. Any interference with this free circulation is liable to reduce the efficiency of the total shipping available and hence to increase the cost of shipping services.' These principles were subsequently incorporated into the OECD Code of Liberalisation of Current Invisible Operations. The Committee is currently studying ways in which the present world shipping structure both within and without the OECD can be equated with the maintenance of the 'free circulation of shipping'. By reason of its threefold function of information, consultation and co-operation, the Maritime Transport Committee has been involved in the shipping aspects of almost every part of the work of the Organisation and has become the principal forum wherein member countries with both shipowner and shipper interests can discuss their common problems and difficulties and harmonize their policies with regard to each other and to the world shipping community. Although shipping is regarded principally as a service industry generating 'invisible' earnings, which accounts for the Maritime Transport Division's location in the Financial Directorate, its work has covered a great many topics which during recent periods have included piracy off Lagos and the Colombian coast, the activities of the Trans-Siberian Railway as a competitor to shipping lines to the Far East, ways of preventing or reducing oil pollution in tanker collisions and the legal problems of containerization and multi-modal transport.

By its very nature, shipping is a worldwide activity, so that the Maritime Transport Division is probably concerned more than many others with problems between the OECD and the rest of the world. Over recent years three different groupings have been involved:

(a) The state trading countries, particularly the USSR, have been competing vigorously and by various means have acquired a considerable part of the general cargo trades of many member countries;

(b) The fleets of flag of convenience countries have grown rapidly, particularly in the tanker and dry bulk carrier sectors;

(c) The developing countries have sought to increase their participation in the seaborne trade of the world, while at the same time trying to keep the freights charged for their cargoes as low as possible.

The Maritime Transport Committee, its General Working Group and its Special Group on International Organisations have enabled member countries to consider jointly how best to react to these pressures and have succeeded, as at the 1979 UNCTAD Conference held in Manila, in establishing and maintaining a common policy and a united front for the developed countries in response to the demands of the developing world.

The OECD also has close working relations with a number of other international organizations as follows:

1. *Relations with inter-governmental organizations.*
The Commission of the European Communities generally takes part in the work of the OECD under a protocol signed at the same time as the OECD Convention. EFTA may also send representatives to attend all OECD meetings. Official relations exist with the ILO, the FAO, the IMF, the IBRD, GATT, the IAEA, UNESCO, UNCTAD, the United Nations Environment Programme, IMCO, the Office of the High Commissioner for Refugees, the European

Conference of Ministers of Transport, the Organization of American States, the Intergovernmental Committee for European Migration and the Customs Co-operation Council. A special arrangement establishing close links with the Council of Europe was concluded in 1962. Working relations exist with about 15 other organizations.

2. *Relations with non-governmental organizations.*
Under a decision of the Council of 13th March 1962 international non-governmental organizations which are deemed to be widely representative in general economic matters or in a specific economy sector may be granted consultative status enabling them to discuss subjects of common interest with a liaison committee chaired by the Secretary-General and to be consulted in a particular field by the relevant OECD committee or its officers. So far, this status has been granted to the Business and Industry Advisory Committee to the OECD, the Trade Union Advisory Committee to the OECD, the International Association of Crafts and Small and Medium-sized Enterprises, the International Federation of Agricultural Producers and the European Confederation of Agriculture.

ORGANIZATION OF THE PETROLEUM EXPORTING COUNTRIES (OPEC)

In 1949 Venezuela approached Iran, Iraq, Kuwait and Saudi Arabia to exchange views and explore avenues for regular and closer communication between them on matters of mutual interest. Ten years later, following a reduction in the price of Venezuelan and Middle East crude oil, the first Arab Petroleum Congress held in Cairo adopted a resolution calling on oil companies to consult the governments of producing countries before making any price alterations. However, the following year the price of oil from Middle East countries was further reduced.

Subsequent consultations among the oil officials of Middle East countries and Venezuela led to the holding of a conference in Baghdad in 1960 attended by representatives of the governments of Iran, Iraq, Kuwait, Saudi Arabia and Venezuela, which brought into being the Organization of the Petroleum Exporting Countries (OPEC). The treaty establishing OPEC was registered with the United Nations in November 1962.

The principal aims of the Organization are the co-ordination and unification of the petroleum policies of member countries and the determination of the best means for safeguarding their interests, individually and collectively. It devises ways of stabilizing prices in international oil markets with a view to eliminating harmful and unnecessary fluctuations, due regard being paid at all times to the interests of the producing nations and to the necessity of securing a steady income to the producing countries, an efficient, economic and regular supply of petroleum to consuming nations and a fair return on their capital to those investing in the petroleum industry. In consultation and co-operation with the other countries of the world, OPEC seeks the establishment of a new economic order based on justice, mutual understanding and a genuine concern for the well-being of all peoples.

Any country with substantial net exports of crude petroleum and interests fundamentally similar to those of member countries may become a full member of the Organization if accepted by a majority of three-quarters of the full members, including the concurrent vote of all founder members, that is to say the countries represented at the first conference held in Baghdad. The Organization now has thirteen members: Algeria, Ecuador, Gabon, Indonesia, Iran, Iraq, Kuwait, Libya, Nigeria, Qatar, Saudi Arabia, the United Arab Emirates and Venezuela. It has its headquarters in Vienna, Austria.

The Conference, which consists of delegations representing the member countries, is the supreme authority of the Organization. At its twice-yearly meetings it formulates the general policy of the Organization and determines the means of its implementation, decides upon any application for membership of the Organization, confirms the appointment of members of the Board of Governors, directs the Board of Governors to submit reports or recommendations on matters of interest to the Organization and decides upon the Organization's budget as submitted by the Board of Governors.

The Board of Governors is nominated by the member countries and confirmed by the Conference. It is responsible for managing the affairs of the Organization, implementing the decisions of the Conference, considering reports submitted by the Secretary General, drawing up reports and recommendations for the Conference and formulating the Organization's budget.

The secretariat, which consists of the Secretary General and a number of specialist departments, carries out the executive functions of the Organization and monitors the economic, legal, technical and political aspects of the petroleum industry. Since 1965, when the Economic and Social Council (ECOSOC) of the United Nations adopted a resolution establishing relations with OPEC, the Organization's secretariat has participated in meetings of United Nations specialized agencies, such as UNCTAD and the Economic Commission for Africa and the Far East (ECAFE). It has also attended the meetings of other important international organizations.

Since its formation in 1960 OPEC has played an important role in placing control over oil production and oil prices in the hands of the producing countries and promoted the harmonization of hydrocarbon policies and legislation in member countries. It has helped its members assess developments in the international petroleum field and has trained nationals in the technical and economic aspects of the industry. It inspired the creation of the Conference on International Economic Co-operation (CIEC) – otherwise known as the North–South Dialogue – between 19 developing countries, including seven OPEC member countries, and eight major industrialized nations aimed at achieving a more equitable distribution of the world's wealth and natural resources. The Organization demonstrated its concern for the plight of those developing countries most seriously affected by recent economic stresses by setting up the OPEC Special Fund, which disburses long-term, interest-free loans to some 45 nations in Africa, Asia, Latin America and the Caribbean. It also recognized the urgency and importance of the food problem in developing countries by allocating $400 million from the Special Fund as OPEC's contribution to the projected International Fund for Agricultural Development (IFAD).

SIMPLIFICATION OF INTERNATIONAL TRADE PROCEDURES BOARD (SITPRO)

SITPRO was set up by the UK government in June 1970 to 'guide, stimulate and assist' the rationalization of international trade procedures and the information flows associated with them. The Board's members come from a wide range of backgrounds and include shippers, carriers, forwarders, insurers, bankers and government officials. The staff is small, consisting of a Chief Executive and Secretary with directors and their assistants responsible for various areas of SITPRO activities. The Board is financed by the

Department of Trade through an annual grant but is independent within its agreed terms of reference.

SITPRO's work falls under several headings. The central problem is that of procedures. Modern transport methods are served by information handling systems which have proved to be inadequate to their task. Traditional systems are costly, complicated and prone to delays and errors, which result in delays to goods out of proportion to their own speed of movement. Procedures therefore have to be rationalized and simplified nationally and internationally. Their point of application in a goods movement is based on traditional cargo intervention points. However, the development of through movement techniques requires the repositioning of official and commercial intervention points, which will in turn modify the relationships and responsibilities of participants. SITPRO's role consists in analyzing the procedures and then collaborating with representative bodies, such as the Joint Customs Consultative Committee, the General Council of British Shipping and the British Shipper's Council, to devise rationalization programmes. As a large part of Britain's exports are manufactured from imported raw materials, SITPRO is actively investigating the possibilities of facilitation in this aspect of international trade.

Procedures are generally represented by documents, which have created their own problems and costs. Every effort has therefore been made to simplify existing documentation and standardize it on the United Nations ECE Layout Key. The United Kingdom now has a fully developed aligned export documentation system and pressure is constantly maintained for the alignment of further forms. As well as developing and maintaining the system, SITPRO provides an advisory service to enable shippers to install systems suited to their needs.

The aligned one-run system of export documentation is based on a 'master' document, on which as much information as possible is entered for subsequent mechanical reproduction in full or in part on individual forms of similar design. This method reduces the time and cost expended on paperwork by eliminating repetitive typing and checking, improves accuracy by standardizing the detailed information shown on documents relating to any one consignment, presents information in a uniform manner, makes for easier document handling and filing and, finally, provides a master reference document.

Paper documents are probably a permanent feature of much international trade, at least as far as small manufacturers and carriers are concerned, but where the rapid movement of goods is of paramount importance, as in air freight, or where data are highly concentrated, as in major seaports, banks or Customs departments, computers are essential tools. However, they require a high degree of standardization if they are to communicate with one another. Even national systems of codes and formats would provide no satisfactory solution and could in fact aggravate the misinvestment inherent in the co-existence of disparate procedures. SITPRO is therefore devoting considerable effort to the establishment of international standards for computer interchange. The analysis that is required to develop EDP applications also has a general reforming effect on traditional procedures. Hence, while it is taking pains to link all procedural improvements to EDP, SITPRO is also streamlining the system of paper documentation. In addition, the Board is developing a technical advisory service designed to ensure that computer users in the United Kingdom benefit from the latest practical experience in adapting their computer systems to deal with international trade procedures and documentation.

The potential benefits of these advances would be lost if SITPRO did not ensure that they were brought to the attention of the international trading community. This is not an easy task, given the relative novelty of facilitation work. SITPRO therefore holds seminars and workshops in particular facilitation applications, such as aligned documentation and customs procedures, and prepares detailed material for use by lecturers and speakers. A series of audio-visual aids is being produced; the first of these cover areas of exporting that are considered to have priority. SITPRO also keeps traders informed of immediate improvements by publishing information bulletins and leaflets as required.

The tangible progress made in the last ten years has been due to co-operation with similar national organizations set up in other countries. Partly as a result of the efforts of SITPRO, foreign trade facilitation bodies now operate in Belgium, Canada, Czechoslovakia, Denmark, Finland, France, The Federal Republic of Germany, India, Ireland, Japan, Kenya, the Netherlands, New Zealand, Nigeria, Norway, Hong Kong, the Philippines, Poland, South Korea, South Africa, Sri Lanka, Sweden, Switzerland and the USA. Bilateral arrangements would, however, be no substitute for full international co-operation. SITPRO has therefore given every support to the work of the former Documentation Working Party in the Economic Commission for Europe in Geneva which, over the last decade, had developed into the Facilitation Working Party with much broader terms of reference. SITPRO also co-operates with UNCTAD in its facilitation programme and sends delegates or advisers to a very wide range of international bodies, such as the International Chamber of Commerce, the Customs Co-operation Council, the International Standards Organization, the International Association of Ports and Harbours, the International Association of Forwarding Agents and about twenty others.

UNITED NATIONS CONFERENCE ON TRADE AND DEVELOPMENT (UNCTAD)

The United Nations Conference on Trade and Development was established by the General Assembly of the United Nations in 1964 to help modify the traditional patterns of international trade so that developing countries would be able to play their part in world commerce. Increased trade, both with the industrialized countries and among the developing countries themselves, was regarded as the key to the accelerated development of these countries and a rising standard of living for their peoples. Today it has 157 member countries and is administered by a Secretary General.

Policy guidelines are laid down at the full Conference sessions, five of which have been held since 1964; the shipping implications of the decisions reached at the fifth session, which was held in Manila in May 1979, are described on pp. 218–219.

The Trade and Development Board has six main committees on commodities, manufactures, invisibles and trade finance, shipping, the transfer of technology and economic co-operation among developing countries. It also has a special committee on trade preferences.

Since its formation, UNCTAD has pioneered important action in the fields of international trade and aid. It conceived the Generalized System of Preferences whereby, since 1971, developed countries have given preferential treatment to imports of manufactures from developing countries; it set the target for official development aid at 0.7 per cent of gross national product; it established a Code of Conduct for Liner Conferences, which defines certain principles to be observed when setting freight rates and determining cargo sharing between shipowners; it drew up a Charter of Economic Rights and Duties of States; and carried out the negotiation of international agreements on primary commodities. In recent years its major concern has been implementation of the Integrated Programme for Commodities, designed to stabilize prices at levels which are remunerative and just to producers and equitable to consumers. It is also devising other means of expanding and diversifying the export trade of developing countries in manufactured and semi-manufactured goods, such as new forms of industrial and trade collaboration arrangements and abolition or control of restrictive business practices.

While trade measures lie at the heart of the development problem, the interdependence of economic issues is such that an integrated approach to policy is required. Questions relating to international financial flows and the international monetary system have continued to engage UNCTAD's attention, especially in the light of the major balance of payments problems of recent years and the need for additional transfers of resources to developing countries. UNCTAD carefully monitors the long-term evolution of financial flows to developing countries, in particular development assistance and balance of payments facilities, analysing problems in these areas in the context of the Development Strategy and the countries' longer-term trade prospects. The problem of the external indebtedness of developing countries continues to concern UNCTAD; in this regard, important decisions were taken at a special session of the Trade and Development Board in March 1978, when agreements were reached to improve net flows of assistance to the poorer developing countries by adjusting the terms and conditions of their past borrowing.

The Committee on Shipping is the main international forum for resolving policy issues relating to participation in world shipping by developing and developed countries. Its present concerns include increased participation in shipping by the developing countries, particularly in the bulk sectors; the adverse effects of the expansion of flag of convenience fleets on the merchant marines of developing countries; the preparation of a draft convention on multi-modal transport; and elimination of port congestion, including technical assistance to improve port efficiency.

Within the UN family, it is UNCTAD that includes insurance in its regular programme of work and deals with all development aspects of that important sector. Under the agreed policy on insurance, UNCTAD aims to promote the insurance earnings of developing countries and to minimize their net outflow of foreign exchange due to the purchase of such services abroad.

The transfer of technology to developing countries has emerged as a subject of primary importance in UNCTAD activities. Acting upon a resolution taken at the fourth UNCTAD Conference, an inter-governmental group of experts has been set up to draft a code of conduct for the transfer of technology, to be negotiated at a special United Nations conference. Furthermore, UNCTAD is playing a prominent role in the revision of the Paris Convention for the Protection of Industrial Property, especially in regard to its economic, commercial and developmental aspects and their relation to technological development in developing countries. It is also working to strengthen the domestic technological capacity of developing countries through the establishment of technology planning within these countries and of centres for the transfer and development of technology at national and regional levels.

By means of studies, meetings and technical assistance activities, UNCTAD supports the programmes of economic co-operation among developing countries adopted in 1976 by the Group of 77 (representing more than 100 developing countries) and by the non-aligned countries. In view of the growing importance attached to the economic self-reliance of developing countries, a Committee on Economic Co-operation among Developing Countries has been established to ensure that these programmes enjoy the support of the developed countries and international organizations.

The expansion of trade and economic relations between developing countries and the socialist countries of Eastern Europe is also a specific concern of UNCTAD. In particular, new forms and mechanisms of economic co-operation, opportunities for trade resulting from the multilateral collaboration schemes of countries belonging to the CMEA, payment arrangements, the experience in East–West trade and its implications for developing countries are being studied in order to impart new dynamism to this flow of trade.

UNCTAD has played a leading role in efforts to provide for special measures in favour of the 31 countries with a total population of some 250 million that have been identified by the United Nations as the least developed on the basis of their low level of per capita income, literacy and industrial activity. UNCTAD is pursuing a wide ranging set of measures, particularly with respect to financial and technical assistance and commercial policy, designed to give special impetus to the development of these poorest countries. In the case of land-locked and island developing countries, UNCTAD action is aimed at improving their transit and transport arrangements and at taking other steps to offset their geographic handicaps.

UNITED NATIONS COMMISSION ON INTERNATIONAL TRADE LAW (UNCITRAL)

The United Nations Commission on International Trade Law was established by the General Assembly of the United Nations in December 1966 in order to further the progressive harmonization and unification of the law of international trade. It has its headquarters at the United Nations offices in New York, where it came into operation in January 1968. At its first session priority was assigned to work on the international sale of goods, international payments and international commercial arbitration. It was later decided that international shipping legislation should also be examined.

Its principal achievement so far has been the preparation of an international instrument on the revision of the Hague Rules, which culminated in the adoption of a new convention on the Carriage of Goods By Sea in March 1978, commonly known as the Hamburg Rules. This work, which took more than seven years to complete, was carried out at the request of UNCTAD, with which UNCITRAL co-operates closely.

UNCITRAL has completed work on a draft convention on the formulation and validity of contracts for the international sale of goods, which was considered for adoption at a diplomatic conference held in Vienna in 1980. A draft convention on international bills of exchange and international promissory notes is also nearing completion. It seems likely that UNCITRAL will now concentrate on the conciliation of international trade disputes, in respect of which a preliminary draft set of UNCITRAL conciliation rules has been produced.

A number of other shipping and international trade organizations are dealt with in Chapter 8 of *Elements of Shipping*, which also includes classification societies.

CHAPTER 14

Political Factors

The international trade scene. Flag discrimination. Liner conferences. Flags of convenience. Subsidies. The future.

THE INTERNATIONAL TRADE SCENE

In the years to come, the international trade scene is likely to change for a variety of reasons, not the least being the increasing influence of UNCTAD and the repercussions of the decisions taken at the fifth UNCTAD Conference held in Manila in June 1979. The shipping industry, which is itself dependent on commerce and yet at the same time an essential determinant of world trade owing to the need for reliable, efficient and cheap transportation, must adapt to the changing circumstances through a process of international co-operation seasoned with an awareness of the commercial realities. The industry and the governments involved must resist the temptation to resort to protectionism, which cannot provide solutions to the problems that have arisen or will arise.

It is against this background that the two major decisions taken at the UNCTAD Conference in Manila should be viewed. The first, whereby the 40/40/20 liner conference code was adopted, is described on pp. 218–219; the second is related to the carriage of liquid and dry bulk cargoes. Discussion revolved around two main points: the right of countries to participate in the carriage of bulk cargoes generated by their own trade and the participation of flag of convenience vessels in the bulk sectors, where their presence is particularly strong.

No overall agreement was reached on the first point as there emerged a major difference between the views of developing countries and those of developed market economies on the fundamental nature of the problem. The latter argued that the bulk market was open to all carriers to compete under conditions of fair competition. They believed that the forces of competition served the best interests of the community at large as well as those of the international shipping industry and its customers. Any attempt to bypass the forces of the market through subsidy, protection or unilateral cargo reservation could only lead to serious structural problems for developing and developed countries alike. Those countries that were experiencing difficulty in achieving increased participation on the basis of sound commercial principles were being assisted by the transfer of technology, training schemes, joint ventures and market orientation provided by international organizations, particularly the International Chamber of Commerce. The developing countries, on the other hand, argued that the so-called 'free market' in bulk cargoes was little more than a myth and claimed that the bulk sector was controlled by cartels and locked into the vertically integrated operations of transnational corporations. The developing nations' campaign for a system of cargo sharing was motivated by a number of factors, such as the need to conserve hard currency, a desire to control sea transport costs in order to boost their export trade, the employment opportunities stemming from an expansion of their fleets, strategic advantages and the greater independence they would enjoy.

A resolution was finally passed recognizing the right of all countries to an equitable participation in the carriage of cargoes generated by their own trade and making a number of recommendations designed to give effect to that right subject to the need to take account of pragmatic considerations. The lack of unanimous support for the resolution precluded any immediate international action on bulk cargoes, but by virtue of the majority vote developing countries were granted authority to introduce unilateral measures and to enter into bilateral agreements with like-minded trading partner countries.

The claims of the developing countries were substantiated in mid-1980 by the UNCTAD Committee on Shipping, whose report on mandatory cargo sharing in the bulk cargo trades indicated that international movements of all the major dry bulk cargoes were controlled to a high degree by a relatively small number of large transport corporations. Grain shipments were completely dominated by five privately owned transnational concerns and iron ore cargoes by corporations which either operated their own fleets or used long-term charters with 'closely related parties'; bauxite/alumina and to a lesser extent phosphate movements were similarly affected. More than two-thirds of these cargoes could be considered captive, creating a formidable barrier to the free entry of any new shipowner. The report concluded that very few shipowners had been able to break into the market, and these had done so 'despite rather than because of the nature of the market'. It confirmed that the dry bulk cargo market was neither free nor competitive.

An example of the UNCTAD cargo sharing formula can be seen in the case of Malaysia, where the Malaysia International Shipping Corporation decided in 1980 to increase its tonnage from 1.3. to 3 million dwt. The national line currently conveys about 10 per cent of the country's trade, whereas to carry 40 per cent of exports Malaysia would need a fleet of at least 40 million dwt. To encourage foreign shipowners to register their vessels in Malaysia, the government recently simplified the registration procedure and introduced a range of concessions, including a twelve-year exemption from profit taxes and a similar exemption on dividend payments up to 10 per cent.

Other developing countries have also taken steps to expand or establish fleets in order to convey a greater proportion of their seaborne trade. One example is Nigeria. In 1958 the Federal Government set up a Committee to examine the possibility of establishing a Nigerian shipping company. The Committee reported favourably and later in the same year the Nigerian National Shipping Line (NNSL) was incorporated with fully paid-up capital of £2 million held jointly by the Federal Government and two shipping companies – Elder Dempster Lines Ltd of Liverpool and Paton Line Ltd of London. In 1961 all non-Nigerian equity holdings were bought out by the Federal Government. Like most developing countries, Nigeria wished to establish a merchant maritime fleet as an effective means of transporting the nations's increasing exports and imports: it aimed to carry at least 30 per cent in NNSL vessels by 1980.

The company commenced operations with three second-hand ships. Over the years the company prospered to the extent that by 1979 it owned fifteen ships. However, with time the older vessels were replaced by modern ships under charter pending the provision of net tonnage. In 1977 the NNSL embarked on a bold expansion programme by signing contracts with shipyards in South Korea and Yugoslavia for the building of 19 vessels, comprising ten 16 000 dwt combi ships and nine 12 000 dwt conventional general cargo ships. All the new tonnage was in operation by 1980, so that by the end of that year the NNSL had a fleet of 26 owned vessels.

The Nigerian National Shipping Line is engaged in shipping operations practically throughout the world. It is a member of five conferences, namely the Far East/West Africa Conference (FEWAC), the Mediterranean/West Africa Conference (MEWAC), the United Kingdom/West Africa Lines (UKWAL), the Continent/West Africa Conference (COWAC) and the America/West Africa Conference (AMWAC).

Another significant political development on the international trade scene has been the expansion of the Eastern bloc's fleet during the past five years. The main growth has occurred in the Soviet general cargo fleet, which totalled ten million tons in 1979, between three and four times the capacity needed to carry the general cargo trade of the USSR; by comparison, the UK fleet amounted to seven million tons in the same year. In the direct cargo liner trade between the United Kingdom and the Soviet Union, Soviet vessels carried 79 per cent of the total tonnage in 1977; the UK flag share came to 17 per cent. Soviet carryings in the bilateral liner trades with the Federal Republic of Germany were 75 per cent (1976), with Japan 97 per cent (1976) and with Belgium 83 per cent (1975). Be that as it may, it is the activities of the Soviet liner fleet on the major trading routes of the world that are causing the greatest concern among Western liner operators. By 1979 some 240 Soviet liners of about 2.4 million dwt were operating regular services in competition with the liner conferences in the UK/Continent–East Africa trade, the UK/Continent–Far East trade, the North Atlantic trades, the Trans-Pacific trades and the UK/Continent–Mediterranean trade. The freight rates they are charging are generally 15–30 per cent below those of the conference with which they are competing – in certain trades the degree of undercutting is even greater. Such low rates, which are often unprofitable by the standards of Western fleets, are made possible by the fact that Soviet ships, being state-owned, enjoy low capital charges, require no hull or machinery insurance, incur very low crew costs and have no social security contributions to bear. Moreover, to the extent that their bunkers are obtained in their home ports, they benefit from rates well below world market levels.

Undercutting by Soviet lines has a dual effect on Western liner operators. First, it draws cargo away from the conferences and secondly it forces them to reduce freight rates for the cargo they do retain to levels which may be uneconomic. With world trade in its present depressed state, the growing Soviet mercantile fleet will increase world laid-up tonnage and further undermine the profitability of long-established cargo liner operators unless action is taken to redress the balance.

The motives for the Soviet expansion into the multilateral liner trades are partly economic, partly political and partly strategic. They have an urgent need to earn foreign exchange because of their massive balance of payments deficit with the Western world. However, their general cargo fleet also provides the means of carrying military personnel and equipment to client nations and establishing a worldwide maritime presence and intelligence system and, in addition, gives the Soviet Union the ability to achieve a dominant position in the principal world trading routes.

The Soviet authorities have declared their wish to avoid a freight rate war and to seek to operate within the established liner conferences, but this clearly depends on their achieving their demands for conference shares. In most cases it has not been possible to reach commercial agreement on the terms under which they could be admitted to conference membership; in one instance a Soviet line was invited to join an open (US) liner conference, but it declined the offer.

Whilst the activities of Soviet shipping in cross trades may appear beneficial to shippers in the short term and whilst the UK government is likely to continue to press vigorously for restraint in the increase in conference freight charges in all trades, it is in the interest of neither to allow such undercutting to continue unchecked. In the short term it is bound to cause instability in the trade, and in the long term it will reduce the efficiency and regularity of the services on which so much of the nation's overseas trade depends. Hence, in the absence of agreement at commercial level, Western ship operators have called upon their governments to take appropriate concerted action to safeguard their shipping interests. It has also been proposed that the EEC Commission monitor the volume of traffic carried between EEC ports by Comecon ships so as to determine whether there is need for some form of control by quota or licence, and that EEC member states consider the joint application of countervailing powers.

The Soviet plan for the five years from 1981 to 1985 provides for continued but slower growth in the merchant marine. In the following decade the fleet will expand by several percentage points each year in order to keep pace with the growth in trade and the scrapping of older vessels. New technology will be introduced and there will be an increase in the amount of traffic moved in containers, Ro/Ro ships, vehicle ferries and barges.

The uses to which oil-producing countries put their oil revenues will have a substantial effect on trade in the remainder of the 1980s. A large proportion of them will be devoted to investment, primarily at home but also abroad. Most of the oil-producing countries have also allocated sums to non-oil developing countries in the form of aid that, as a percentage of GNP, often far exceeds the amounts given by industrialized countries. Such aid and the additional financial assistance provided by the OPEC Special Fund will have a profound effect on world trade, and in particular on the dry cargo shipping market.

The need to provide early financial and economic relief for developing countries was exemplified by the report of the Independent Commission on International Development, which was published in 1980. The four key elements in the Commission's proposed programme of action are a large-scale transfer of funds to the third world, an agreement on the security of energy supplies and conservation, an efficient world food programme and reform of the world financial system including the means of financing development. Such proposals would release a new assured flow of funds to the developing countries, which would thus be able to plan with greater confidence and would have additional revenue to purchase imports from the industrialized countries.

FLAG DISCRIMINATION

Flag discrimination comprises a wide variety of acts and pressures exerted by governments to direct cargoes to ships flying the national flag, regardless of the commercial considerations which normally govern the routing of cargoes. Such activities dislocate the competitive nature of the shipping industry because they often divert trade to a less efficient carrier and obscure the real cost of the service. The Merchant Shipping Act, 1974, empowers the UK government to take counter-measures against foreign governments where UK shipping or trade interests are affected or where such action is required to meet Britain's international obligations. Orders can be made to obtain information, regulate the carriage of goods, levy charges on ships, refuse admittance of ships to UK ports and approve or reject agreements.

The following are the more important forms in which flag discrimination can be exercised:

(a) Import licences. Some countries have used the licensing system to ensure that cargo is carried in ships flying their national flag. This tends to encourage reciprocal action, which further hinders the growth of trade, and can delay the shipment of goods if the relevant services are irregular.

(b) Discriminatory customs dues and other charges, such as harbour, lighthouse, pilotage and tonnage dues, consular fees and taxes on freight revenue. Such practices are particularly prevalent in countries where the ports are in state ownership.

(c) Administrative pressures. In some countries official cargo is automatically conveyed in vessels flying the national flag.

(d) Routing of gifts and other non-commercial cargoes. Under certain aid programmes half of the goods are carried in ships of the donor country, with complete disregard to commercial considerations.

(e) Exchange control. The manipulation of exchange control offers countless ways of making shipment in national vessels either obligatory or so commercially attractive that it has the same effect.

(f) Bilateral trade treaties. Many countries have entered into bilateral trade treaties which include shipping clauses reserving all or most of the trade between the two countries to ships of the two flags.

Some of the forms that flag discrimination can take are illustrated in Table 14.1, which relates to the situation in 1980.

It must be appreciated that the discriminatory practices illustrated in Table 14.1 are subject to frequent change and may be greatly influenced by the outcome of international conferences such as the UNCTAD Conference held in Manila in 1979.

LINER CONFERENCES

Under the liner conferences system, which has long been an established feature of the shipping industry, a group of shipowners of one or several nationalities serve a group of ports on a given route. The sailing pattern is agreed by the conference members with a view to ensuring that a regular schedule is maintained throughout the year. All members charge identical tariffs and grant no rate concessions

Table 14.1   Cargo preference in favour of national flag carriers

Cargo preference laws	Other preference practices
Algeria	
The government requires export contracts for both oil and LNG to contain a 50 per cent cargo clause giving preference to Algerian flag vessels.	Algeria and Brazil have a maritime, navigation and transportation agreement covering all traffic between their ports; it excludes petroleum and bulk cargo shipments. Traffic between French and Algerian ports is reserved for French and Algerian flag ships. Algeria has bilateral agreements with the USSR, Bulgaria, the German Democratic Republic, Guinea, China and the Republic of Cape Verde that divide cargo on a 50/50 or 40/40/20 basis.
Argentina	
The 1973 Merchant Marine Law reaffirmed the 1969 law establishing the 'right' of Argentine flag vessels to carry 50 per cent of all goods exported or imported by state and municipal governments, companies in which the state has a holding of at least 50 per cent and non-official imports and exports financed by any state credit institution or enjoying any form of import duty reduction, tax concession or exchange control relief. It also requires a minimum of 50 per cent. Argentine flag carriage of all goods under any international commercial trade agreement.	Argentine flag vessels are exempt from consular and similar fees. The government reserves the right to deny port facilities to foreign ships which do not operate under approved agreements. Under the 1973 law the government has the power of approval over all freight conference agreements involving Argentine overseas commerce. Any freight conference which appears to place limitations on Argentine ships (below 50 per cent carriage) will not be recognized. Argentina has 50/50 bilateral agreements with Uruguay, Peru, Brazil, Chile, Colombia and the USSR. In the event of a shortage of national-flag ships it is necessary to obtain a waiver for transport in third-flag carriers. Three US companies have equal access agreements with Argentina covering the southbound movement of government-controlled cargoes.
Australia	
Trade between New Zealand and Australia must be carried in New Zealand or Australian flag ships.	

Table 14.1 continued

Cargo preference laws	Other preference practices

Brazil

All goods imported or exported by federal, state, municipal or public administration departments, public enterprises and mixed-economy firms and all imports and exports enjoying tariff concessions, preferential internal fiscal treatment, national finance or international loans must be carried in Brazilian flag ships. The same applies to all ordinary paper (excluding special paper and pulp) unless special arrangements are made.

The government has a monopoly on the transport of petroleum and petroleum products; small companies existing before the law was passed are exempt.

Provision is made for a waiver of cargo preference under the following circumstances:

Up to 50 per cent of the total weight of import or export cargoes obligatorily linked to transportation in Brazilian flag ships can be liberated in favour of the flag of the exporting or importing country provided the buying or selling nation concedes at least equal treatment to Brazilian flag ships.

When exportation or importation of merchandise subject to liberation is made to or from a country that is not served by ships of both the countries involved, the Brazilian Superintendency of Merchant Marine will effect prior liberation of cargoes covered by Decree Law 666, designating the transporter. Should no ship of the Brazilian flag or the flag of the importing or exporting country be in a position to take the cargo, the Brazilian Superintendency of Merchant Marine can, at its discretion, permit the cargo to be

Brazil has advantageous rates of exchange for carriage costs on national lines.

Foreign shipping companies cannot operate from Brazil unless they are members of a conference to which a Brazilian company belongs.

An exporter who ships aboard a Brazilian vessel has taxes on production and circulation credited to him for the purpose of buying raw materials for his products.

SUNAMAM (National Merchant Marine Superintendency) 1970 provides for 50/50 US–Brazilian carriage of coffee and cocoa.

Brazil has 50/50 cargo-sharing agreements with Argentina, Chile, Peru, Uruguay and Nigeria when flag vessels are available.

All trade between Brazil and Mexico must be carried in national flag ships on a 40/40 basis; each nation is allowed to cede 10 per cent to third-flag vessels, with preference given to countries of Latin American Free Trade Association; vessels chartered by Mexico or Brazil enjoy the same status.

Brazil and Algeria have a maritime, navigation and transportation agreement covering all traffic between their ports; it excludes petroleum and bulk cargo shipments.

Brazil regulates the conferences in which it participates to ensure increased carriage for its own flag.

Three US lines have sailing, pooling and equal access agreements with Brazilian lines.

Brazil issues shippers an 8 per cent tax credit, based upon cost of merchandise plus freight, on frozen orange juice if the shipper uses Brazilian flag vessels. If the

Table 14.1 continued

Cargo preference laws	Other preference practices
transported by a third-flag ship specifically designated.	shipper uses foreign flag vessels, the credit is based upon the cost of merchandise only. The US has negotiated equal access with Brazilian lines under this law.

Cameroon

Cameroon Shipping Lines enjoy the exclusive right to transport all imports for the government, public collectives and state-owned companies.

All importers and exporters who do not present at customs a Cameroon Shipping Lines bill of lading or a certificate of dispensation shall be fined 15 per cent of the value of the merchandise: CIF for imports and FOB for exports.

All contracts for private imports and exports must give priority to Cameroon Shipping Lines or obtain a waiver from the company for any shipping it cannot handle.

Chile

Since 1969 all cargoes of the state, state-owned enterprises and bodies in which the state has an interest or part interest have had to be carried in state-owned vessels; the same applies to 50 per cent of imports and exports other than nitrate and most ores, bulk cargoes and oil.

If a state-owned vessel is not available, the goods may be carried in a Chilean-owned ship. If none are available, exceptions will be made.

If a trading partner grants 50 per cent carriage between the nations, exceptions will be made.

Provision was made in 1975 for 50 per cent of export cargoes to be carried on flag ships of the country of destination provided that the country recognized the equal rights of Chilean vessels.

For five years ships will be considered Chilean if operated by Chilean lines.

The Ministry of Transport has issued new procedures on cargo allocation whereby 50 per cent of export cargo,

Foreign lines may obtain status as 'associated' carriers and acquire the right to participate in transport and compete for cargo on the same basis as Compania Sudamericana de Vapores, the shipping line with minority state interest. (Two US companies have such pooling agreements.)

Chile has 50/50 cargo-sharing agreements with Argentina and Brazil, subject to availability of national flag ships.

Table 14.1 continued

Cargo preference laws	Other preference practices

whether US bound or way-port, will be reserved for Chilean flag shipping, and 50 per cent will be open to shippers' free choice. If space on a Chilean flag ship is not available within a set period of time cargo can be transported by a foreign flag ship without having to request a waiver from Chilean flag companies.

China

Self-reliance in shipping is a government policy. No details of cargo reservation laws, as such, are available outside China. However, the Chinese maritime authorities have directed that at least half of the country's seaborne foreign trade should move in Chinese flag ships, all of which are operated by the China Ocean Shipping Company, a state-owned and controlled monopoly. Special taxes are imposed on exports and passengers departing from Chinese ports on foreign flag ships unless exempted for specific national flag ships by a maritime agreement. Preference is given to Chinese subsidiary companies operating ships under Panamanian and Hong Kong flags. Exports are shipped on a CIF and CF basis, imports on an FOB basis. In each instance this allows China to control the flag under which goods are shipped. In 1975 71 per cent of China's overseas commerce was carried in its own ships.

Colombia

The 1969 cargo preference law requires not less than 50 per cent of general import and export cargoes on routes served by Colombian ships to be hauled on such ships, providing that the requirements of Article 2 of Decree No. 1208 are met.

Decree No. 1208 reserves no more than 50 per cent of bulk, liquid and

Imports are on an FOB basis; freight and insurance are to be paid in Colombian currency, of which a proportion is non-transferable.

Colombia has 50/50 bilateral shipping agreements with Argentina and Uruguay.

Table 14.1 continued

Cargo preference laws	Other preference practices

refrigerated import and export cargo to Colombian flag vessels. Reserved cargoes are stipulated only when they do not conflict with previous government agreements and foreign loans.

Decree No. 1670 orders that shipments to all government entities (autonomous, semi-autonomous and of mixed private and public nature) must comply with the 50 per cent reservation law above.

Latin American shipowners registered in the Latin American Association of Shipowners can participate in transportation of reserved cargoes on the same terms as Colombian vessels provided that equal treatment is given to Colombian ships in those countries.

Dominican Republic
Legislation has been passed reserving for national ships 40 per cent of general import and export freight, 50 per cent of import freight privileged with fiscal exoneration by the Incentive and Industrial Protection Law, 50 per cent of all cargo exported by state enterprises and 60 per cent of liquid, bulk and general cargo imported by government-controlled institutes, state-owned enterprises and those enterprises in which the state is the main stockholder.

Ecuador
In 1974 the National Council of the Merchant Marine and Ports raised the percentage of Ecuadorian general cargo reserved for national flag ships from 30 to 50 per cent.

The Hydrocarbons Law of 1971 reserves 50 per cent of all oil cargo to national flag vessels.

All government cargo, as well as cargo

Table 14.1 continued

Cargo preference laws	Other preference practices

shipped by organizations in which the government has more than a 50 per cent capital investment, must be carried aboard national flag ships.

Egypt

30 per cent of imports and exports must be carried in Egyptian vessels.

In 1976 the Council of State decreed that all seaborne shipments entering or leaving Egypt that pertain to state business, public institutions, public organizations and their affiliates must be arranged and supervised by the Egyptian Company for Maritime Transport or the foreign agents of that company.

Egypt has a 50/50 bilateral agreement with India.

France

A Decree of April 1931, as amended in August 1970, requires that two-thirds of French oil imports be carried in French flag vessels or in ships of which the charter parties have been approved by the Ministry of Fuel and the Ministry of Transport (Merchant Marine).

Legislation of 1935 and 1936 states that 50 per cent of coal imports destined for the public services or subsidized enterprises and 40 per cent of such imports not destined for the above cited services or enterprises should be carried by French registered vessels.

French lines do not compete against each other in any one conference; joint companies have been established with the shipping lines of other EEC countries to ensure orderly markets.

The government has statutory authority to restrict freedom of French ship-owners to charter vessels; the chartering of all ships over 500 gross tons must be reported to the government, which may offer opposition on the grounds of national interest.

France and the Ivory Coast have a maritime co-operation agreement providing for reciprocity between the two nations regarding cargo sharing, tariffs, freight forwarding and freight handling.

Traffic between French and Tunisian ports is restricted to French and Tunisian flag ships.

Traffic between French and Algerian ports is reserved for French and Algerian flag ships.

Table 14.1 continued

Cargo preference laws	Other preference practices

Gabon

The government reserves 50 per cent of refined petroleum product exports for vessels of the state-owned shipping company Sonatran.

Federal Republic of Germany

Shipowners and operators may claim a 50 per cent reduction in the corporate tax on income earned from shipping services in foreign trades.

German flag vessels receive tax-free fuel.

The government is empowered to restrict the conclusion of freights contracts and charters between residents and carriers that are residents of countries which exclude German ships from free competition.

Germany has a 50/50 cargo-sharing agreement with South Korea.

Ghana

All imports and exports of industrial and commercial goods are reserved for the state-owned shipping company.

All cargoes ordered by the Ghana Supply Commission (government purchasing organization) are handled by Black Star Line as shipping agent. Cargoes go on the first available conference ship.

Discriminatory shipping and insurance clauses annexed to import licences require importers to use vessels of state-owned lines.

Greece

Greece and the USSR have signed a shipping agreement which provides for the development of bilateral relations.

Guatemala

Legislation of 1971 reserves all import cargoes to Guatemalan national flag lines and fixes a penalty of 50 per cent of the total freight charges for violation.

In 1971 tax exemption was granted for import cargoes carried by national carriers under the Industrialization Promotion Act, exports of timber and certain other goods to the USA, goods imported duty-free under the Industrial

Table 14.1 continued

Cargo preference laws	Other preference practices
	Development Law and government imports.
	Guatemala has a 100 per cent surcharge on imports from certain countries with which it has an adverse balance of payments unless carried on national flag ships or associated lines.
India Shipments for government account must be carried in Indian flag ships. The government is exerting cargo preference pressure on the oil import trade. National refineries give preference to Indian flag lines, which are to transport 90 per cent of all crude as compared with 30 per cent in April 1976. Export–Import Bank cargoes not conveyed on US flag ships must be carried on Indian flag ships.	Trade agreements with the German Democratic Republic, Iran, Poland, Peru and Rumania contain a 'best endeavour' clause to allocate bilateral cargoes to flags of either country on the basis of equality of tonnage and earnings. India has a 50/50 bilateral agreement with Egypt and the USSR. India and Bulgaria have initialled a cargo sharing agreement allocating equal quantities of cargo to their respective flag vessels; no income tax will be levied by either country upon the freight earnings from cargo moving between ports of their countries. The India, Pakistan and Bangladesh conference observes 40/40/20 cargo sharing.
Indonesia 45 per cent of European cargoes are allocated to Indonesian flag vessels. The Indonesian Freight Board has unlimited authority to discriminate in favour of national flag carriage at any time in the future. The Minister of Sea Communications has ruled that transhipment of goods for Indonesia must be in Indonesian-owned ships using only Indonesian transhipment ports. Indonesian-owned coasters will be used for transhipment from Bangkok, Thailand, and Kompongsom, Cambodia and Kompong Som, Kampuchea.	In 1971 a tax was imposed on foreign shipping at a rate of 4 per cent of the gross revenue from sales made anywhere in the world for transport of passengers and freight within or from, but not to, Indonesia. A law of 1964 provides that all requests for shipping space for export of Indonesian commodities be channelled through Indonesian shipping boards. This is designed to give national shipping companies priority. Indonesia has a bilateral agreement with the USSR. Indonesia and Singapore have a

Table 14.1 continued

Cargo preference laws	Other preference practices
If national vessels are unavailable, third-flag carriers may be licensed to carry transhipments.	cargo-sharing agreement whereby 55 per cent of cargo from Indonesia must go on Indonesian vessels and 45 per cent on Singapore ships.
Iran All government imports must move on Iranian ships.	Iranian Line ships have preferential berthing in Iran.
Iraq First preference is given to Iraqi flag ships.	
Israel	Requirements for the use of Israeli vessels to carry meat to Israel have been negotiated in a series of bilateral agreements between Zim Israeli Navigation Lines and foreign exporting nations.

Ivory Coast	Legislation passed in 1975 regulates maritime transport on the 40/40/20 cargo-sharing principle.
	    Only freight rates negotiated and ratified by the government are applicable in the Ivory Coast.
	    A maritime co-operation agreement between the Ivory Coast and France provides for reciprocity between the two nations regarding cargo-sharing, tariffs, freight forwarding and freight handling.

Japan	Japanese operators are granted tax credits against earnings in the foreign trades. All industries are eligible for tax exemption on 1.5 per cent of the total export sales of shipping services or 40 per cent of net export income earned by selling shipping services, whichever is lower. This applies to invisible exports only; under the GATT, Japan cannot offer tax benefits or monetary incentives on visible exports.

Table 14.1 continued

Cargo preference laws	Other preference practices
	Japan has bilateral agreements with China, Taiwan and South Korea. Utilization of government financing or licensing services often results in the direction of commercial cargoes to Japanese flag carriers; e.g. for years tobacco cargoes from the USA have been shipped exclusively in Japanese flag ships. The close relations between government and industry necessarily result in a shipping policy that is essentially a 'ship Japanese' programme.
Kuwait According to the Middle East Economic Digest (16th September 1977) Kuwait has decreed that 100 per cent of its natural gas exports to the USA and 50 per cent to Japan must be shipped in Kuwait vessels. (At the time of the report, however, Kuwait had no LNG carriers.)	Crude oil sales contracts include a clause requiring that Kuwaiti tankers or those owned in part by Kuwaiti interests receive preference.
Mexico Traffic of PEMEX (the state petroleum company) is reserved for national flag vessels.	In 1963 an export tax was imposed on bee honey at a rate of 1 per cent if shipped by Mexican flag vessels and 3 per cent if shipped otherwise. A decree of 1st January 1966 provides subsidies for products intended for export if shipped in Mexican flag vessels or foreign flag vessels under charter to Mexican shipping companies. Subsidies of 50 per cent of the freight rate are granted for manufactured products intended for export and subsidies of 25 per cent of the freight rate are granted for semi-manufactured products or manufactured products not for end consumption. The government subsidizes the cost of its vessels' fuel to the extent of 50 per cent of the total cost.

Table 14.1 continued

Cargo preference laws	Other preference practices
	Legislation of 1966 grants a subsidy of 25 per cent of the freight rate to Mexican producers who ship their products to areas bordering the USA, Guatemala and Belize by rail, ship or air.

Legislation of 1967 encourages exports of cotton by granting a 97.7 per cent reduction in the export tax to shippers who use Mexican flag vessels or vessels chartered by national shipping companies.

Mexico has a 40/40/20 bilateral agreement with Brazil; preference is given to Latin flag lines.

Preferential treatment in other areas is given on the basis of administrative action rather than law:

Approval of applications for import licences subject to proviso that goods in question be imported in Mexican flag vessels.

Where goods are restricted by currency quotas, the cost of sea transportation is not charged against the quota if the goods are imported on national flag vessels.

Many state-owned agencies insist that their imports be carried on national flag ships.

Morocco
40 per cent of imports and 30 per cent of exports must be shipped on national flag vessels.

Nicaragua
Under legislation of 1972 cargoes bought or sold by the state shall be transported exclusively by Nicaraguan shipping enterprises. 50 per cent of commercial cargoes shall be carried in Nicaraguan flag ships and 50 per cent in those of its trading partner; should the other party not provide shipping services, the Nicaraguan share may rise to 80 per cent.

Table 14.1 continued

Cargo preference laws	Other preference practices
Nigeria Legislation of 1972 reserves 50 per cent of all foreign trade to national flag vessels.	Nigeria has a 50/50 bilateral agreement with Brazil.
Pakistan 50 per cent of all US–AID and World Bank aid cargoes must be shipped on national flag vessels.	Cargo preference is practised among participants in international shipping conferences which reserve a portion of the conference trade to Pakistani ships. Pakistan has a 50/50 bilateral shipping agreement with Poland. Pakistan participates in a conference with India and Bangladesh which observes 40/40/20 cargo sharing.
Peru Legislation of 1970 reserves 30–50 per cent of Peruvian exports and imports (calculated on a monthly basis) for Peruvian flag ships. Imports exempt from customs duty must be carried in national flag ships when available. Legislation of 1974 gives Corporacion Peruana de Vapores, a national line, the preferential right to transport imports and exports, of the Peruvian government, public corporations or corporations in which the government has a major interest; it requires lines of other nations to have loading contracts with CPV for any portion of such cargoes which CPV cannot carry. Legislation of 1976 guarantees that CPV shall receive preference in the carriage of all government cargoes, national and local.	Under legislation of 1969 preference in the carriage of cargoes enjoying import duty exemption shall be given firstly to Peruvian flag vessels, secondly to foreign flag vessels chartered to Peruvian companies and finally to foreign flag vessels associated with Peruvian companies. Legislation of 1957 provides that national flag ships shall pay 50 per cent of regular fees for ship clearances and for certification of consular invoices and bills of lading. Dry docking fees are 5 cents per ton for Peruvian ships and 15 cents per ton for foreign ships. Peruvian flag ships pay about 40 per cent less than foreign flag ships in Callao and 50 per cent less in other ports for mooring and unmooring. Wharf demurrage, charges for repair, docking and fuelling are less for Peruvian flag ships than for foreign flag vessels. Peru has 50/50 bilateral agreements with Argentina, India and Brazil whereby the two parties have a right on equal terms to transport the cargoes and share the freight receipts derived from their bilateral trade.

Table 14.1 continued

Cargo preference laws	Other preference practices

The Philippines

Legislation of 1976 requires any company which receives any subsidy, tax concession, assistance, contract or subcontract from the government to use Philippine flag vessels for all import and export cargo and personnel transport to the maximum extent service by such ships is available. Overall preference on the carriage of imports is given to Philippine flag vessels.

All imports under control of government agencies and corporations must be shipped on national flag vessels unless they are not readily available.

Import licences will be issued for government cargo only when it is imported on national flag ships, unless none are available.

Legislation of 1975 provides that the government will take all steps necessary, including provision of direct incentives, to enable Philippine flag vessels to carry a substantial and increasing share of foreign trade. It states that Philippine flag vessels and those owned, controlled or chartered by Philippine nationals shall carry a share of cargo at least equal to that carried by its trading partners.

All imports of US agricultural commodities under Section 402 of the US Mutual Security Act and US PL 480 which are in excess of the 50 per cent required to be carried in US flag ships must be shipped in Philippine flag ships when available.

All purchases of Philippine imports must be made on an FOB basis and all freight payments must be made in pesos.

Exporters will be able to deduct from their taxable income an amount equivalent to 150 per cent of overseas freight expenses and charges in Philippine ports incurred in shipping export products, provided they use Philippine flag carriers. Enterprises registered with the Board of Investments will be allowed to deduct from their taxable income 200 per cent of shipment costs incurred in transport of their products and raw materials to and from foreign ports provided that they use Philippine flag vessels for their shipments.

Portugal

The Merchant Marine Secretariat has prepared a draft law stipulating that:

   1. Where no bilateral agreement exists all imports and exports exceeding 10 tons by entities owned or partly owned by the government must be carried on Portuguese flag ships;

Portugal and the USSR have a 50/50 cargo-sharing agreement. The 'right' of other countries' ships to participate in trade between the ports of Portugal and the USSR shall not be affected, however.

Portugal and Mozambique have agreed that all trade between the two

Table 14.1 continued

Cargo preference laws	Other preference practices
2. Where a bilateral agreement exists, as much of the cargo as possible should be reserved for Portuguese flag ships;	countries shall be reserved for Portuguese flag ships.
3. All imports exceeding 10 tons financed by bank credits or guarantees must be carried on Portuguese ships.	
4. In all the above provisions, FOB terms must be obtained for imports and CIF terms for exports.	

Saudi Arabia

Legislation of 1975 requires that 5 per cent of Saudi exports (primarily oil) be carried in Saudi vessels, rising to 50 per cent by 1980.	Saudi vessels have a lower bunkering rate than foreign flag vessels.
Overall, 25 per cent of trade is reserved for national flag vessels when financial and other terms are competitive.	

South Africa

All government cargo from Europe to South Africa must move on South and Southeast African conference lines, of which SAFMARINE is a member.

South Korea

Under the Shipping Promotion Law it is mandatory for exporters and importers to use Korean flag ships exclusively. Waivers are allowed only if no Korean vessel is available.	The government encourages the use of Korean flag ships by awarding some government procurement contracts on an FOB basis rather than a CIF basis.
With completion of its first container ships, Korea demanded that container cargo move in Korean flag vessels. If no suitable Korean flag vessel is available in three days, cargo may move on foreign flag vessel.	A preferential interest rate for importing raw materials for export production is extended to cover freight costs when imports are carried on Korean flag ships.
Legislation of 1976 states that imports of crude oil, iron ore, lumber, grain and fertilizer will be carried in national flag ships, subject to availability.	South Korea has bilateral agreements with the USA, the Federal Republic of Germany and Japan.

Table 14.1 continued

Cargo preference laws	Other preference practices
Spain	
All imports of crude oil, tobacco and cotton for domestic consumption must be shipped in Spanish vessels if capacity is available.	
Sri Lanka	
The Ceylon Shipping Corporation has a monopoly on all cargo imports for government and state-owned corporations.	In 1972 Sri Lanka and China signed a joint shipping agreement, which included the provision that 'both countries will have a fair and equal opportunity in the carriage of commodities'.
Taiwan	
	It has been agreed that 50 per cent of total trade between Taiwan and Japan shall be carried in national flag ships.
Tanzania	
	Since 1976 income tax has been levied on the gross receipts of foreign shipping lines accruing from outbound shipping freight and passengers. The tax does not apply to transhipment traffic.
	Tanzania and China have a joint shipping agreement.
Thailand	
Legislation of 1972 provides that double duty must be paid on certain types of imported goods unless they are carried in ships licensed by a special interdepartmental committee.	
Turkey	
All public-sector cargo must be carried in national flag ships.	The Maritime Bank exerts pressure on exporters and importers to ship commercial cargoes on Turkish ships when available.
Legislation of 1975 states that all imports should be carried by national flag ships whenever possible. When none are available, any other line may ship the goods after obtaining a 'nomination certificate'.	
Uruguay	
Legislation of 1977 reserves a minimum of 50 per cent of export cargo for	The Executive has authority to establish rebates to be granted for cargo exported

Table 14.1 continued

Cargo preference laws	Other preference practices

Uruguayan flag vessels.

Import cargo must be carried on national flag lines whenever available; availability will be determined by the Executive in consultation with the Ministry of Transport and Public Works. Import registrations must indicate the means of transport.

Vessels registered elsewhere may be used only with authority from the Ministry of Transport and Public Works and on the following conditions;

1. That they are included in international commercial agreements with Uruguay;

2. That they are included in agreements or freight conferences in which Uruguay participates.

Preference will be granted to foreign vessels which realize equal conference traffic with Uruguayan flag lines, provided that the rates quoted do not exceed those offered by non-conference lines on the same route.

The Executive can extend preference to exports of merchandise, assets or products which benefit from fiscal exemption and to those whose financing or guarantee is channelled through institutions forming part of the national banking system.

Uruguayan vessels are defined as those 51 per cent or more owned by Uruguayan citizens.

On routes in which Uruguayan flag vessels do not participate, waivers will be granted, provided reciprocity of cargo is agreed.

Infringement carries a penalty of from 10 to 100 per cent of the freight value generated by the shipment in question.

USSR

in national flag vessels. The exporter may deduct the corresponding freight rebates from his taxes.

The government reserves the right to decide upon the validity of all conference agreements involving import and export cargo. The Executive can disqualify national and foreign enterprises from operating in Uruguayan ports if the conferences in which they participate have not been duly approved.

All general merchandise is subject to an import surcharge; cargoes arriving on Uruguayan ships receive a 10 per cent rebate.

Goods shipped from US Gulf ports where Uruguayan flag vessels call pay an extra 5 per cent surcharge; shipments from US East Coast ports where no Uruguayan ships call do not pay a surcharge.

Merchandise arriving in Uruguay for use by state entities, as well as certain exports, is entitled to 'fiscal exemptions' only when shipped in Uruguayan flag ships.

Trade with LAFTA countries is considered as coastal trade; cargoes from LAFTA countries are exempt from the consular fee if they arrive in Uruguayan vessels.

Uruguay has 50/50 cargo-sharing agreements with Argentina, Brazil and Colombia; an agreement with Bolivia contains a discriminatory clause.

The USSR sells goods on a CIF basis and buys on an FOB basis, so that in the first

Table 14.1 continued

Cargo preference laws	Other preference practices
	case the exporter and in the second the importer selects the carrier, which is usually the national flag line, unless a bilateral shipping agreement provides otherwise.
Venezuela The Law for the Protection and Development of the National Merchant Marine requires that 50 per cent of all exports and imports, including oil, be carried in national vessels, which are defined as ships at least 75 per cent owned by Venezuelan nationals. The government hopes to reach this goal by 1985. The transport of not less than 10 per cent of exports and imports of petroleum and its derivatives is currently reserved for Venezuelan flag ships; the proportion will gradually rise to 50 per cent. Transport of ore, wheat and other free-flowing cargo shall be treated likewise, both as imports and exports. The government has suggested that preference should be given to state-owned Compania Anonima Venezolana do Navigacion (CAVN) in the shipment of cargoes controlled or contracted by the government.	The Venezuelan Pilotage Law allows the Executive to grant Venezuelan ships exemptions of up to 50 per cent of the charges established by the Law. In addition, national flag ships pay 50 per cent charges set by the pilotage regulations of individual ports. CAVN operates joint shipping services with several 'associated' lines from Europe and Japan; imports partially or totally exempt from import duties must move on CAVN or 'associated' line ships, thereby assuring CAVN of a definite share of the cargo in areas where it maintains a service.
Yugoslavia	The Yugoslav National Bank grants exporters an export premium of 20 per cent on ocean freight to US North Atlantic ports and 30 per cent on that to other ports if shipment is made via a Yugoslav port on a Yugoslav flag ship. If no Yugoslav flag ship is available a certificate to that effect must be obtained from the Association of Yugoslav Shipowners.
Zaire The Compagnie Maritime Zaïroise has	

Table 14.1 continued

Cargo preference laws	Other preference practices
the monopoly of export shipping from Zaire and the monopoly of all imports purchased with the assistance of the Bank of Zaire. It may bestow a portion of this operation on other companies of its choice.	

to shippers of large volumes of goods. However, immediate or deferred rebates are given provided shippers do not use services outside the conference. Income is pooled and subsequently divided in accordance with criteria laid down by members; some conferences operate a gross receipts pool, in which each member bears his own expenses, whereas others have a net receipts pool into which only the profit element is paid.

In view of the common tariff policy, competition among conference members is restricted to the field of service quality. Many critics consider their rates to be too high and the service semi-monopolistic, particularly as governments and trade associations tend to be closely associated with liner conference policies. It must be conceded, however, that the service achieve a high standard, a factor which is generally more important to shippers than the tariff, provided it is not prohibitive.

The subject of liner conferences is described in greater detail in *Elements of Shipping*. Nevertheless, in the context of this chapter it is appropriate to examine the results of the 1979 UNCTAD Conference as an example of the effect of politics on liner conferences.

One of the important decisions to emerge from the fifth session of the UNCTAD Conference was the United Nations Code of Conduct for Liner Conferences. Earlier in the 1970s UNCTAD had proposed the 40/40/20 rule giving each of the trading partner countries the right to carry 40 per cent of the liner cargoes generated by their own trade and leaving the remaining 20 per cent for third-flag carriers; in fact, the code would allow considerable flexibility in reaching agreement on cargo shares. At the 1979 session a sufficient number of countries accepted the code, but their fleets do not yet represent the required proportion of the world general cargo fleet for it to enter into force.

The countries of the EEC were among those that accepted the

code in 1979. They indicated, however, that they would not apply the cargo-sharing provisions in intra-Community shipping or between member countries and other OECD countries that adopted the code, as they intended to preserve a commercial regime within OECD trades. However, they would not exclude developing countries from bidding for the 20 per cent share. The net result will be a steady increase in the amount of liner cargo carried by the national lines of developing countries.

While many consider that the Convention on a Code of Conduct for Liner Conferences offers a basic economic framework for liner shipping, there is still much disagreement about its cargo-sharing provisions. Many are fundamentally opposed to any governmental cargo-sharing scheme and hold that an agreed regime for the conduct of liner conferences should be based on self-regulation through strong shippers' councils, thus avoiding unnecessary government regulation.

Over the long term the composition of liner conference membership is likely to change, especially in trades involving developing countries and where cross trade operation is prevalent. The time scale of such changes will depend on the ability of developing countries to expand their fleets and acquire the management expertise to operate them.

FLAGS OF CONVENIENCE

Shipping companies are subject to income and profits taxes in the state in which they are domiciled. In this respect they are no different from any other undertaking. However, the shipping industry is more sensitive to the level of taxation than others owing to the enormous cost of ship replacement, which is continuing to rise. Today this is one of the main reasons for registering ships under so-called flags of convenience. The main countries to offer such facilities are Liberia, Panama, Singapore, Cyprus and Somalia, which have a declared open registry policy and thereby encourage the registration of vessels whose beneficial owners reside elsewhere. In 1979 ships sailing under these flags accounted for about 31 per cent of the world fleet (see Table 1.6).

The flags of convenience have incurred the displeasure of UNCTAD, which is concerned at the fact that the fleets of developing countries increased only slightly during the last decade as a proportion of the world fleet; in 1978 they accounted for 8.6 per cent, compared with the share of about 85 per cent in the case of the fleets of developed market economies registered under their own flags or under flags of convenience. Between mid-1976 and mid-1978 the developing countries increased their share of the world's deadweight tonnage from 6.7 to 8.6 per cent, but about three-quarters of the increase was attributable to growth in the fleets of 13 countries which had made more rapid progress than the majority in expanding their merchant marine. On the basis of this, a report presented at the fifth UNCTAD Conference concludes that the employment of seamen from developing countries on vessels sailing under flags of convenience is one of the factors impeding the development of these countries' shipping fleets. It concedes that free flag shipping helps keep transport costs down, but this in itself makes national flag vessels unable to compete for cargoes, thus preventing countries from exercising their right to carry a fair share of their export trade in their own ships. Greater opportunities would open up for developing countries if flag of convenience operations were phased out. It was therefore agreed to reconvene an intergovernmental working group to consider this question.

The viewpoint presented by UNCTAD is at variance, however, with a report commissioned by the Sea Transport Committee of the US Council of the International Chamber of Commerce and published in 1980. The survey, which aimed to identify the underlying economic issues for different categories of emergent nations, states that open registry operations provide readily available shipping services at a lower price than would be the case if shipowners were obliged to operate under their own national flag. In the event that flag of convenience operations were phased out it is doubtful, according to the report, that it would be accompanied by an even redeployment of ships to a wide range of developing countries on a trade related basis. Many of the vessels affected would probably be re-registered under quasi-flags of convenience in lower cost OECD countries such as the United Kingdom, Greece and, perhaps in the future, Spain. The extent of increases in charges to ship users, including developing countries, would depend on the degree to which OECD countries were prepared to continue to subsidize shipping, either directly or indirectly by granting tax concessions. The much smaller proportion of open registry shipping that might be redeployed in developing countries under joint venture arrangements would mainly go to the richer and more politically stable nations. The report concludes that the extent to which cost could be kept under control in these circumstances would again depend on the tax concessions offered and it points out that it is concessions of this very kind that attract owners to open registries now and that have drawn criticism from UNCTAD.

Many other countries believe that, far from interfering with the efficient allocation of shipbuilding, ship operating and seafaring resources throughout the world, the existence of open registries has directly served the national interests of various developing and developed nations. Moreover, they consider that there are legal and political arguments supporting current international law on the sovereign rights of nations to establish vessel registries and to control vessels so registered.

Further evidence that conflicts with UNCTAD's desire to withdraw flags of convenience has come from the Liberian Government Bureau of Maritime Affairs. It stresses that a switch to national flag policies would restrict trading potential and increase freight charges, thus reducing a developing country's economic growth in favour of developed countries. Moreover, the capital invested in a merchant fleet would not yield a very high return and could be used to better advantage if it were invested in other directions in other countries. The report contends that open registry brings positive benefits in terms of economic growth and employment in developing countries. It compares the manning levels on Liberian tankers operating with crews from low cost employment areas with those on tankers with high cost crew members. The average complement on 66 tankers with crews from Northern Europe, Spain and Italy was 32, whereas on 69 tankers with low cost crews from Taiwan, the Philippines, India, Bangladesh and Indonesia it was 37; the labour input was therefore 15 per cent higher if cheaper labour was used. It supports the view that with the freedom to use low cost labour, there is a tendency to create more jobs.

The study concludes that the abolition of the open registry would have a serious adverse effect on world trade and would generally disregard financial and investment considerations.

It is significant that by early 1980 Greek shipowners were tending to register their vessels under the Greek flag rather than under those of Liberia or Panama. This move had been engendered by changes in Greece's taxation laws and the owners' desire to avoid difficulties with the International Transport Workers' Federation. Nevertheless, the flag of convenience fleet was still primarily controlled by the United States, Hong Kong, Greece and Japan, which together account for over 70 per cent of the total.

At present it is difficult to predict the likely outcome of the open registry controversy; much will depend on the ultimate economics of the case and the availability of capital for developing countries to build up their fleets, but politics will undoubtedly play their part.

SUBSIDIES

Over the past decade the shipping industries of many countries have shown a return on capital of between 3 and 4 per cent, compared with yields of 15 per cent and more in some other industries. Indeed, in several cases virtually no capital return has materialized owing to poor trading conditions. The situation is aggravated by differences in the cost of labour; the fleets of industrialized countries are finding it increasingly difficult to compete with those from countries with low wage scales despite attempts to reduce crew complements. These circumstances have encouraged protectionism and nationalism, trends that have been reinforced by the resolutions passed at the 1979 UNCTAD Conference. We have already examined the UNCTAD liner conference code and the question of flag discrimination; we should not overlook another factor tending to distort free competition in the shipping industry, namely the granting of state subsidies.

Subsidization can take various forms:

(a) Building subsidies, either as a percentage of the total building cost or as a fixed sum. This technique is sometimes used as an incentive in 'scrap and build' schemes. Such subsidies are usually subject to certain conditions and are often granted as a means of giving the country's shipyards orders that would otherwise have been placed abroad on the basis of cost and time criteria. Policies of this kind are particularly prevalent in countries with state-owned fleets, whose development is considered vital to the nation's economy and trade as they contribute to their invisible exports and save hard currency. Building subsidies are also available, however, in countries whose fleets are not state-owned. Some countries grant subsidies on vessels to be built in a foreign yard; this is most likely to occur if the country has no shipyards of its own. It must be borne in mind that few shipowners today have sufficient funds to build vessels without drawing on loans and state subsidies.

(b) Shipyard subsidies are becoming increasingly prevalent in view of the depressed state of the shipbuilding industry throughout the world. Such subsidies apply to both new construction and repair work irrespective of whether the vessels are registered in the country concerned or abroad.

(c) Interest-free or low interest loans to finance the building of new ships. The conditions imposed may include a requirement to employ a domestic shipyard. Such subsidies may form part of a 'scrap and build' scheme whereby, for example, two new vessels might be built to replace three existing ones more than fifteen years old.

(d) Operating subsidies granted to shipping companies either to make good the loss incurred in a particular year or to finance their operations over a specified period.

(e) Conventions. These are annual sums paid to a shipping company to keep tariffs at a reasonable level on services that are essential to the economic and social well-being of a community, such as the services between mainland Scotland and the Hebrides, the Orkneys and Shetland. Conditions are usually attached to the grant, such as the requirement to provide a service throughout the year and a minimum number of weekly sailings in each direction.

(f) The funding of fleet insurance by the state. This method of subsidization is used in many Eastern bloc countries and also extends to the social security contributions of the crew.

(g) Bunker rate discounts for vessels on the national register.

The subsidization of shipping may serve national aspirations and objectives in a number of ways. Maintenance of the subsidized services may conserve the country's scarce reserves of foreign currency and may also boost invisible earnings by operating in a cross trade. Subsidies may enable countries with high wage scales to compete on equal terms against those with lower labour costs. The main argument advanced in favour of subsidies, however, is that they permit the development or maintenance of a country's fleet and shipyards, with all that that implies in terms of employment, prestige and independence.

On the other hand, subsidies tend to inflate world shipping capacity to a level that trade alone cannot support, thus destroying the commercial freedom of the seas in some sectors; a subsidized fleet can undercut competitors in the knowledge that losses will be covered. Moreover, in granting subsidies on ships ordered by Eastern bloc countries and in providing developing countries with ships at less than their true commercial cost the governments of Western industrialized countries are supplying vessels that could well undermine their own fleets. Subsidies also tend to encourage uneconomic ship operation, as the knowledge that the state will make good any losses removes the incentive to minimize costs. Above all, subsidies promote the growth of nationalism and flag discrimination.

There can be no doubt that subsidization will continue to increase in the next decade as the practices of nationalism and protectionism escalate. Industrialized countries that have not hitherto pursued policies of extensive subsidization may find themselves compelled to advance further in that direction in order to sustain their fleets at a reasonable level.

THE FUTURE

The remainder of the 1980s will undoubtedly be a period of great change, but it will also present opportunities that shipping entrepreneurs must grasp if they are to succeed. Ship management techniques will continue to improve in all areas, as the provision of competitively priced sea transport will remain essential to the development of world trade. More effective budgeting and marketing techniques and, where practicable, the development of shipboard management will be required. The importance of training in all areas of shipping and trade will grow. Manning levels, economic ship propulsion and ship design and efficient port operations will remain dominant factors in the search for improved ship productivity. International organizations, in particular IMCO, OPEC, the ILO, BIMCO, UNCITRAL and UNCTAD, will play a more prominent role in the field of shipping.

World consumption of energy, especially oil, will have a major bearing on the size of the world tanker fleet, which is likely to remain stable or even contract. Cargo liner trades, on the other hand, will probably expand. As indicated above, the need to recycle some of the oil revenues, particularly to third world countries, will become paramount in the interest of sustaining and developing world trade. The growth in trade will be more marked in the Orient than among Western countries. The decisions of the 1979 UNCTAD Conference will have a profound effect on international shipping; developing countries will play a more important role in world trade and their fleets will carry a larger share of cargoes. Eastern bloc countries may also increase their presence in the industry. The merchant navies of established maritime nations such as the United Kingdom are likely to show a corresponding decline as their participation in cross trades diminishes. Politics will continue to influence the world of shipping, with the commercial freedom of the seas receding in the face of growing protectionism. It is highly unlikely that state involvement in shipowning in the Western industrialized countries will come about as a result of planned nationalization; it is more likely to occur by reason of the fact that governments not only provide direct finance for the shipbuilding industry but also guarantee massive shipbuilding loans to shipowners – loans that are increasingly subject to renegotiation or default. State control – or at least influence – over shipping exists in all maritime nations, since loan agreements and debt structures give lenders the right to exert a direct influence on the actions of shipowners. As a large proportion of mortgage loans are guaranteed by the government, it is the state as ultimate lender that is increasingly having to take direct or indirect control of fleets and shipping companies.

High professional standards are essential if the shipping industry is to remain viable and foster international trade, thereby raising living standards throughout the world. It is hoped that this book will make a modest contribution towards attainment of that objective and that it will form the basis of further study.

Addresses of Organizations and Institutes Engaged in the Fields of Shipping and International Trade

Baltic and International
Maritime Conference
19, Kristianiagade
DK–2100 Copenhagen
Denmark

Baltic Mercantile and Shipping
Exchange
St Mary Axe
London EC3

British Overseas Trade Board
(BOTB)
1, Victoria Street
London SW1H 0ET

Chartered Institute of
Transport
80, Portland Place
London W1N 4DP

Council of European and
Japanese National Shipowners'
Associations (CENSA)
17/18, Bury Street
London EC3A 5AH

Freight Transport Association
(FTA)
Hermes House
157, St John's Road
Tunbridge Wells
Kent TN4 9UZ

General Council of British
Shipping (GCBS)
30/32, St Mary Axe
London EC3A 8ET

Institute of Bankers
10, Lombard Street
London EC3

Institute of Chartered
Shipbrokers
25, Bury Street
London EC3A 5BA

Institute of Export
World Trade Centre
London E1 9AA

Institute of Freight Forwarders
Ltd
Suffield House
9, Paradise Road
Richmond
Surrey TW9 1SA

Institute of Marine Engineers
76, Mark Lane
London EC3

Institute of Marketing
Moor Hall
Cookham
Maidenhead
Berks SL6 9QH

Institute of Road Transport
Engineers
1, Cromwell Place
Kensington
London SW7 2JF

Institute of Transport
Administration
32, Palmerston Road
Southampton SO1 1LL

Inter-Governmental Maritime
Consultative Organization
(IMCO)
101–104, Piccadilly
London WIV 0AE

International Association of
Independent Tanker Owners
(INTERTANKO)
Radhusgaten 25
PO Box 1452–VIKA
Oslo
Norway

International Cargo Handling
Co-ordination Association
(ICHCA)
Abford House
15, Wilton Road
London SW1V 1LX

International Chamber of
Commerce (ICC)
38, Cours Albert 1 er
75008 Paris
France

International Labour Office
(ILO)
CH–1211 Genève 22
Switzerland

International Monetary Fund
(IMF)
Washington DC
20431
USA

Lloyd's Register of Shipping
71, Fenchurch Street
London EC3M 4BS

Organisation for Economic
Co-operation and Development
(OECD)
Maritime Transport Committee
2, Rue André Pascal
75775 Paris Cedex 16
France

Organization of the Petroleum
Exporting Countries (OPEC)
Obere Donaustrasse 93
1020 Vienna
Austria

Royal Institute of Naval
Architects
10, Upper Belgrave Street
London SW1

Simplification of International
Trade Procedures Board
(SITPRO)
Almack House
26–28 King Street
London SW1

United Nations Commission on
International Trade Law
(UNCITRAL)
United Nations
New York
NY 10017
USA

United Nations Conference on
Trade and Development
(UNCTAD)
Palais des Nations
CH–1211 Genève 10
Switzerland

Further Recommended Textbook Reading

Branch, A.E. (1979), *The Elements of Export Practice*, 1st Edn, Chapman and Hall, London.

Branch, A.E. (1982), *A Dictionary of Shipping/International Trade Terms and Abbreviations* (2600 entries), 2nd Edn, Witherby & Co. Ltd., London.

Branch, A.E. (1981), *Elements of Shipping*, 5th Edn, Chapman and Hall, London.

Packard, W.V. (1979), *Voyage Estimating*, 1st Edn, Fairplay Publications Ltd.

Packard, W.V. (1980), *Laytime Calculating*, 1st Edn, Fairplay Publications Ltd.

Schmitthoff, C.M. (1976), *The Export Trade*, 8th Edn, Sweet & Maxwell, London.

Watson, A. (1979), *Finance of International Trade*, Institute of Bankers, London.

Ship Diagrams

Diagrams III to XI follow, illustrating many of the vessels referred to in the text.

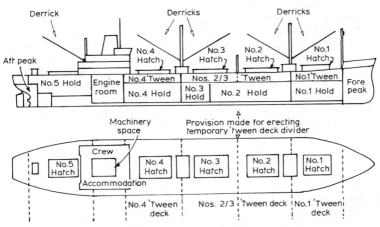

Diagram III   SD 14 Mark IV 15 000 dwt general cargo vessel

This type of vessel is built by Austin and Pickersgill of England. She has a crew of 30, a speed of 15 knots and a loaded mean draught of 8.84 m. Her length is 140 m and her beam 21 m. Her gross register tonnage is 9100 and her net register tonnage 6100. The total grain cubic capacity exceeds 764 000 ft³; total cargo deadweight tonnage is 14 000. This vessel is very versatile in operation and is employed to carry traditional tramp bulk cargoes, viz. grain, timber, ore, coal etc. More than 50 ships have been built to this broad specification. Austin and Pickersgill have pioneered a number of general purpose-built vessels for the tramp market; others include the SD 18 (a multi-purpose general cargo vessel of 18 000 dwt), the SD 9 (a general cargo vessel of 9000 dwt) and the B 26 (a seven-hold bulk carrier of 26 000 dwt with a service speed of 15 knots).

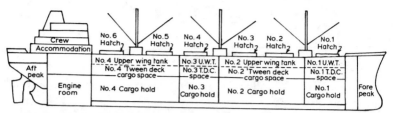

Diagram IV   Freedom-type ship with 'tween deck accommodation

This is a modern tramp vessel built in Japan. It combines the essential features of a single deck bulk cargo carrier with those of a closed shelter deck ship. It can operate efficiently in dry cargo tramp trades such as grain, coal, potash, phosphate rock, bauxite and iron ore, as well as general cargoes, palletized and container cargoes. The ship has a crew of 30, a speed of 14 knots and an overall length of 145 m. Her beam is 21 m and her loaded mean draught about 9 m. Total grain capacity is 705 000 ft³ and cargo deadweight tonnage 15 000. In common with the SD 14, the Freedom-type vessel is a multipurpose dry cargo carrier. More than 50 have been built to this broad specification.

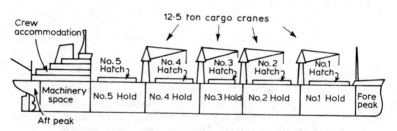

Diagram V   Bulk carrier 30 000 dwt

This single deck vessel, built by Austin and Pickersgill of England, is a 30 000 dwt bulk carrier with a draught of 10 m and a speed of 15 knots. The crew totals 34, her overall length is 179 m and her beam 28 m. Each crane has a capacity of 12.5 tonnes and the vessel is ideal for grain and other bulk cargoes. The gross register tonnage is 18 500.

230

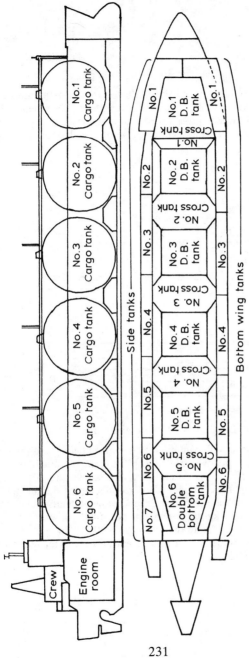

Diagram VI Liquefied natural gas (LNG) carrier

The development of the liquefied natural gas carrier fleet was very significant in the early 1970s but demand for this tonnage has fallen away in
recent years. Such purpose-built vessels have crew accommodation and
machinery aft.

231

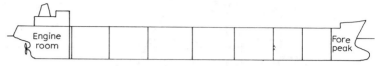

Diagram VII   Oil tanker

Tankers form a substantial proportion of the total world mercantile fleet. A vessel of 25 000 dwt would have an overall length of 170 m, beam of 24 m and draught of 13 m. The gross register tonnage is 15 000 with the net register tonnage 10 000. Her speed is 15 knots. Such a vessel would be called a parcels tanker.

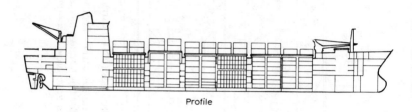

Profile

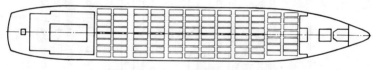

Upper deck container arrangement

Diagram VIII   Container ship

This vessel is a purpose-built container vessel engaged in ocean-going cargo liner services with a capacity of 500 20 ft ISO containers. Each hold of the cellular ship is fitted with a series of vertical angle guides adequately cross-braced to accept the containers. Her overall length is 120 m, her beam 17 m and her loaded draught 5 m. Accommodation is aft and she has a speed of 14 knots. Her gross register tonnage totals 4000 and her net register tonnage 2200. Her cargo deadweight tonnage is 3000. This type of vessel is found in the short sea trade and can also act as a feeder to deep sea container ships of some 2500 TEU.

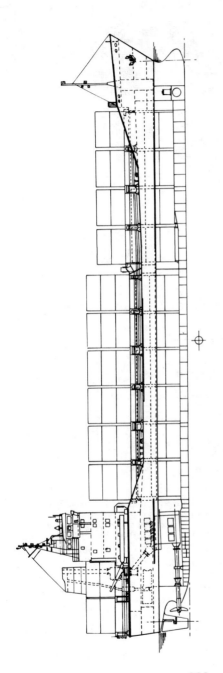

Profile

Length overall	104·15 m
Breadth moulded	16·50 m
Depth moulded	8·10 m
Load draft	5·54 m
Deadweight (estimated total/cargo)	4120 – 3700 t
Containers (cellular and deck 8'0" or 8'6")	300 TEUs or 139 at 40 ft
Container electric sockets for refrigeration or heated tanks	50 with individual remote monitoring
Gross tonnage	1599
Net tonnage	900
Main engine	Doxford 58 JS 3
Power	5000 bhp at 220 r pm
Service speed	15 knots

Diagram IX   Container vessel engaged in the UK–Mediterranean–Middle East trade

Container tonnage continues to grow and the type of vessel illustrated is therefore becoming more popular. It offers all the benefits of containerization and is a handy size of ship capable of operating in many container trades.

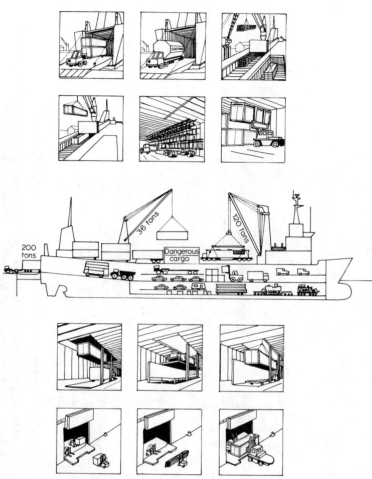

Diagram X   Omni carrier – roll on/roll off – lift on/lift off and side-loading
vessel (combi carrier)

This modern vessel, called a 'combi carrier', is operated by DFDS Nordana
Line in the US Gulf–US East Coast–Mediterranean–Caribbean/Central
America trade. It conveys general cargo in containers, trailers and other
unitized consignments, break bulk cargo and heavy equipment up to 200
tons. The stern ramp of 200 tons' capacity can be used for the rapid loading
and unloading of containers on trailers or heavy fork lift trucks. Side loading
facilities permit simultaneous operation by two fork lift trucks handling
palletized cargo. There are two derricks, one of 36 tons' capacity and one of
120 tons.

The vessel has an overall length of 135 m, beam of 25 m and draught of 7 m;

234

her speed is 15 knots and she has a crew of about 20. Her gross register tonnage is 4500 and her net register tonnage 1750. Metric deadweight tonnage comes to 8000.

The ship can convey a total of 516 TEUs on the upper, main and lower hold decks. Bale capacity exceeds 18 500 m³, whilst lane capacity to accommodate trailers totals 1400 m. The combination of cargo facilities can be adjusted to reflect market demand for the carriage of containers, vehicles, heavy lifts, break bulk consignments, etc.

This type of vessel is very versatile in operation and cargo capacity mixture. It is likely to become very popular in cargo liner trades in the 1980s. The vessel is generously provided with lifting gear and cargo transhipment equipment, thereby aiding rapid turnround and helping to overcome any inadequacies in port facilities.

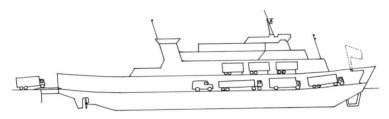

Diagram XI   Ro/Ro vessel

Ro/Ro vessels represent one of the ship types that have shown the fastest growth in numbers in recent years; this trend is likely to continue throughout the 1980s. They operate in both the short sea and deep sea liner cargo services conveying vehicular traffic which, depending on the vessel design, may include road haulage vehicles, road trailers, coaches, trade vehicles, accompanied cars, containers on trailers, etc. Passenger accommodation is also provided in short sea trades.

The vessel illustrated is found in the short sea trade and has an overall length of 130 m and a beam of 22 m. Her deadweight tonnage is 2000, gross register tonnage 9000 and net register tonnage 3200; her speed is 20 knots. She can convey up to 60 Ro/Ro vehicles each 15 m in length. Bow and stern loading provide drive-through facilities. The vessel can load and discharge simultaneously on both decks, thereby speeding up turnround. A mezzanine deck is available to convey cars and the upper garage deck can accommodate 122 cars or 28 Ro/Ro vehicles. Clearance between the main and upper decks is 4.5 m.

The vessel design aids rapid turnround; most of the ships have main deck loading and discharge facilities at both bow and stern. Conversely, much space is wasted between the vehicle decks in comparison with a cellular container ship, as broken stowage obtains.

Index

Oil tanker, 232
Omni carrier, 63
OPEC, 185–187, 199, 224, 227
Open account, 100, 102, 108, 109
Operating expenses, 46
Operating subsidies, 223
Operation of shipboard management, 152–154
Organization of shipboard management, 151, 152

P & I Clubs, 70
Packaging, 21
Pakistani cargo preference laws, 212
Panama canal, 69, 96
Panamanian fleet, 5–12
Par, 29
Parcels tanker, 37, 232
Passenger certificate, 63
Passenger fares, 81, 82
Payload, 40
Payments on open account, 100
Personnel cheque, 100
Personnel department, 152
Peruvian cargo preference laws, 212
Philippine cargo preference laws, 213
Piggy back operation, 123, 124
Planned economy, 22, 23
Planning, 132–135
Plying limits, 66
Political factors, 134, 194–225
Port operation, 74–76
Portuguese cargo preference laws, 213
Post Office receipt, 105
Preferential trading groups, 23–26
Premium rate, 29
Pricing (market), 146, 147
Problems caused by fluctuations and imbalances in trade, 71–73
Promotions, 143–146
Purchasing department, 152

Radio officers, 57–58
Rate of exchange, 26
Rates, 77–86
Rebates, 84
Red clause credits, 107
Relationship between world seaborne trade and world mercantile fleet, 3–12
Relationship of international trade to function of shipping, 1, 2
Relative importance of speed, frequency, reliability and cost of sea transport, 73, 74

Reservation system, 147
Revenue budget, 136–140
Revocable credit, 102–105
Revolving credits, 106, 107
Road haulage freight rates, 78, 79
Role of international organizations, 156–193
Ro/Ro vessels, 37, 45, 52, 62, 82, 120, 133, 166, 235
Rubber, 23
Rubber Trading Association, 17

Safety, cost and construction factors, 31–34
Sailing schedules planning, 64–70
Saleback, 49, 50
Saleform sundry form, 92
Sales conferences, 144
Saudi Arabian cargo preference laws, 214
Saudi Arabian fleet, 5
SEABEE, 127
SD, 14, 229
SDRs, 178–181
Seasonal traffic, 66, 67
Seasonal traffic fluctuations, 71, 72
Sea Transport Account, 5
Selling rate, 26–28
Services offered by freight forwarders, 21, 22
Services of train ferries, 125, 126
Ship agency and chartering procedures, 92–95
Shipboard management, 70, 149–155
Shipbroker, 21, 22
Shipbuilding nations, 10–12
Ship capital requirement, 44, 45
Ship design, 31–42, 75, 147
Ship finance, 47–51
Ship investment criteria, 44–54
Ship management, 47, 48, 129–148
Ship management companies, 131, 132
Ship manning, 56–64
Ship operation, 55–76
Shipper councils, 72, 86
Shipping company, 129
Shipping company consortia, 129–131
Shipping Finance Study Group, 50
Ship propulsion, 32
Ship registry, 46
Ship's agent, 94, 95
Ship stability, 36
Shipyards, 34–40, 52, 53, 70
Shipyard subsidies, 223